Union Divided

MUSIC IN AMERICAN LIFE

The Music in American Life series documents and celebrates the dynamic and multifaceted relationship between music and American culture. From its first publication in 1972 through its half-century mark and beyond, the series has embraced a wide variety of methodologies, from biography and memoir to history and musical analysis, and spans the full range of musical forms, from classical through all types of vernacular music. The series showcases the wealth of musical practice and expression that characterizes American music, as well as the rich diversity of its stylistic, regional, racial, ethnic, and gendered contexts. Characterized by a firm grounding in material culture, whether archival or ethnographic, and by work that honors the musical activities of ordinary people and their communities, Music in American Life continually redefines and expands the very definition of what constitutes music in American culture, whose voices are heard, and how music and musical practices are understood and valued.

For a list of books in the series, please see our website at www.press.uillinois.edu.

Union Divided

Black Musicians' Fight for Labor Equality

LETA E. MILLER

UNIVERSITY OF ILLINOIS PRESS
Urbana, Chicago, and Springfield

Publication of this book was supported in part by a grant from the Judith McCulloh Endowment for American Music, and the Joseph Kerman Fund and General Fund of the American Musicological Society, supported in part by the National Endowment for the Humanities and the Andrew W. Mellon Foundation.

© 2024 by the Board of Trustees
of the University of Illinois
All rights reserved
1 2 3 4 5 C P 5 4 3 2 1
♾ This book is printed on acid-free paper.

Library of Congress Cataloging-in-Publication Data
Names: Miller, Leta E., author.
Title: Union divided : Black musicians' fight for labor
  equality / Leta E. Miller.
Description: Urbana : University of Illinois Press,
  2023. | Series: Music in American life | Includes
  bibliographical references and index.
Identifiers: LCCN 2023020347 (print) | LCCN
  2023020348 (ebook) | ISBN 9780252045561
  (hardback) | ISBN 9780252087677 (paperback) |
  ISBN 9780252055225 (ebook)
Subjects: LCSH: Musicians—Labor unions—United
  States. | Musicians, Black—Labor unions—United
  States. | American Federation of Musicians—History.
  | Discrimination in the music trade.
Classification: LCC ML3795 .M524 2023 (print) |
  LCC ML3795 (ebook) | DDC 780.89/96073—
  dc23/20230620
LC record available at https://lccn.loc.gov/2023020347
LC ebook record available at https://lccn.loc.gov/2023020348

This work is dedicated to the memory of my husband, Alan K. Miller, who offered his boundless support to me both emotionally and intellectually for fifty years and who urged me to write this book.

Contents

Acknowledgments ix

Abbreviations xiii

Chapter 1. Prelude 1

Chapter 2. The Origins of the American Federation of Musicians and Its Place in the History of Organized Labor 9

Chapter 3. The Formation of Black AFM Locals, 1897–1927 28

Chapter 4. Early Black Locals: Three Case Studies 46

Chapter 5. From the Glories of the '20s to the Despair of the '30s 60

Chapter 6. The 1940s: Change Is in the Wind 84

Chapter 7. Leading the Pack: The 1953 Los Angeles Merger 97

Chapter 8. Mergers from 1954 through 1966: State Labor Laws and the Battle of Chicago 112

Chapter 9. After Chicago 132

Chapter 10. Coda 146

Notes 155

References 183

Index 201

Acknowledgments

I am very grateful to the Emeriti Association at the University of California, Santa Cruz, for honoring me with a generous Edward A. Dickson Emeriti Professor Award. This financial support helped fund my travel and other research costs. As I investigated the fascinating, yet at times troubling history discussed in this book, I enjoyed extraordinary cooperation from officials at all levels at the American Federation of Musicians (AFM). None of them attempted to gloss over or excuse missteps or unwise decisions by the federation; indeed, all of those with whom I corresponded eagerly offered assistance in exposing the difficult path the musicians' union followed in terms of ensuring racial equity. Assistant AFM secretary Jon Ferrone expressed enthusiasm when I began the project and put me in touch with Daniel F. DeRienzo, Membership Services Representative in the New York office. I cannot thank Dan enough for the incredible support he provided by looking up numerous details for me. Without Dan's help, I could not have completed this work.

Other AFM officials met with me or responded to email requests. Especially helpful in this regard was William (Bill) Moriarity, who served as president of the enormous Local 802 in New York for eleven years (from 1993 through 2003) and was also associated with Local 2 in St. Louis earlier in his career. Bill not only met me and provided me with crucial information, but he also read an early draft of the book and offered very valuable advice. Other AFM officers who helped my work include Sue-Ellen Hershman-Tcherepnin and Mark Pinto from Boston's Local 9-535, Candace Lammers from Hartford's Local 400, Steven Hoover from St. Louis's Local 2, and Marc Sazer from Los Angeles's Local 47. My 2007 article on racial segregation in the San Francisco AFM formed the basis for the discussion of that city's local throughout the present book. During the research process for that article, I also was pleased by the exceptional cooperation of officers at San Francisco's Local 6, particularly Gretchen Elliott, Alex Walsh, and Melinda Wagner. For that preliminary work, I was also helped by AFM national officers Lew Mancini and Bob Crothers, John Grimes from Boston's Local 9-535, Gordon Stump from Detroit's Local 5, Dan Stevenson from Des Moines's Local 75, and Warren Johnson from Seattle's Local 76-493.

I conducted a number of in-person or phone interviews with other AFM officers or members. I am grateful to these individuals for giving me their valuable time and their input into the complex history of the AFM: Earl Watkins (San Francisco; now deceased), Gordon Bowman (Boston), Anita Dixon (Kansas City), Otis Ducker and Gene Tournour (Washington, DC), Henry Francis and Fred Williams (Boston), William May (Newark), and Lovie Smith-Wright (Houston). I was also privileged to have been able to contact David Keller, whose thesis and book on Seattle's Local 493 was immensely helpful to this project, and Terry Perkins, author of an article in *Downbeat* on the situation in Kansas City. Both Keller and Perkins kindly answered my questions and provided additional information.

In addition, I could not have completed this book without the help of numerous library staff members. Many thanks to the librarians at my own institution, the University of California, Santa Cruz, who cheerfully processed my many requests for materials. I would also like to extend special thanks to three librarians who went far beyond the call of duty to help this project: Therese Dickman, at the National Ragtime and Jazz Archive at Southern Illinois University at Edwardsville (SIUE), Allee Monheim at the University of Washington Special Collections, and Lori Schexnayder at Tulane University's Special Collections. Dickman hosted me for an extended and very fruitful visit to SIUE, whose library houses a great deal of unpublished material regarding St. Louis's Local 2. Monheim arranged for me to visit UW's Special Collections remotely on several occasions, during which I was able to read manuscript materials regarding Seattle's Locals 76 and 493. Schexnayder provided a remarkable service in having her staff scan hundreds of pages of unpublished documents regarding New Orleans's Locals 174 and 496, allowing me to read these documents at a time when travel was highly restricted due to the COVID-19 epidemic. Other librarians and archivists were exceptionally helpful as well, including: Alan Medlock and Zachary Palitzsch at the State Historical Society of Missouri; Cynthia Millar, Special Collections librarian at the St. Louis Public Library; Alan Wierdak at the George Meany Archive, University of Maryland College Park (who provided me with the invaluable correspondence between Meany and James Petrillo); David Olson at the Columbia Oral History Project; Gina Bardi at the San Francisco Maritime National Historical Park Research Center; and John Short at Washington University, St. Louis.

Three anonymous readers solicited by the University of Illinois Press read earlier versions of this book and provided extremely helpful suggestions. In addition to Bill Moriarity (mentioned above), David Anthony, Professor of African and African American History at UCSC kindly read the preliminary version of this book and gave me amazingly detailed and helpful feedback. All of the suggestions by these five readers were most welcome and significantly enriched the book.

Abbreviations

AFL: American Federation of Labor (founded 1886)
AEA: Actors' Equity Association (union of stage actors founded in 1913)
AFM: American Federation of Musicians (founded 1896)
BSCP: Brotherhood of Sleeping Car Porters (AFL union headed by A. Philip Randolph)
CIO: Congress of Industrial Organizations (founded 1935)
CMHI: Chicago Musicians for Harmonious Integration (a group of "rebel" musicians from Chicago's Local 208 who joined white Local 10 in 1963)
CMS: Chicago Musical Society (precursor to Local 10)
CNLU: Colored National Labor Union (founded 1869)
FDR: Franklin Delano Roosevelt (32nd president of the United States)
FEPC: Fair Employment Practices Committee (Federal agency, established in 1941)
IEB: International Executive Board (of the AFM)
IM: *International Musician* (monthly magazine of the AFM)
LMD: Living Music Days (AFM program to combat unemployment in the Great Depression)
MCI: Musicians' Committee for Integration (from Local 47, Los Angeles)
MMPU: Musical Mutual Protective Union (New York; founded 1863)
MNPA: Musicians' National Protective Association (founded 1871)
MOWM: March on Washington Movement (1941–47)
NAACP: National Association for the Advancement of Colored People (founded in 1909)

NLM: National League of Musicians (founded 1886)
NOLA: New Orleans, Louisiana
NLU: National Labor Union (founded 1866)
WPA: Works Progress Administration (agency of the New Deal employing millions of jobless Americans during the Depression in the 1930s; started in 1935; renamed in 1939 as the Work Projects Administration)

Union Divided

CHAPTER 1

Prelude

On March 31, 1971, Hal Davis, president of the American Federation of Musicians (AFM), wrote to the members of Philadelphia's "colored" Local 274 to inform them of a drastic action taken by the federation's International Executive Board: effective the next day, their local's charter would be unilaterally cancelled. Only a dozen years earlier, Local 274 had been one of more than fifty Black AFM locals, which energetically and effectively represented African American musicians throughout the country. By 1971, however, Local 274 was the last survivor of its type. It had repeatedly declined to merge with Local 77, its white counterpart, but its resistance ultimately proved futile.

Most of the fifty-plus Black locals in the AFM had formed in the 1910s and 1920s and Philadelphia's history was no exception. In 1915 African American musicians in the city secured a charter as Local 591. That union dissolved in 1930 due to financial troubles, but five years later, in the depths of the Great Depression, Local 274 replaced it.[1] The force behind the new Black local was bandleader Frank Fairfax (1899–1972), who spearheaded the collection of the needed funds and recruitment of the required number of members.[2] The chartering of Local 274 in 1935 reinforced the carefully considered and widely held opinion on the part of Black musicians that operating within a racially segregated local offered benefits beyond those likely to accrue to them in a multiracial organization. Indeed, Local 274 became one of the most active of the Black unions (officially called "colored locals") and it operated successfully until the national action of 1971 put it out of business.

To be clear, nothing in the AFM's charter or bylaws called for segregated locals. The numerous Black locals that took shape during the first three decades of the twentieth century formed as a result of proactive petitions from the Black musicians themselves, who saw economic, cultural, and musical advantages from establishing their own unions. With the permission of the much larger white (or primarily white) locals in their areas, Black musicians undertook to organize independently, thereby securing—as we will see—better access to jobs and guaranteed representation at AFM conventions. The motivations of these Black musicians were complex: sometimes a response to overt racism, but also an attempt to counter disadvantages accruing to them from the prioritization of highbrow culture—a trend toward cementing cultural hierarchies in music, theater, literature, and the visual arts that Lawrence Levine[3] powerfully describes as taking place during the years after the AFM was founded. The effect of this overwhelming cultural change and its role in prompting the formation of Black locals will be explored in more depth in chapter 3.

The AFM acceded to the requests of the African American artists as long as the closest existing local agreed. The territories these locals controlled, however, were for the most part identical to those of the corresponding white locals,[4] a situation that led, in numerous cases, to jurisdictional conflicts and interracial clashes. Competition became particularly fierce in the 1930s when musicians suffered not only from the general economic depression, but also from the advent of sound films in the late 1920s, eliminating lucrative jobs in theaters, the most prestigious of which were held by whites. Furthermore, this double hit on musical employment came on the heels of Prohibition (1920), which forced the closure of many clubs that hired musicians.

After the Second World War, with increasing attention to civil rights and the eventual enactment of governmental mandates to eliminate segregation in all areas of U.S. life, the AFM faced growing pressure to undo its support of racially separated locals. Following the *Brown v. Board of Education* decision in 1954 and the Civil Rights Act of 1964, the federation initiated an active policy of amalgamating the Black and white locals that controlled overlapping territories. But undoing the long history of separation proved much more difficult than one might expect. In a few cases, Black locals favored merger but white locals resisted. In most other cases, however (Philadelphia being one of the most vocal), the Black locals were reluctant to surrender their autonomy and force their members to become a small minority in a large white pool. In numerous Black unions, younger members pressed for amalgamation while older members worked to preserve the independent institutions they had built over many years. Indeed, it was not at all clear that integration would benefit Black musicians. Their largely monoethnic locals offered them control over their livelihoods, support for valuable cultural affinities, opportunities for inspiring musical collaboration, and a unity of purpose and action that integration could destroy.

Local 274 held out to the bitter end, arguing that it was not in fact segregated.[5] Indeed, by the 1960s some of these locals were no longer monoethnic. Among Local 274's five hundred members at the end of its life, fifty were white.[6] In other cities as well, some white musicians had begun enrolling in "colored" locals for musical or economic reasons (for instance, to facilitate playing in interracial ensembles, to benefit from more competitive pay scales, or to take advantage of laxer enforcement of rules against playing with nonunion colleagues). Furthermore, as Local 274's officers pointed out, the 1964 Civil Rights Act did not explicitly prohibit dual locals separated by race. To quote the prolix language of Title VII:[7]

> It shall be an unlawful employment practice for a labor organization . . . to limit, segregate, or classify its membership or applicants for membership, or to classify or fail or refuse to refer for employment any individual . . . [in a way that] would deprive or tend to deprive [that individual] of employment opportunities, or would . . . adversely affect his [or her] status as an employee or as an applicant for employment, because of such individual's race, color, religion, sex, or national origin.

Local 274 argued convincingly that its existence hardly deprived its members of employment; in fact, it enhanced their opportunities.

The AFM found itself in an unenviable position, to say the least. To further the goal of ending racial segregation, it would be forced to counteract the wishes of Philadelphia's Black musicians. Indeed, Local 274 had rejected several proposals by the federation aimed at alleviating the disadvantages its members anticipated through merger with Local 77, which had 5,020 members at the time (ten times as many as Local 274). Among the membership of Local 77 were twenty African Americans.[8] When negotiations reached a stalemate, the federation decided to take unilateral action; the International Executive Board (IEB) chose the path of eliminating segregation by terminating 274's charter.

In May 1971 the former members of Local 274 challenged the AFM's action in court, arguing that the merger deprived them of control over their own affairs, forced them to relinquish their meeting house and liquor license, and failed to ensure them a meaningful voice in union affairs.[9] As part of the legal procedure, James Adams, the Black president of 274, enlisted the testimony of one of his local's white members.[10] In addition to demonstrating 274's interracial membership, this action suggests that even at this late date, the local's president may have judged that the testimony of a white man would potentially carry more weight or greater integrity—or at least would have more impact—than that of an African American. Despite the arguments of the Local 274 members, however, on June 30, 1971, the judge ruled in favor of the federation.[11] Frank Fairfax, still an active member of Local 274, moved in May 1971 to Local 77 and became Assistant to the Project Chairman of the Music Performance Trust Fund and Secretary of its Clef Club.[12]

With the demise of Local 274, the AFM ended a pattern of racial separation that had begun seventy-four years earlier with the admission of the first Black local in St. Louis. (This local had actually formed two years prior to the founding of the AFM in 1896 and was incorporated into the national organization the following year.) But the problems of systemic racism didn't disappear with the dissolution of Local 274. As we will see, the AFM continued to grapple with the ramifications of the mergers and amended its rules in order to stimulate greater representation by African Americans. Even today, both the federation and its constituent locals continue to examine their practices and policies, as well as their (sometimes troubled) histories. On the national level, for example, the AFM has implemented a Diversity Council and rewarded the efforts of creative individuals who enhance the committee's goal through a Diversity Awards program.[13]

This book describes and evaluates the AFM's labyrinthine path toward ethnic equitability and inclusion by tracing the origins of its racially separated unions, their growth and successes in the 1920s, the challenges they faced and the federation's often-difficult responses during the Great Depression, and the ultimate dismantling of this segregated policy, beginning with the first merger in Los Angeles in 1953. As suggested by the previous discussion, the establishment of dual unions separated by race but competing in the same territory is a far more complex phenomenon than simply a brazen refusal to admit members due to skin color—although such overt racist actions were certainly manifest in some cities. Many other factors complicated the decisions both to organize separately and, ultimately, to end such separation. Of course, the systemic racism that has characterized U.S. society since the first slaves were brought to the New World in 1619 affected the decisions made by the federation, its Black members, and its constituent locals. But other factors, such as genre-based audition requirements, the skills required for different musical expressions, varying approaches to musical creation, rules regarding national representation, and sometimes prohibitive pay scales, all contributed to the complicated decision-making process. Black musicians, like all musicians, sought the best employment opportunities they could secure, and pursued the most advantageous means they could envision to reach that goal. The solutions of the Black locals, which evolved and changed during the course of the twentieth century, arose from a commitment to ensuring employment and competitive wages for members, even if these solutions were not uniformly successful. This book is the story of their struggle.

As the present work critically examines the history of a large institution (the AFM), it seems appropriate in this introductory chapter to situate it in the context of recent scholarship in labor history, which has tended to move away from the dispassionate study of such institutions in order to focus instead on the lived experiences of workers and their interactions with their communities.[14] In response to such legitimate concerns, I have attempted to enliven and enhance the institutional history of the AFM with reflections from the musicians themselves. Scattered throughout the book are the voices of individuals, at times those of well-known performers such as Fate Marable, Hayes Pillars, Red Saunders, Clora Bryant, and Jackie Kelso, but more often those of lesser-known figures who struggled to make a living through their art and either benefitted from, or suffered at the hands of, their labor representatives. Most of the artists quoted in these pages are no longer alive, but many have left us reflections of their experiences in the form of interviews. Occasionally these interviews are published: a particularly rich source for the present work is the book *Central Avenue Sounds*, which presents the recollections of nineteen musicians who lived and worked in Los Angeles's predominantly Black neighborhood before its lively musical scene virtually disappeared following the merger of the Black and white locals. More often, though, the interviews survive only as audio recordings or rough transcripts buried in the special collections departments of libraries. The voices of these working musicians add personal experience to the details of organizational postures. Readers will hear the reflections of performers such as pianist Sid LeProtti and the members of his So Different Orchestra in San Francisco the 1910s; drummer Earl Watkins, who recalled the union battles of the 1930s in San Francisco and eventually became an officer in the merged union; Elijah "Lige" Shaw, Lloyd Smith, and Eddie Randle, who played in theaters and on riverboats in St. Louis; Milt Hinton, who informs us about the segregated club scene in Chicago; and Powell Barnett, who was a key figure in the unions (both Black and white) in Seattle. I myself conducted about a dozen interviews with unionists who were heavily involved in the last stage of the integration process, when mergers were hammered out by officials of Black and white locals. Several of these musicians were in their nineties, but their recollections of the painful negotiation process leading to amalgamation were still fresh; and the time that had elapsed since the mandated mergers gave them the perspective to evaluate the situation with insight. Their voices enhance the objective narrative by introducing a personal viewpoint regarding the difficulties, rewards, and challenges of the union's attempts at achieving racial equitability.

One central question addressed in the present study is how musicians benefitted from unionization in the first place, an issue that underlies the very formation of the AFM. The federation's predecessor and competitor, the National League of Musicians (NLM), had struggled with the tension surrounding musicians' identification as laborers rather than (or in addition to) artists, and therefore hesitated to align itself with the powerful American Federation of Labor (AFL), the AFM's parent body. The NLM, as we will see, was so hampered by this fundamental debate that it brought about its own demise.

The highbrow/lowbrow hierarchy that solidified at the end of the nineteenth century affected all of the arts and influenced other unionization efforts, such as that of the Actors Equity Association (AEA), which formed in 1913 and affiliated with the AFL six years later.[15] The motivations for the actors to organize bear some similarities to those of the musicians. Actors debated, for example, their fundamental identification as laborers or artists (which was, as in the NLM, a fundamental controversy hindering previous theatrical organizations, such as the Actors' Society of America).[16] Actors experienced wage problems similar to those that plagued musicians (such as inadequate compensation for rehearsals and vast pay differentials between the few stars and the rank and file), and they saw the benefits of cementing contractual obligations from managers. But ultimately the formation of the AEA arose from a development quite different from the experiences of musicians, namely, the consolidation and commercialization of the American theater as a "standardized commodity" under the control of national booking agencies such as the Theatrical Syndicate and the Shubert Brothers (or, in vaudeville, under magnates such as Benjamin Franklin Keith).[17] This national solidification fundamentally changed the nature of theatrical productions throughout the country and undermined the autonomy of local presenters. The musicians, on the other hand, remained fragmented, with most individuals piecing together a living through part-time work in local clubs, theaters, skating rinks, dance halls, riverboats, circuses—in short, anywhere that music could function as a desirable enhancement to nonmusical activities. Some longer-term employment was available, of course, notably in the theaters for silent films, the most desirable job market for non-orchestral performers in the period before sound films. Radio offered some steadier employment as well, and many U.S. symphony orchestras began to form at the end of the nineteenth century and the beginning of the twentieth: Boston (1881), Chicago (1891), Philadelphia (1900), Seattle (1903), San Francisco (1911), Cleveland (1918), and others. Symphony musicians also needed labor protection, because in the early years there were no long-term contracts, no assurances of continued work, exploitation in terms of required hours of rehearsals, and so on. Furthermore, there was no assurance whatsoever that these large and expensive performing ensembles would even be financially secure enough to survive.[18] Race is intimately linked to these issues of employment. The orchestras were bastions of white talent. Black musicians, on the other hand, sought job security in other areas and their talents often focused on a fundamentally different method of musical creation: improvisation as opposed to the interpretation of a fixed score. In chapter 7 we will see how those opposing methods of musical performance ultimately informed each other in the 1950s in the fruitful interactions that took place in Los Angeles leading to the first union merger. At the outset, however, the organization of musical labor faced the formidable task of servicing through a single union such diverse musical performers and their needs. The AFM was remarkably successful in navigating that challenge. By the 1920s the union controlled the work of about 90 percent of performing musicians throughout the country, according to the testimony of several contemporaneous sources. As we will see, it did so by striking a balance between local autonomy and central control. In fact, the very fragmentation of the musical work scene aided the union in its efforts; the AFM did not have to negotiate with powerful national employer organizations.

My research, which began with the publication of a detailed account of the problematic history of San Francisco's Local 6 and its two (successive) Black competitors,[19] has thankfully benefitted from enthusiastic cooperation on the part of union officials throughout the country. I have encountered no resistance to unmasking the (sometimes painful) historical record, and no attempts to justify or excuse racist actions of the past. In fact, the overall response has been to provide whatever documentation survives, and to celebrate those victories that led to greater equity, while still recognizing the urgent work left to do.

Some locals have begun to explore the historical issues on their own. San Francisco and Boston provide two examples. In 2004 Local 6 (San Francisco) commemorated the forty-fourth anniversary of its amalgamation with Black Local 669 by holding a joyous, if rather belated, celebratory event. Officials there eagerly offered me access to their archives and made my completed article that detailed their history available to the membership. In Boston, the president of Local 9-535, Sue-Ellen Hershman-Tcherepnin, conducted a series of oral histories, interviewing fifty members who recalled the Black local; excerpts appeared in the organization's newsletter, *Interlude*.[20]

Such efforts at investigating and exposing racist actions of the past (whether overt or subconscious) are increasingly common both within and outside of the AFM. Many institutions today are actively taking responsibility for the behaviors of their predecessors. One exemplary effort among many is an in-depth series published in the *Kansas City Star* in 2020. "For much of its early history—through sins of commission and omission," wrote editor Mike Fannin, the *Star* "disenfranchised, ignored and scorned generations of Black Kansas Citians.... We are sorry.... Even the Black cultural icons that Kansas City would one day claim with pride were largely overlooked. Native son Charlie 'Bird' Parker didn't get a significant headline in The Star until he died, and even then, his name was misspelled and his age was wrong."[21] To rectify this history, the paper published a six-part series based on thorough research by its reporters. Although we can never reverse troublesome actions of the past, it is my hope that the present book will add to the extensive critical dialogue by shining a spotlight on the historical record within the musicians' union, and will lead to continued revelations and inquiries by others. I have examined the trajectories of numerous segregated AFM locals that once existed, but certainly not all of them; thus, I welcome others to embellish my tale.

The AFM's story of racial separation is closely linked to the troubled history of Black labor relations in general and to the uncomfortable role into which African Americans were often thrust as scabs when whites staged labor strikes. From the outset, the AFM was a constituent member of the American Federation of Labor (AFL), which, during most of its early history, confronted—and chose to dodge—outspoken efforts by Black workers to enact principled measures against racism. For this reason, our story begins with a look at the instigation of the musicians' union and its relation to the problematic history of race relations within the AFL, the largest and most powerful labor organization in the country.

CHAPTER 2

The Origins of the American Federation of Musicians and Its Place in the History of Organized Labor

The American Federation of Musicians was not the first national organization of musical performers, but it was the first, and ultimately the only, successful one. The union's meteoric rise after its founding in 1896 and the control it soon exerted over musical employment ranging from large organizations offering contractual arrangements to small groups playing single engagements was due in large part to its affiliation with the American Federation of Labor (AFL) and the willingness of the AFM's organizers to identify with workers in unrelated fields.

In contrast to other (unsuccessful) musicians' organizations, the AFM's founders recognized that the principal motivation for establishing a national federation coincided with that of workers everywhere: namely combatting workplace exploitation. For musicians, such exploitation was manifest in low wages, long hours, employers who skipped town without paying their workers, rehearsals running way past scheduled times, unpaid rehearsals, lack of long-term employment commitments, and similar grievances. In addition, the AFM took shape under pressure from the AFL itself, which for a decade had courted the most prominent existing organization, the National League of Musicians, only to meet with repeated rejection. Samuel Gompers, the first president of the AFL, and his executive board endeavored to enlist as many member organizations as possible in order to strengthen the organization's clout within the wage-labor system in the country. In addition, however, Gompers had a special attraction to music—albeit to the highbrow classical repertoire—and he saw clearly the intersection of the interests of musical and nonmusical wage earners. It was, in fact, at Gompers's initiative that the AFM organized.

Figure 2.1. Samuel Gompers (1850–1924). (Photo by Harris and Ewing. Library of Congress Prints and Photographs Division, Harris & Ewing photograph collection.)

The National League of Musicians (1886–1904) and its Predecessors

As early as 1863, a local union, called the Musical Mutual Protective Union (MMPU), formed in New York, but it had no national presence.[1] Eight years later a union in Philadelphia initiated the first attempt to unite organizations in several cities, resulting in the short-lived Musicians' National Protective

Association (MNPA), founded in June 1871.[2] That group lasted less than a decade, failing at its biggest challenge: that is, gaining the confidence, and thus the affiliation, of unions elsewhere in the country. Musicians in U.S. cities were isolated enough at this time that a national federation did not seem useful.

The second national organizing attempt was far more effective. In 1886, the same year in which the AFL was founded, a local union in Cincinnati called a meeting of seven similar bodies in the East and Midwest—Boston, Chicago, Cincinnati, Detroit, Milwaukee, New York, and Philadelphia—resulting in the formation of the National League of Musicians (NLM). The newly formed AFL immediately jumped into action; in 1887, one year after both unions organized, the AFL invited the NLM to join.

The NLM, however, declined.[3] The main issue from its point of view was whether musicians were artists or laborers—the same question that arose a few decades later in the unionization of stage actors (described in chapter 1), and even in the organization of vaudevillians.[4] Gompers's vehement arguments in favor of the common interests between musicians and workers in other fields stemmed both from his interest in the AFL's expansion and from his own position of empathy. He had much more than a passing knowledge of music and understood well the NLM's hesitation. His grandfather had exposed him to classical music concerts as a child, where, he later recalled, he "lived in another world and quivered with the beauty of tone and melody or grew tense when the music dropped in[to] minor or developed in some grand effect. . . . Music appeals to my whole nature as does nothing else," he wrote in his autobiography. "Many a time to find relief from the strain of struggle of the labor movement I have sought music. The beauty of wonderful music would hold me speechless, motionless."[5] Gompers bought a violin with money he was supposed to have used for dress fabric for his wife; and he came to enjoy evenings of music-making with friends by playing the violin or singing. His daughter Sadie, who unfortunately died from the "Spanish flu," engaged in serious vocal study.[6]

Gompers thus spoke from a certain degree of experience and with sincere concern for the interests of performers when he wrote that "musicians employed in orchestras and bands were in a sort of No Man's Land that lies between the professional worker and the wage-earner." He argued that professional instrumentalists—those who depended on musical employment for their livelihood—needed protection from amateurs who would undercut them. "People to whom music was only a diversion or part-time work were willing to accept employment on terms impossible for the musician who depended entirely upon his music for income."[7]

Year after year the AFL invited the NLM to affiliate; and just as consistently the NLM refused—a decision its officers and members would come to regret. To some degree the issue was one of class. The NLM musicians saw themselves as a "self-validated elite," and through their elevation of classical and semiclassical music above popular music, they "proclaimed and perpetuated a hierarchy in musical culture"[8] that would later challenge race relations within the AFM. The NLM also suffered from too much local autonomy. There were, for example, no transfer memberships, which disadvantaged traveling bands who therefore declined union affiliation. The institution of an audition requirement based on the Western classical tradition (another sign of the new stratification of art into "high" and "low" manifestations in this period) also encouraged rivals to perform at reduced wages. Despite these drawbacks, however, the NLM expanded quickly and by 1896 it claimed about a hundred affiliates throughout the country with a total membership of about nine thousand.[9]

Meanwhile, the AFL began to encourage some local unions without ties to any national organization to affiliate with it independently. Among the "roughly two thousand charters listed in the AFL's charter records before 1899," writes Dorothy Cobble, "two indicated racial separation."[10] One of these groups was a musical organization, the Great Western Union of Colored Musicians of St. Louis, Missouri[11] (chartered independently by the AFL on May 18, 1894). Three years later, this Black organization would become the first "colored local" in the AFM.

The Founding of the American Federation of Musicians (1896)

Increasingly frustrated by the NLM's refusal to affiliate with the AFL, Gompers announced in 1895 that continued rejection would lead him to support a rival union. He and James O'Connell, third AFL vice president, attended the NLM convention in Washington, DC, in April 1896[12] and for one final time invited the NLM to join forces with the American Federation of Labor. The vote was tied and therefore constituted a rejection. Gompers then called a convention of all musicians' organizations associated with both the NLM and the AFL, as well as independent groups throughout the country, to be held October 19–22, 1896 in Indianapolis.[13] Twenty-six locals, seventeen of them affiliated with the NLM,[14] sent delegates. Among the non-NLM attendees was John R. Fields, representing the small independent Great Western Union of Colored Musicians of St. Louis.[15] The convention delegates authorized formation of the American Federation of

Musicians; they drafted a constitution and bylaws, and elected officers.[16] Owen Miller from St. Louis (but not from the Colored Musicians group) became the AFM's first president; he had worked closely with Gompers to bring about an association with the AFL.[17] Gompers recalled Miller as "a well-trained musician who knew a number of the great European artists and had intimate knowledge of many of their lives."

> He [Miller] had pondered over the economic problem of musicians which he realized was fundamental in determining their advancement. He decided that their problem was essentially the same as that of other wage-earners and courageously advocated identification with the American labor movement.[18]

On November 6, 1896, the AFL issued a charter to the AFM, which, in turn, began chartering its own locals early the next year. By the time the *Official Proceedings* of the first AFM convention were published, the organization had forty-eight affiliated locals, among them No. 44, the "Great Western Union (Colored)" of St. Louis with John R. Fields as president.[19] There was, of course, another local from St. Louis, AFM Local 2, the group with which president Owen Miller was affiliated. Both St. Louis locals received their charters in February 1897. Thus began the AFM's pattern of chartering dual locals separated by race but having jurisdiction over the same territory. According to the *Official Proceedings* of the second AFM convention in 1897, (Black) Local 44 had 37 members and (white) Local 2 had 335.[20]

In 1896, the same year in which the AFM was founded, the U.S. Supreme Court issued a landmark—and devastating—decision: In *Plessy v. Ferguson* the court approved of separate but (ostensibly) equal institutions for Blacks and whites throughout the country. (They proved, of course, to be anything but equal.) Virulent Negrophobia was on the rise in the South during the 1890s; lynchings of Blacks, for instance, hit their highest point in 1892.[21] The 1890 census, showing a lower growth rate for African Americans than for whites,[22] even led some to predict the inevitable extinction of the Black population.[23] By the turn of the century, racial Darwinism—which postulated that racial characteristics "lie at the root of all social difficulties and problems"[24]—was widely accepted and used to justify policies of repression. The AFM made no such declarations, but at the same time, the formation of its separate Black locals after 1902 was certainly reflective of, and coincident with, racist trends in the society at large.

Musically, this decade saw the rise of the coon song, which often portrayed Blacks not only as ignorant and lazy, but also as ambitionless and libidinous in the guise of dishonest drunkards and gamblers. Whereas minstrelsy had often cast Blacks as outlandish, it had not typically presented them as physically threatening.[25] Many coon songs, on the other hand, depicted Blacks as treacherous savages, threatening violence against whites. "The subliminal message was clear," notes James Dorman. "Blacks are potentially dangerous; they must be controlled and subordinated by whatever means necessary. They must also be segregated."[26]

Meanwhile, the NLM vainly sought to fight back against the ascendancy of the AFM. It revoked the charters of any affiliates that associated with the AFM and tried to block AFM members from attending NLM meetings. By these actions, however, the NLM only accelerated its own demise. In 1898 it had only nine locals at its annual convention and by 1902 three were left: New York, Philadelphia, and Baltimore. In 1904 the NLM disbanded.[27]

The AFM, in contrast, moved quickly to establish its authority over musical employment and to unite its affiliates under common rules. Formation of new locals was easy, requiring only fifteen professional musicians in any unorganized territory—and the federation defined a "professional" loosely as any musician "who receives pay for his musical services."[28] Members needed to be instrumentalists and U.S. citizens (or intended citizens). Both men and women could join. Within four years, the number of locals had more than doubled: the *Official Proceedings* of 1899 lists ninety-two affiliates.[29]

In 1906, John Commons wrote that the AFM already had 424 locals and exerted "more complete control of their business throughout the United States and Canada than that enjoyed by any other large union in the American Federation of Labor."[30] Gary Fink gives the following impressive membership numbers:

1896: 4,000
1904: 22,000
1912: 50,000
1920: 70,000
1929: 146,326 (a peak not reached again until 1944).[31]

Federation policies governed musical work throughout the nation to such an extent that in 1948 Vern Countryman wrote that "virtually all musicians in the United States who play for hire are members of the AFM."[32] Other sources support this claim of nearly universal control over instrumental musical performance. For example, in 1929 Anna Green wrote, in her University of California master's thesis in economics, that San Francisco's Local 6 "enjoys practically 100% control over the so-called 'steady' engagements and approximately 90% control over the casual engagements."[33]

Indeed, the AFM skillfully developed policies and procedures that ensured union representation in the wide range of performance situations enjoyed by working musicians. The effectiveness of the union for large ensembles, in which musicians could expect steady employment and contractual arrangements, is obvious. The organization could, in these cases, negotiate terms governing the same types of concerns as in other fields; that is, it could increase wage scales, enforce limitations on work hours, secure contractual agreements, and so on. Similarly, the AFM could negotiate favorable terms for musicians employed in theaters or in broadcasting. But the federation extended its control far beyond these areas of employment, to regulate casual work in clubs, restaurants, dance halls, entertainment centers—any venues that hired musical ensembles on a temporary basis. The fragmentation of the music scene and the variety of conditions governing employment in various geographic regions allowed the AFM to establish dominance, as there was no unified opposition. The federation wisely allowed a considerable degree of local control over wages and working conditions while imposing rules to recognize different types of employment and different regions in the country. In short, the organization authorized local authority in many areas, but also imposed national standards under a unified banner; it was, as Vern Countryman notes, able successfully to "strike a compromise between adequate national authority and effective local representation."[34]

In 1948–49 Countryman published a detailed legal analysis of the AFM in the *University of Chicago Law Review*, in which he analyzed the carefully forged policies that led to this nearly universal control. One major contributing factor was the AFM's contracting scheme, initiated in 1913. Casual ensembles were hired for performance not by the venue itself, but by local independent contractors, who acted as middle men, but who were most often members of the hired ensemble.[35] The contractor assumed responsibility for negotiations with the venue, collection and distribution of payment, enforcement of working hours and required number of performers, and other details.

Locals, for their part, exerted exceptional constraints over union membership and working conditions. They initially evaluated applicants through an individualized and locally controlled audition process, and they also set pay scales, which could vary depending on the type of employment, the size of the venue, the nature of the performance, and other factors. These pay scales differed radically from one community to the next. The powers held by the locals directly influenced the racial composition of their membership, as the officers and examining committees could exclude musicians who did not meet the standards they devised. Because the AFM was able in effect to enforce a closed shop for most casual engagements throughout the nation, the denial of union membership by a local union could bar musicians from most jobs. The solution, in the view of many African American musicians who failed to meet the admission requirements of their locals, was to form their own segregated locals, through which they could satisfy the requirement of union membership imposed by employers while enforcing their own competitive pay scales and admission requirements.

Representation at the national convention was also a product of compromise: Every local was guaranteed at least one delegate and one vote for its first hundred members. Above a hundred, the local gained an additional vote for each hundred members or majority fraction thereof. At the same time, the constitution capped the total number of delegates for any one local at three and the total number of votes a local could cast at ten.[36] For example, a local with 151 members had two votes; but if a local had 3,000 members, it could only cast ten votes. (These rules regarding the number of delegates and votes have substantially changed over the years.)[37]

The AFM also solved the matter of touring musicians—another major weakness of the NLM. A musician who was a member of an AFM local for six months or more could play in another jurisdiction by taking out a transfer card and paying local dues, which were minimal. Traveling bands charged employers a 10 percent tax, which went in part to the local in whose jurisdiction the performance took place, in part to the federation, and in part to the performers.[38]

The AFM successfully battled rivalry with military bands and foreign musicians, instituted booking agency licensing requirements, and reduced competition with amateur performers. The organization also forged agreements with other unions, such as the International Alliance of Theatrical Stage Employees, binding members of both unions to sympathy strikes. Through such agreements, union workers exerted exceptional control over theaters and clubs. Sympathy strikes continued to be an extremely powerful negotiating tool until they were outlawed by the Taft-Hartley Act of 1947, limiting union prowess to such a degree that the AFM began to lose its broad control over casual engagements.

Organized Labor and Race

From the start of labor's national organization in the mid-nineteenth century, race was an ongoing area of intensive debate. Because the issues for labor are fundamentally economic, race and economic class—as well as race and caste, as Isabel Wilkerson ominously reminds us[39]—are intricately linked. Race is fluid: skin pigmentation ranges incrementally from pale to dark, and the definitions of both Black and white have evolved according to the efforts of the dominant culture to impose repressive measures on those they judge to be beneath them. Class can and has been bridged, though often with considerable difficulty. But caste has been virtually impermeable in the United States, even for those in the most prestigious positions politically or economically; and it continues to persist in numerous acts of conscious or subconscious bias occasioned by the perceived physical manifestations of race.

Since the seventeenth century, Blacks have been forced into the lowest caste of U.S. society. Black labor was unpaid for nearly 250 years and whites justified constraining African Americans to the bottom of the labor pyramid through Wilkerson's eight foundational pillars underpinning a caste system: evocation of divine will and the laws of nature, assumption of heritability, control of mating, fear of pollution, maintenance of occupational hierarchies, efforts at dehumanization, imposition of terror techniques, and a belief in inherent white superiority.[40]

The Civil War created for the first time an enormous *paid* Black workforce. The end of the conflict led to the liberation of nearly four million slaves, a huge increase in the workforce even if we consider only the men (as women entered the working world in small numbers at the time). Although these freedmen had no experience with wage-labor, they sought jobs in competition with whites while still confronting disdain and exclusion on the part of even the poorest among the dominant racial caste.[41] For a brief moment in time the North implemented policies aimed at achieving greater racial equality, but the withdrawal from Reconstruction following the destructive Compromise of 1877 led to the re-establishment of white supremacist rule in the states of the former Confederacy and the reversion to quasi-slavery in the form of the repressive Black Codes.

The rapid growth of organized labor during and after the Civil War led to the formation of craft unions throughout the country, none of which welcomed Blacks.[42] Placing additional stress on the labor market, the annual influx of immigrants in this period also rose dramatically, from 130,000 in 1860 to 460,000 by 1873.[43] In the musical world, immigrants from Germany swelled the ranks of instrumental performers, reinforcing the trends toward the sacralization of "high art" at the end of the century. In the opera world, a similar influx of Italians swamped the native workforce, with major stars dominating the stages from coast to coast.

Most of the new union members resided in the Northern states and found employment as skilled craftsmen; the unions for the most part excluded laborers and agricultural workers, the primary occupations among Blacks. Even in nonagricultural work, Blacks faced racial exclusion. As the United States transformed from a rural/agricultural to an urban/industrial society, employers typically prioritized the hiring of native white workers, even those in the poorest classes who were often the most virulently racist, as they viewed immigrants and non-whites as threatening competition.[44]

The intensification of racism during this period was hardly confined to the South or to select industries. In response to fear of competition from the freed slaves, white workers in general began to "define themselves by their whiteness," as David Roediger emphasizes. Even if these workers earned a low wage, they were "compensated in part by a . . . public and psychological wage" by defining themselves as "not slaves" and not Black. "Whiteness was a way in which white workers responded to a fear of dependency on wage labor and to the necessities of capitalist work discipline." Although job competition and economic well-being figured strongly into the equation, Roediger emphasizes that the basic underlying issue was one of caste. The white worker developed a "self-conscious social category mainly by comparing himself to Blacks."[45] Indeed, as a number of recent studies on whiteness have shown, self-awareness of race as a fundamental, defining, and essentialized trait among white laborers arose in response to the emergence of paid Black labor.

From an organizational standpoint, the AFL was founded on, and devoted to, the principle of skilled craft unionization. As we will see, the federation adhered to this concept despite the ongoing problems it created, among the most important of which was racial exclusion by some of its most powerful constituents. An alternative approach, which would emerge much later in the guise of the CIO in 1935, but which had attracted adherents for decades, was industrial organization. Organizing by industry (e.g., all of the auto workers or all of the mine workers) held major implications for Blacks, as such unions recruited members working at all skill levels. The AFL's adherence to the craft principle, however, was historical and enduring. (The AFL and the CIO, which were at first antagonistic, merged in 1955.) Throughout its early history, the AFL paid lip service to racial equity while tolerating exclusionary rules by some of its members—most notably the railroad unions—in its unbending devotion to craft unionization.

Precursors to the AFL also grappled with white workers' antipathy toward admitting Black members. The National Labor Union (NLU), founded in 1866, twenty years prior to the AFL, placed the question of Black membership on its first agenda. Adherents argued that admitting Black members was not only ethical, but also economically astute, as efforts by white skilled workers to gain benefits through strikes had repeatedly been hampered by management's hiring of Blacks as scabs. African Americans, inexperienced in the wage-labor market after years of slavery and excluded from employment in numerous areas due to racist policies, naturally accepted the offers of employment, even though they were often summarily dismissed once the strikes ended. A 1934 article in San Francisco's Black newspaper, *The Spokesman*, colorfully summarizes the issue, which was still current:

> If [African Americans] work, they are traitors to labor; if they remain idle, they are traitors to their stomachs.... Union labor never seems to need the loyalty of Aframerican workers until it calls a strike. As long as the unions are getting what they want, any person darker than a sunburned Swede is blackballed the moment he sticks his head in the meeting room. But when the union boys want to wrest a few extra hours or dollars from the "bosses," the atmosphere becomes thick with mellow friendship, warm invitations, and loud hurrahs for "our black brothers."[46]

The NLU delegates reached no consensus at that first convention in 1866 nor at subsequent ones, until finally in 1869 they began to actively court African Americans, encouraging them to form separate segregated unions, which could then join the larger federation. Nine Black delegates were actually seated at that 1869 convention, but the report from that year urged "our colored fellow members to form [their own] organizations in all legitimate ways to send their delegates from every state in the Union to the next Congress."[47] The NLU thereby established a model for future labor organizations, including the AFL and the AFM, to form locals explicitly segregated by race. A plea for equal treatment of Blacks by Baltimore caulker Isaac Myers at that 1869 convention met with outright rejection.[48] Thus, asserts Rayford Logan, "the first large-scale exclusion of Negroes by private organizations in the post-bellum period was the handiwork of organized labor."[49]

Two months after this 1869 meeting, African American laborers formed their own Colored National Labor Union (CNLU). Myers became its first president. The NLU formally dissolved in 1873; the CNLU ceased most of its activity around the same time and eventually folded.

The Knights of Labor, which organized in 1869 and grew into the largest labor federation in the country during the nineteenth century, adhered from the outset to a more progressive agenda than other organizations in many areas. In terms of racial diversity, a statement in the group's journal in 1891 expressed this ideal: "The noble Order of the Knights of Labor teaches equal privileges to all, special favors to none, as in our local assemblies women are on equality with men; there is no discrimination on account of race or sex."⁵⁰ (Interestingly, the organization did exclude Chinese workers, however.)

Under the banner of "an injury to one is the concern of all," the Knights actively recruited African American members—although it is difficult to ascertain exactly how many joined because the Proceedings of its General Assembly do not distinguish delegates by ethnicity. Some locals were racially segregated; others (primarily in the North) were racially inclusive.⁵¹ Frank Ferrell, the Knights' most prominent Black leader, estimated that in 1887 there were more than four hundred all-Black locals with a total membership of about sixty thousand. Considering the multiracial locals as well, he projected the total African American membership at ninety to ninety-five thousand.⁵² Significantly, in terms of the present study, some Black workers in the Knights encouraged the establishment of segregated organizations. In a foreshadowing of a later argument supporting segregated locals in the AFM, some Southern Black Knights of Labor groups lobbied for segregated district organizations to give them control of the district offices and ensure "more Black representation at the state and General Assemblies."⁵³

In 1886 Ferrell attended the Knights' convention in Richmond as part of the delegation from New York. Upon arrival, the New York delegates discovered that the hotel they had booked would not accommodate Blacks. Thereupon the delegation canceled its reservation and moved to a hotel that would. In addition, a subsequent visit to a local theater by the same delegation provoked protests about a Black man seated in a prime audience location. Angry patrons left the theater and instituted a boycott. These incidents prompted the Knights' leader, Terence V. Powderly, to spotlight Ferrell by giving him the honor of introducing Powderly at the opening meeting (see Figure 2.2). Outraged editorials, condemning Powderly in particular and the Knights in general, appeared in the local papers. Powderly countered with a lengthy response, published in full in the *Richmond Dispatch* and in part in other papers. "My sole object in selecting a colored man to introduce me," he wrote, "was to encourage and help to uplift his race from a bondage worse than that which held him in chains twenty-five years ago—viz. mental slavery."⁵⁴

Although Powderly's actions may have been quite bold for their time and place, they were also limited as well as patronizing. Despite the hysterical claims in numerous press articles, Powderly made clear that he had no intention of promoting social equality, "for that cannot be regulated by law.... Every man has the right to say who shall enter beneath his roof."⁵⁵ Herman Bloch suggests that Black distrust of organized labor resulted di-

Figure 2.2. Machinist Frank J. Ferrell introducing Terence V. Powderly, the head of the Knights of Labor, at the union's convention in Richmond, Virginia, 1886. (Wood engraving.)

rectly from such "social antipathy," espoused even by sympathetic whites like Powderly, which was "so overwhelming that Negroes with trades were rarely organized."[56]

Powderly appointed some Black organizers for the Knights, but they often met with hostility and even violence.[57] Recruiter John F. Clark organized Blacks into secret assemblies in order to avoid violence, and Hiram F. Hover (often given erroneously as Hoover) scheduled his organizational meetings for African Americans between midnight and dawn with guards stationed at the doors. Hover suffered major physical injury in 1887 from a shotgun blast intended to kill him.[58]

The Knights' loose organization, inadequate funding, resistance to mass strikes, and appeals for workers' self-discipline led to the organization's decline. Furthermore, the Knights failed miserably in their well-intentioned efforts to stem overt racism in the South, and white members left the organization in large numbers.[59] By 1890 membership had sunk to about one hundred thousand and the Panic of 1893 marked union's de facto demise, though it did not officially disband until 1949.

Meanwhile, a new national union took shape in the same year that the Knights reached their apex—1886. The American Federation of Labor would soon overshadow all other attempts at labor organization and take on the battles of workers ranging from railroad employees to plumbers to musicians. But although the AFL aggressively advocated for labor-friendly policies and managed to secure significant benefits for workers, its failure to take a strong stand on racial inclusion disadvantaged Black workers from the start. The federation's tepid endorsement of racial equality did not result in any significant reform until the government-ordered integration legislation of the mid-twentieth century finally forced action.

The AFL's Ineffective Policies on Race

Because the American Federation of Musicians operated under the auspices of the American Federation of Labor, its racial policies were necessarily affected by those of the umbrella organization. Understanding the rationale for the AFM's segregated local policy requires an examination of the context in which it originated—a context that involves not only musicians, but also (and perhaps even more importantly) workers in other affiliated unions. This chapter thus ends with an overview of the AFL's troubled history of dealing with the nation's large and influential African American workforce.

Learning from the failures of the National Labor Union and the Knights of Labor, the AFL aimed to be expansive in its reach and to exert strong control over its member unions. In order to bolster its effectiveness, it enlisted as many skilled craft groups as possible. However, this very policy of widespread admission also drove the AFL to tolerate (admittedly with discomfort) the exclusionary racial policies of some of its affiliates.

The AFL also faced sociological barriers to enlisting Black workers: to wit, their disinclination to join the labor movement at all. In 1913 Booker T. Washington described in some detail the causes for Blacks' distrust of organized labor.[60] African American workers were leaving the rural South in droves to move to cities, primarily, he says, to access educational and cultural opportunities. Emerging from a history of legalized slavery followed by the economic slavery that accompanied the end of Reconstruction—namely, sharecropping and Black Codes—these new citizens were unused to looking for work. "Work has always looked for [them]," Washington wrote. Blacks were also suspicious of organizations "founded on a sort of impersonal enmity to the man by whom he is employed." When, in addition, some unions denied them membership, these workers not only became further alienated, but also developed—from economic necessity—into "professional strike-breakers."[61]

The fraught relationship between the AFL and African American workers persisted uneasily for decades as the federation tried to balance its desire for widespread control of the labor market with fundamental ethical imperatives. In the early years the organization attempted, with limited success, to enforce a policy of racial inclusivity. In a test case cited by nearly every writer describing the history of Blacks and labor in the United States, the AFL in 1890 refused to admit the Machinists' Union due to a "whites only" clause in its constitution. The 1890 convention report describes instructions given to the machinists to expunge the offending restriction. It also contains a broader policy statement that the federation cited repeatedly in ensuing years: "This Convention . . . looks with disfavor upon trade unions having provisions which exclude from membership persons on account of race or color."[62] Samuel Gompers tried to hold fast to the denial of membership unless the machinists acted on this "respectful" request. He even visited the machinists' 1893 convention with the aim of forcing a constitutional change.[63] In the same year, the AFL reaffirmed its opposition to racial exclusion: "Resolved, that we here and now reaffirm as one of the cardinal principles of the labor movement that the working people must unite and organize, irrespective of creed, color, sex, nationality or politics."[64] The machinists, however, refused to comply.

Gompers and the AFL Executive Committee organized a rival machinists' union and told the original one that it would be admitted only "if it abrogated the anti-Negro clause."[65] The union's president promised action, but then retreated, citing opposition from the membership. In 1894 Gompers was defeated for the AFL presidency. The next year, under the temporary leadership of James Duncan (who was acting as AFL president for a few months while the new president, John McBride, was ill), the federation admitted the machinists through a ruse: The union expunged the whites-only clause from its constitution, but added to its ritual a pledge to be taken by all new members that they would only nominate whites for admission. The following year Gompers won back the presidency and remained in that position until his death in 1924, but the damage had been done. Other unions, such as the blacksmiths, soon instigated similar ritual protocols.

"The more Gompers attempted to induce organizations to accept Negro workers," writes Gerald Grob, "the stronger and more intense the opposition grew."[66] Faced with the prospect of losing a number of powerful affiliated unions, Gompers finally had to admit that his demands for racial inclusion were unrealistic. "The race prejudice exists to such an extent," he wrote to George Norton in 1892, "that it seems it were better under the circumstances, to give the white men and the colored men the opportunity of organizing separate unions rather than to have them not organize at all."[67] Gompers struggled with the race issue on both ethical and practical grounds. "If we fail to organize and recognize the colored wage-workers we cannot blame them very well if they accept our challenge of enmity and do all they can to frustrate our purposes," he wrote in another personal letter. "Thus if common humanity will not prompt us to have their co-operation, an enlightened self-interest should."[68]

At numerous conventions over the next two decades (notably 1897, 1910, 1917, and 1918)[69] the AFL verbally reaffirmed its opposition to racial exclusion, but was never willing to take the one action that would have definitively reinforced that verbal commitment, that is, ousting those unions insistent on barring African American members. Time and again, resolutions appeared on the AFL's convention agenda, only to be defeated or relegated to the dustheap of investigative committees.[70] Especially outspoken on this matter was A. Philip Randolph, head of the (Black) Brotherhood of Sleeping Car Porters (BSCP), a union launched in 1925 and finally chartered by the AFL in 1935.[71] Randolph became increasingly vocal during the 1930s, insisting that the AFL expel unions with whites-only constitutional provisions. Most of the affected organizations were railroad unions and thus closely connected to Randolph's own workers. But votes at the AFL conventions repeatedly resulted in tabling resolutions to expel these unions, or referring such resolutions to study commissions where they languished. By 1946 there were still nine unions in the country, with an overall membership of 707,556, that constitutionally excluded Blacks (five associated with the AFL and four independent). Eight were railroad unions.[72] As late as 1959, after the AFL had amalgamated with the CIO, Randolph was still fighting the same battle. As we will see in chapter 8, he specifically condemned the AFM's segregated union structure even if Black musicians supported it.[73]

The imperfect solution that Gompers and the AFL's Executive Board eventually implemented was the establishment of so-called Federal Unions comprised entirely of Black workers. An amendment to the federation's constitution, as described in the *Proceedings* of 1900, permitted the chartering of "colored central labor unions, local unions, and federal labor unions if it seemed 'advisable and to the best interest of the trade union movement to do so.'"[74] In his annual report to the membership that year, Gompers addressed this new policy.

> In some parts of the South, central bodies chartered by the American Federation of Labor have refused to receive and accord seats to delegates from local unions composed of negro workers.... This matter has been one of considerable correspondence, with the result that the thought has been developed for the formation of central bodies composed of representatives of negro workers' unions exclusively; that they be permitted to work under a certificate of affiliation from the American Federation of Labor; that there should be a general council representing both central bodies upon any matter of importance.[75]

Notably, Gompers also repeated two arguments made by the leaders of earlier national federations: namely, that the AFL advocated employment equality but took no stand on social equality, and that the failure to organize Black workers would not only be unethical but also antithetical to the economic interests of whites. "The American Federation of Labor has upon all occasions declared that trade unions should open their portals to all wage-workers, irrespective of creed, color, nationality sex, or politics."

> Even if it were not a matter of principle, self-preservation would prompt the workers to organize intelligently, and to make common cause. In making the declaration we have, we do not necessarily proclaim that the social barriers existing between the whites and blacks could or should be felled with one stroke of the pen; but when white and black workers are compelled to work side by side under the same adverse circumstances and under equally unfair conditions, it seems an anomaly that we should refuse to accord the right of organization to workers because of a difference in their color. Unless we shall give the negro workers the opportunity to organize, and thus place them where they can protect and defend themselves against the rapacity and cupidity of their employers; unless we continue the policy of endeavoring to make friends of them, there can be no question but that they will not only be forced down in the economic scale and be used against any effort made by us for our economic and social advancement, but race prejudice will be made more bitter to the injury of all.[76]

Under the new policy implemented in 1900, organizations composed of Black workers could obtain separate AFL charters; but members of these unions remained under the authority of the overall parent union. Blacks could thus unionize in crafts with whites-only clauses in their constitutions, but the larger dominant white union retained overriding control. This highly imperfect solution resulted from Gompers's years-long struggle to balance the intransigence of some of his member unions with the moral imperative of racial equality. Ultimately, he relented and helped develop this compromise position, thus maintaining the power of the federation through the inclusion of influential unions, while offering a limited opportunity to Black workers.

Bernard Mandel offers a harsh assessment of Gompers's actions. In Mandel's opinion, by developing policies that allowed for the persistence of racism in some unions, Gompers "sacrificed both his principles and the Negro workingmen, as well as the broader interests of the whole labor movement, to the short-sighted and selfish demands of the aristocratic officialdom of the craft unions, whose spokesman he had agreed to be."[77] Other historians are more sympathetic, recognizing the pressures that led Gompers to accede to segregated organizations.[78]

Unsurprisingly, the new union structure did little to relieve the plight of Black workers. These Black unions came into existence by agreement with the white parent bodies, which negotiated on their behalf, often providing ineffective representation at the bargaining table. As Dorothy Cobble notes, members paid "inflated dues to the Federation for minimal institutional support in negotiations with employers, and lacked equitable voting representation in Federation affairs."[79]

In 1919, the AFL, still confronting recalcitrant whites-only unions, amended its policy again, but continued to reject the option of expelling the offending organizations. The new process authorized completely separate Black unions, called Federated Unions, chartered directly by the AFL but *not* under the thumb of the white parent union.[80] Although the action was heralded in some newspaper reports as ending the AFL's color line,[81] this new policy constituted only marginal improvement in the federation's approach to racial exclusion.

Year after year, Black representatives submitted resolutions at AFL conventions demanding the removal of "whites only" clauses from union constitutions. The fate of two resolutions in 1920 illustrates the recalcitrance of the offending unions and the reluctance of the AFL to assume a strong moral stance. Resolution 5, submitted by the (Black) Freight Handlers, Station and Express Employes' [sic] Union No. 16220 of Richmond, addressed the

Brotherhood of Railway Clerks. Noting that there were about one hundred thousand Black employees serving under the supervision of the "whites only" Railway Clerks but barred from full membership, and assuring white members that "we are not trying for, nor do we want what is called 'social equality,'" they urged passage of a resolution demanding that the words "only white" be stricken from the Clerks' constitution and that Black workers be admitted to full membership. Alternatively, read their appeal, the Clerks should "allow the Black workers to establish a Brotherhood of their own." The review committee did not concur with the resolution, noting that the AFL could not "interfere with the trade autonomy of affiliated national and international unions" and that Black workers, by the ruling of 1919, could organize under direct AFL charters.[82]

Resolution 37, submitted at the same 1920 convention, pitted the Black Railway Coach Cleaners against the Brotherhood of Railway Carmen. It demanded that the AFL "prohibit any International Organization from adopting racial lines in their constitution." Once again, the weak response of the convention was a "recommendation" that the Carmen "eliminate from their constitution all reference to the admission of colored workers."[83]

Gompers kept trying, to no avail. In 1921, for example, after the AFL's Law Committee again disapproved of resolutions barring racial exclusion on the grounds that the organization couldn't interfere with "the trade autonomy" of its affiliated unions,[84] the convention instructed the Executive Council to call a meeting of the affected organizations. Gompers wrote repeatedly to these unions but never succeeded in organizing the requested meeting.

On the positive side, Eric Arnesen argues that despite the severe limitations, Black workers benefited to some extent from the AFL's new separate organizational structure, as it authorized them to control their own resources and engage directly in collective bargaining.[85] Earl Lewis even suggests that in some cases workers may have "preferred all-black locals," not only "because the social climate dictated such a structure," but also because "through them, they retained some element of control and power."[86] As we will see in the next chapter, these arguments rang true with Black musicians when they began to form separate locals of the AFM during the teens and twenties. Even though the musicians' union never had any exclusionary whites-only policy, Black musicians in the early twentieth century found that through separate locals they could more effectively lobby for equal rights, equal consideration, and most importantly, equal opportunity.

CHAPTER 3

The Formation of Black AFM Locals, 1897–1927

Once the AFL began forming Federated Unions for African American workers in 1900, the musicians' union initiated a similar process, approving the creation of independent all-Black locals. But whereas the AFL's Federated Unions represented an attempt—albeit a weak and rather ineffective one—at counteracting constitutional bans on Black workers in some of its affiliates, the AFM's role was simply to authorize the formation of segregated locals that were proposed by the Black musicians themselves. Eric Arnesen appropriately calls the AFM's structure "biracial unionism."[1]

That Black musicians provided the impetus for racially separate AFM unions is not at all to discount or diminish the deleterious effect of systemic racism. In fact, such attitudes and the resulting internal policies in some locals played a significant role in making a dual local structure attractive to African Americans. The national body, for its part, agreed to charter these locals with the caveat that the nearest existing (white) local give its approval.

First to take advantage of this opportunity were the African American musicians of Chicago, who formed Local 208 in mid-1902, followed in the fall of the same year by musicians in New Orleans and a month after that by those in East Liverpool, Ohio.[2] Of course, the AFM already had one Black local: Number 44, the "Great Western Union (Colored)" of St. Louis, which had formed independently prior to the establishment of the AFM, as noted in the previous chapter. The new locals chartered in 1902, however, set the scene for an explosion of such organizations over the next quarter century. It is not surprising that the musicians in Chicago and New Orleans led the way; both cities boasted of a large active African American music scene whose members explored the latest trends in popular culture.

The subsequent fate of these two Black locals was quite different, however. Local 242 in New Orleans lasted only three years. The federation suspended its charter in 1905 for nonpayment of dues[3] and another Black local did not form in that city until 1926. Similarly, the charter for the local in East Liverpool, Ohio, lapsed in 1906. Local 208 in Chicago, on the other hand, enjoyed a continuous existence until 1966, when it merged—after considerable struggle—with (white) Local 10. In the interim, Local 208 became the largest and most powerful Black union in the federation.

Table 3.1 shows all of the Black locals chartered up to 1927—sixty-six in all—with details of their subsequent histories. Fifteen of these locals (23 percent) survived without interruption until amalgamation with the white unions in their areas. These cases are designated in the table by the notation "continuous until merger" in column 4. Notable among them is Local 767 in Los Angeles (chartered in 1920), which in 1953 became the first Black local to merge with its white counterpart. Conditions in Los Angeles made the case for merger particularly strong, but even there, some of the older members of the Black local resisted. The complex negotiations and the fallout in terms of the decline of the lively Central Avenue music scene will be the subject of detailed discussion in chapter 7.

Even a cursory examination of this table shows that most of the Black locals had complex histories. In many cases charters lapsed because membership fell below the prescribed level, or the AFM's International Executive Board (IEB) revoked charters due to poor management or alleged failures to adhere to various policies. When a charter lapsed, its number was reassigned to another local in a different city. If a new local then arose in the original city, it received the next available open number, which could be higher or lower than that of the previous local. For example, Black Local 635 in Dayton received a charter in 1913. Column 4 shows that its charter was "erased" in 1929. Then a new Black local formed in 1939 and was assigned the (lower) number 473.

Because locals disappeared and new ones received charters each month, keeping track of the history of the AFM's locals is a complex task. Obfuscating matters further, the federation's unpublished *Charter Book* uses a variety of terms to document the disbandment of a local: "lapsed" or "expired" indicates that membership had fallen below the prescribed threshold or that the local was out of compliance with federation guidelines. "Suspended" has a similar meaning but particularly suggests nonpayment of dues. Charters that were "revoked," "erased," or "canceled," on the other hand, suggest direct action by the IEB in response to accusations of poor management or rule violations. (As we will see, such accusations often arose out of the

Table 3.1. Black Locals Chartered by the AFM between 1897 and 1927 (Officially Called "Colored Locals" in AFM Documents)

Year Chartered	Local No.	City	Subsequent Activity and/or Later Black Locals	Merger w White Local (Year/Local #)
1897	44	St. Louis, MO	1932: Charter revoked; becomes subsidiary. 1944: Black local 197	1971 w Local 2
1902	208	Chicago, IL	Continuous until merger	1966 w Local 10
	242	New Orleans, LA	1905: Charter suspended. 1926: Black local 496	1970 w Local 174
	253	E Liverpool, OH	1906: Charter lapsed	(no merger)
1903	305	Buxton, IA	1919: Charter lapsed	(no merger)
1908	471	Pittsburgh, PA	Continuous until merger	1966 w Local 60
1910	550	Cleveland, OH	Continuous until merger	1962 w Local 4
1912	589	Columbus, OH	Continuous until merger	1960 w Local 103
1913	635	Dayton, OH	1929: Charter erased. 1939: Black local 473	1970 w Local 101
1914	675	Springfield, IL	Continuous until merger	1966 w Local 19
1915	591	Philadelphia, PA	1930: Charter suspended. 1935: Black local 274. 1971: Charter canceled	(no merger)
	535	Boston, MA	Continuous until merger	1970 w Local 9
1916	702	Jacksonville, FL	1920: Charter lapsed. 1942: Black local 632. 1959: Charter revoked	1959: mbrs join Local 444
	185	Parkersville, WV	Continuous until merger	1965 w Local 259
1917	533	Buffalo, NY	Continuous until merger	1969 w Local 43
	627	Kansas City, MO	1932: Charter revoked. 1933: Charter reinstated	1970 w Local 34
	706	Pittsburg, KS	1926: Charter revoked	(no merger)
1918	543	Baltimore, MD	Continuous until merger	1966 w Local 40
	458	Seattle, WA	1924: Charter revoked, replaced by Black local 493	1958 w Local 76
	666	Martins Ferry, OH	1932: Charter revoked. 1946: Black local 692. 1950: Charter canceled	(no merger)
	584	Paducah, KY	1929: Charter erased, then restored. 1932: Charter revoked, then restored. 1935: Charter revoked	(no merger)
	538	Evanston, WY	1928: Charter revoked	(no merger)

Table 3.1. (continued)

Year	Local	City	Notes	Merger
1919	708	Atlantic City	1934: Charter revoked, becomes subsidiary.* 1945: Charter reinstated	1969 w Local 661
	168	Dallas, TX	Continuous until merger	1965 w Local 147
	242	Youngstown, OH	Continuous until merger	1969 w Local 86
	465	Mobile, AL	1933: Charter canceled. 1942: Black local 613	1968 w Local 407
	305	Charleston, WV	1923: Charter surrendered	(no merger)
	745	Sioux City, IA	1926: Charter revoked. 1927: Black local 743	1960 w Local 254
1920	753	Denver, CO	1932: Charter revoked. 1938: Black local 623	1960 w Local 20
	767	Los Angeles, CA	Continuous until merger.**	1953 w Local 47
	702	San Antonio, TX	1924: Charter lapsed. 1947: Black local 658	1965 w Local 23
	632	Des Moines, IA	1939: Charter revoked. 1945: Black local 799. 1947: 799's charter revoked; Black local 740 established. 1956: Charter revoked	1956: Integration w Local 75
1921	558	Omaha, NE	1924: Charter lapsed, then restored	1967 w Local 70
	781	Memphis, TN	1924: Charter revoked	(no merger)
	782	Springfield, OH	1932: Charter returned	(no merger)
	783	Topeka, KS	1926: Charter revoked. 1947: Black local 665	1968 w Local 36
	799	Indianapolis, IN	1924: Charter revoked. 1931: Black local 300 chartered then revoked	(no merger)
1922	775	Richmond, VA	1928: Charter revoked. 1929: Black local 38. 1940: becomes subsidiary. 1945: Black local 695. 1959: Charter canceled	(no merger)
	710	Washington, DC	Continuous until merger	1967 w Local 161
	520	Trenton, NJ	1930: Charter revoked, then restored. 1932: Charter revoked	(no merger)
	813	Zanesville, OH	1928: Charter revoked, then restored; 1929: Charter erased	(no merger)
	814	Cincinnati, OH	1970: Charter canceled	(no merger)
	548	Wilkes Barre, PA	1926: Charter revoked	(no merger)
	602	Terre Haute, IN	1928: Charter revoked	(no merger)
1923	449	Wilmington, DE	1933: Charter revoked. 1939: Black local 641	1968 w Local 311
	676	Norfolk, VA	1928: Charter surrendered. 1945: Black local 702	1966 w Local 125
	523	Gary, IN	1929: Charter revoked. 1938: Black local 622.	1956 w Local 203
	648	San Francisco, CA	1934: Charter revoked. 1935: becomes subsidiary. 1946: Black local 669	1960 w Local 6
	722	Cairo, IL	1927: Charter revoked	(no merger)

Table 3.1. (continued)

1924	286	Toledo, OH	Continuous until merger	1970 w Local 15
	486	New Haven, CT	Continuous until merger	1966 w Local 234
	587	Milwaukee, WI	Continuous until merger	1966 w Local 8
1925	335	Jacksonville, IL	1928: Charter moved to Hartford, CT. 1930: Charter lapsed. 1931: Charter restored; 1961: Charter revoked	(no merger)
	495	Sacramento, CA	1926: Charter revoked	(no merger)
	570	Erie, PA	1928: Charter lapsed	(no merger)
1926	177	Lafayette, IN	1928: Charter lapsed	(no merger)
	513	Houston, TX	1931: Charter revoked. 1950: Black local 699	1966 w Local 65
	548	Annapolis, MD	1929: Charter erased	(no merger)
	681	Salt Lake City, UT	1929: Charter revoked	(no merger)
	695	Chester, PA	1930: Charter revoked	(no merger)
	496	New Orleans, LA	(See Local 242, 1902 above); 496 continuous until merger	1970 w Local 174
1927	482	Beaumont, TX	1928: Charter lapsed	(no merger)
	718	Harrisburg, PA	1935: Charter revoked	(no merger)
	733	Birmingham, AL	1936: Charter revoked, then restored	1969 w Local 256
	740	Muskogee, OK	1929: Charter revoked	(no merger)
	722	San Diego, CA	1936: Charter revoked	(no merger)

* Atlantic City: prior to the revocation in 1934, there was a lapse, then a reinstatement, a revocation, a restoration, and another lapse. Thanks to Dan DeRienzo for this information.

**Los Angeles: The 1953 merger of Locals 767 and 47 was the first among all segregated locals.

The information in this chart derives from three sources: (1) the secretary's reports in the annual *Official Proceedings*; (2) reports in the AFM's monthly magazine, the *International Musician* (IM); and (3) information entered in the AFM's unpublished *Charter Book*. In some cases, information from these sources conflicts. In those cases, I have tried to determine the most reliable dates. Often the dates in the *Charter Book* differ by a year from those given in the *Official Proceedings* or the *IM*. The problem might be a difference between the issuance of a lapse or revocation and the date when it took effect. In minor instances such as these, I have adopted the date given in the *Charter Book*. Thanks to Dan DeRienzo at the national AFM office, who checked the AFM's *Charter Book* for a multiplicity of conflicting dates or missing information. This unpublished *Charter Book* was not available for me to consult directly. Without Dan DeRienzo's help, I would not have been able to resolve numerous conflicts and questions.

Charter terminology: "lapsed" or "expired" = membership below prescribed threshold; out of compliance. "Revoked," "erased," or "canceled" = poor management of local; violations, etc. "Surrendered" = local approaches the AFM's International Executive Board (IEB) to discuss termination. "Suspended" = lapsed (particularly because of nonpayment of dues). "Returned" = surrendered.

white local in the area, which could conveniently use this tactic to eliminate the direct competition posed by the Black local.) Charters "surrendered" or "returned" indicate preemptive action by the local, which approached the International to discuss termination. No further explanation of the reasons for dissolution appears in the *Charter Book*, but occasionally there are discussions in the minutes of the International Executive Board meetings, printed in the federation's monthly magazine, the *International Musician* and in the *Official Proceedings* of the annual conventions.

In numerous cases no Black locals replaced those that dissolved: see, for example, East Liverpool, Ohio; Buxton, Iowa; Pittsburg, Kansas; Evanston, Wyoming; Charleston, West Virginia; Memphis, Tennessee; Wilkes Barre, Erie, Chester, and Harrisburg, Pennsylvania; Terre Haute and Lafayette, Indiana; Cairo, Illinois; Sacramento and San Diego, California; Salt Lake City, Utah; Annapolis, Maryland; and others. In these cases, of course, there was never any merger with the white local in the same city because the Black local had permanently disappeared. Column 5 contains the indication "(no merger)" in these instances.

In many other cases, however, new Black locals (with different numbers) formed several years later. For example, Local 465 in Mobile, Alabama received a charter in 1919. It survived until 1933, when its charter was canceled. In 1942, Black Local 613 received a charter in the same city and in 1968 it merged with (white) Local 407, as shown in column 5. Readers can examine column 4 to see similar cases: for instance, Sioux City, Iowa; Topeka, Kansas; Wilmington, Delaware; Norfolk, Virginia; and Houston, Texas. In other cases, however, the second Black local failed to survive as well (e.g., Martins Ferry and Zanesville, Ohio; Trenton, New Jersey). In a few cases, racial integration took place without formal merger agreements (a situation discussed in chapter 8).

Cincinnati (Local 814) and Philadelphia (Local 591, superseded by Local 274) are special cases. Both Black locals refused to merge with the white locals in their cities and the AFM was forced to cancel their charters in the final stage of the merger process in order to end segregation in the federation. The situation in Philadelphia has already been described in detail in chapter 1. Cincinnati followed a similar path.

Four locals listed in Table 3.1 became "subsidiaries" of their corresponding white locals during the 1930s: St. Louis, San Francisco, Atlantic City, and Richmond. (Eight more subsidiaries also formed in other cities in the same period.) These cases mark a nadir in relations between the Black groups and the national organization. The IEB revoked their charters and their members became nonvoting participants in the much larger white locals in the same city. The Black locals in question simply disappeared from the listings in the *Official Proceedings*. Although their members technically became part of the white local, the Black musicians had no voting rights, no access to union facilities, and no voice in decision-making. Unfortunately, some sources—even a few that are otherwise dependable—erroneously confuse "subsidiary local" with "colored local."[4] It is crucial to draw a distinction. "Colored" locals were independent bodies, had the same rights as (predominantly) white locals, and arose at the urging of Black musicians. Subsidiaries resulted from mandates by the federation and involved severe restrictions. As one member of St. Louis's Subsidiary 2 asserted, they amounted to taxation without representation.[5] In chapter 5 we will look in detail at two cases: St. Louis's Subsidiary Local 2, which formed after the IEB revoked Local 44's charter in 1932 at the request of (white) Local 2, and San Francisco's Subsidiary Local 6, which formed in 1935 following a lawsuit filed by members of Black Local 648.

The number of subsidiaries was always small, and in 1944 the AFM abolished all of them. There were, at that time, a dozen. Thereafter, new Black locals formed in most of these cities and in at least one case, the members of the subsidiary became full voting members of the parent organization (see chapter 6).

The AFM's aggressive recruitment efforts in the early twentieth century led to the chartering of locals in some quite small towns; in most cases, these units did not survive for long. One intriguing example is Buxton, Iowa, the majority of whose residents were African American. Buxton was established by the Consolidation Coal Company (owned by the Chicago and North Western Railroad), which aggressively recruited Black workers, many from the Southern states. By 1905, 2,700 of Buxton's 4,691 residents were African American.[6] The town was a thriving municipality with numerous professionals, state-of-the-art recreation facilities, a baseball team, and many musical organizations, including choral groups, a glee club, and several bands. The most prominent ensemble was the Buxton Band, which traveled throughout the region, but the town's cornet band was also popular; the *Iowa State Bystander*, a Black newspaper founded in Des Moines in 1894, highlighted one performance of the group on Emancipation Day, 1901.[7] The AFM issued a charter to Buxton's musicians in 1903.[8] By the time the charter expired in 1919, the town had only four hundred residents. It is now a ghost town.

Applications by Black musicians to form independent, racially separated locals became most numerous in the years following the First World War.

Table 3.1 above graphically illustrates the explosion of such Black locals in this period: from 1918 to 1927 there were often five or more of them chartered each year. The reasons why the Black locals took shape in this period (or indeed why they developed at all) are complex and multifaceted. These motivations are explored in general below and fleshed out in detail in the chapters that follow. One might assume that combatting racism was the overriding factor, but as we examine individual cases we will note that practical concerns often emerge as predominant. In fact, in contrast to Chicago, where Black musicians faced direct refusal for admission by Local 10, most other locals were racially integrated until the African Americans broke away to form independent organizations. Indeed, the issues of race and employment opportunities in the AFM became so intertwined that Black musicians felt a need to establish their own unions in order to ensure fair treatment in the marketplace. Because the AFM's structure gave locals wide latitude and exceptional control over workplace negotiations, African American musicians determined that it was in their best interests to establish segregated units. Furthermore, Black musicians identified closely with the struggles of Black AFL workers outside of music.

In a discussion of the breakaway by African Americans from the multiracial local in Boston in 1915, Stephen Laifer generalizes (and oversimplifies) their motivation as a desire "to have their own identity."[9] This benign statement, though defensible, belies a number of far more practical considerations, however. Eric Arnesen, discussing labor unions in general in this period, succinctly summarizes them: "Black trade unionists," he argues, "might view separate locals as a way of avoiding abusive treatment by whites, controlling their own resources, strengthening their position, and reaping the fruits of collective action."[10] In the case of the AFM, the benefits noted by Arnesen translate into three specific advantages: defining the skill level and musical experience required to become a member (that is, managing the audition process), controlling pay scales, and securing representation at national conventions.

Motivations for Establishing Segregated Locals (1): The Audition and Its Role in Defining Musical Professionalism

Although a resolution at the AFM's first convention defined a "professional musician" as anyone "who receives pay for his musical services," the federation also instituted, at that same convention, a test of an applicant's musical expertise. "Every local," states this resolution, "shall appoint or elect an Examination Board to pass upon the eligibility of applicants for membership"[11]—that is, locals were to administer entrance auditions.

This requirement resembles those by other craft unions, which would typically demand proof of expertise before granting admission. However, in the case of the musicians, tension arose between those who favored limiting membership to artists with proven skills and those who wished to include all working musicians,[12] a disagreement reminiscent of the concerns of the NLM and one that would lead to a major crisis within the AFM in 1920.

Some relaxation in the enforcement of the audition requirement was evident as early as 1904, when AFM president Joseph Weber wrote that "every Instrumental Performer receiving remuneration for his services is eligible for membership."[13] This broad statement allowed for the admission, without audition, of some "professional" musicians—that is, those "receiving pay for musical services."

Being "eligible" for membership, of course, did not guarantee automatic admission, and in the federation's early years the audition was administered throughout the country. Individual locals determined the nature of the examination and in many—perhaps the majority of—cases, they prioritized music reading fluency, knowledge of Western classical works, and sight-reading. Furthermore, they determined on a local basis the level of demonstrated skill required to pass, a judgment that might be subjective and could potentially allow for the consideration of nonmusical issues such as race, even when locals denied such prejudice.

The emphasis on musical literacy and familiarity with the Western classical canon reflects the hierarchization of high/low artistic expressions cited in chapter 1. As Lawrence Levine has eloquently recounted, the eclecticism pervasive in all the arts earlier in the nineteenth century, manifest in programs mixing vastly diverse expressions that attracted heterogenous audiences, gave way near the century's end to a stratification of artistic valuation that prioritized highbrow culture not only in music, but also in theater, museums, and other cultural institutions. Performances of Shakespeare, for example, had previously attracted large and diverse audiences by accepting alterations of, and abridgments to, the text in order to make the works comprehensible to audiences with various educational backgrounds. Popular parodic treatments also attracted diverse attendees, but depended on the audience members' familiarity with the Bard's works. Combination programs typically mixed genres; Shakespeare might share the stage with popular theatrical acts and even acrobatics. These bowdlerized productions declined near the end of the century in favor of purist interpretations directed to select, "refined" audiences. The emphasis changed from entertainment to education.[14]

Why did this sacralization of "high art" take place? One factor noted by Levine was the influx of foreign immigrants, who brought with them perceptions of hierarchical rankings in music, art, and theater. Indeed, the substantial immigration to the United States of musicians in this period, particularly German instrumentalists and Italian vocalists, encouraged the elevation of the Western canon to a semireligious status—a divine art with cleansing and uplifting properties. Influential publications such as *Dwight's Journal* encouraged such stratification of musical styles, as did forceful personalities such as conductor Theodore Thomas, who strived mightily to "uplift" the general population through the cult of classical music, presented for the edification of audiences and supported by wealthy patrons. The AFM was thus torn by conflicting allegiances. On the one hand, union officials strove to enlist as many musicians as possible. On the other hand, the aesthetic preferences of the era directed attention to the educational value of "good" music and the audition requirements prioritized knowledge as exemplified by musical literacy, with a bow to the white-dominated musical culture.

The audition's determination of the applicants' level of professionalism frequently revealed the nature of their individualized training. Black musicians often developed proficiency through nontraditional instructional paths; at times they were even self-taught. Their skill was often manifest in the imaginative ways they could vary a melodic line and its harmonic underpinning through improvisation in much the same way as nineteenth-century theatrical performances built new works around creative reinterpretations of Shakespeare. Expert improvisation requires exceptional aural skills, namely the ability to listen to a musical passage, commit it to memory, and then communicate it with creative variation. These musical accomplishments differ in many respects from the equally demanding technical and musical skills required for accurate realization and interpretation of a fixed score. The prioritization of the latter in the typical AFM audition reflected the sacralization of "high" musical culture enhanced by European immigration at the end of the century. How, in the context of the new aesthetic valuation, should the skill of Black improvisers be appropriately evaluated and compared to those with traditional training and current musical priorities?

Race thus complicated the old issues that had undermined the NLM. In addition, an inherent tension arose between the perception of musicians as skilled craftspeople or as employees in an industry, or, as was frequently the case, both.[15] More crucially, the audition requirements raised the fundamental question of the definition of professionalism and in the process challenged the effectiveness of unionization for musicians with a wide range of training and varying aims in terms of artistic expression. In view of the AFM's overriding control over casual employment, however, Black musicians could not simply ignore the union. Membership was a necessity for them to piece together a living through work in these venues.

How applicants' acquired skills should be measured in terms of mastery of various genres and in consideration of the performance venues they found most gratifying became a fundamental issue driving the formation of many Black locals in the federation. With their own locals, Black union officials could test applicants for their facility on their instruments without prioritizing music reading skills; they could assess mastery of popular music styles; and they could relate the union's employment efforts to the most appropriate and desirable available opportunities. In terms of Arnesen's practical considerations listed above, Black musicians might well have viewed the implementation of their own audition criteria as "avoiding abusive [read: racially biased] treatment by whites."

By the mid-twentieth century, the audition requirement had changed substantially. It first became a formality in many cities[16] and then the AFM made it optional. From 1955 onward, the bylaws read: "Locals *may* [italics mine] appoint or elect an Examination Board to pass upon the eligibility of applicants for membership."[17]

The debate between limiting membership to artists with proven skills versus welcoming all working musicians lay at the heart of the federation's most serious crisis, a revolt by its largest affiliate, New York's Local 310 (which was later replaced by Local 802). The disagreement was sparked in 1920 by a theatrical wage settlement negotiated by the federation that the local found inadequate, but on a deeper level it reflected 310's discomfort with the AFM's attempts to favor increased membership numbers over demonstrated skills. The New York local's "compliance with the universal membership law had always been grudging,"[18] notes Vern Countryman.

In addition, the local had become impatient with the transfer cards; New York was inundated with them as musicians throughout the country sought to perform temporarily in the nation's largest city. Local 310 started rejecting some of those transfers. In response, the federation dissolved Local 310 in July 1921, and the next month chartered a new local (802) upon petition from a thousand city musicians. To the chagrin of Local 802, however, the International Executive Board assumed ongoing control over the appointment of the local's governing board. On May 8, 1922, Local 310 appealed the revocation of its charter to the federation and two years later initiated an action in New York Superior Court seeking its reinstatement. Both efforts failed.[19] The dispute between Local 802 and the International continued for another thirteen years; it was not resolved until 1934.[20]

Motivations for Establishing Segregated Locals (2): Pay Scales

A second motivation for establishing segregated locals was the opportunity to institute competitive pay scales. With independent locals, the Black musicians could charge lower fees than the white locals and thereby attract desirable work (undercutting their competitors in the process). In Arnesen's terms, they could control their own resources.

In fact, in the society at large in this era, the prevailing assumption was that Black workers would be paid less than whites. One report from a slightly later time provides an instructive example. In the early 1940s, the AFM negotiated pay raises with the Ringling Brothers Circus. Richard Leiter asserts with some pride that the union would not countenance discriminatory treatment, but his concluding remarks tell a rather different story, underscoring the assumption of a racially determined pay differential: "Eventually the salaries of the white musicians were raised from $47.50 to $54.00 per week, while those of the Negroes were increased from $26.50 to $30.50."[21] (In addition, African Americans only played in sideshows.)

Such wage disparities based on race were common throughout the country and could only be breached occasionally by bold action. For instance, Lloyd Smith, saxophonist and flutist from St. Louis, recalls that jobs on riverboats in the 1920s paid about $35 a night to Black musicians but $50 to whites.[22] Smith and his Black colleagues in a band led by Fate Marable decided to confront the ship's captain about the wage differential and demand the same pay as whites in similar bands. The captain refused their demands and Smith left the job—but only temporarily, as it turned out. "About a week later, the people began to call for the flute," Smith recalled. The captain called Smith back at a rate of $60, which infuriated his band colleagues. "I came back, he gave me sixty dollars a week and the white band make fifty and they [the other Black musicians] was making thirty-five. Fate was making five dollars more as the leader."[23]

Smith's success was not common, however, and segregated locals could provide Black musicians with the opportunity to work at rewarding jobs in a highly competitive field. In a multiracial local, contractors would have to pay all members the same wage for the same type of work regardless of race (or any other factor, for that matter). Blacks legitimately feared that employers would decline to hire them in such circumstances. With their own locals, however, they could determine their own scale. They might have to work for less, but at least they could work.

Many Black locals decided that setting up a lower fee scale than their white competitors was necessary both to counter systemic racism and to offset the outsized influence enjoyed by the much larger white locals. Unsurprisingly, agreeing to play at a lower rate than that charged by white musicians in the same venues led to major conflicts. The white locals typically tried to demand that Black locals adopt their pay scale. Black musicians resisted, reasonably countering that doing so would undermine their chances to work. These wage differentials led to numerous formal complaints by whites to the national office. Among many examples was Seattle, discussed in the next chapter.

Motivations for Establishing Segregated Locals (3): National Representation

A final reason for establishing independent Black locals concerned representation at the national conventions. Because every local was guaranteed at least one delegate and one vote, the new Black locals secured a guaranteed voice on the national scene. If their membership exceeded 150, they would acquire a second vote, and the number of votes increased for every majority fraction over a hundred. By 1926, Chicago's Local 208 had 400 members and therefore four votes; Local 44 in St. Louis had 154 members and two votes. Thus, Black musicians could, in Arnesen's terms, strengthen their position and "reap the fruits of collective action."

Interestingly, however, an examination of the attendance at the conventions during the 1920s shows that many Black locals did not take advantage of their opportunity to send representatives. In 1926, for example, delegates from only four of the Black locals listed in Table 3.1 above appeared at the convention: Local 208 (Chicago), Local 44 (St. Louis), Local 535 (Boston; 110 members, 1 vote), and Local 589 (Columbus, Ohio; 155 members, 2 votes). We can only guess why the others failed to appear, but it is likely that the smaller AFM locals did not have sufficient funds to cover travel and housing expenses for delegates, and individuals would naturally be reluctant to bear the considerable expense of subsidizing their own trips. This situation changed dramatically in later years. In 1946, for example, forty-one representatives from thirty-two Black locals attended the convention.[24]

The AFM's rule that to form an independent local required acquiescence from the nearest existing local offered the opportunity for white unions to block the establishment of Black locals, arguing that they would create unfair competition. In the next chapter we will examine the situation in San Francisco, where Local 6 refused to grant permission in 1916 and prevented a Black local from forming until 1923.

The New York Local Squelches Attempts to Form a Black Affiliate

New York presents a more complex situation. Its local has often been praised in writings about the AFM for maintaining a racially integrated union throughout its history. A deeper exploration of its history, however, reveals that the New York white unionists, through deft negotiating, thwarted the formation of a Black local.

Unlike other cities, Black musicians in New York had the option of an alternative representative body during the second decade of the twentieth century. The famous Clef Club, founded by James Reese Europe in 1910, not only provided a social and performance space for Blacks, but also acted as an effective labor exchange—a direct challenge to AFM Local 310's lively hiring hall. Eileen Southern describes the Clef Club and the slightly later Tempo Club, also founded by Jim Europe, as organizations that "combined the functions of a musician's union and a contracting service."[25] Fueling the Clef Club's success in providing work for Black musicians was the high demand for their services throughout the city. "Any Clef Club member not working on a steady engagement could just go to the clubrooms where the phone would soon ring bringing a call from one of the hotels or restaurants," recalled Tom Fletcher in 1954. "The colored musicians . . . had every amusement place outside of legitimate theaters sewed up."[26] A 1915 editorial by the NAACP's James Weldon Johnson substantiates Fletcher's claim. Johnson commented acerbically on a complaint by a white New York musician that "the Negro musician is to-day engaged at most of the functions given by society, especially its dances."[27] Johnson retorted that the overwhelming preference for Black musicians stemmed from their expertise, their musical ability, and "a certain abandon" that they put into their performances. There was plenty of work available and the Black performers did not have to acquiesce to an audition process prioritizing Western classical repertoire.

Fletcher recalled that in this period Jim Europe, the Clef Club's president, explored the possibility of founding a Black local in New York comparable to Chicago's Local 208, of which he was a member. Europe reputedly wrote to the governor to investigate securing a charter for an independent Black local but learned that he would need permission from New York City's Local 310.

To this end, Black musicians in March 1914 met with officials from 310, who, instead of giving their permission, offered them "a special dispensation" that included a "modified" audition and an offer to spread out the payment of the $100 initiation fee over four years.[28] The Black musicians were divided over this proposal, some of them suspecting that the officers of 310 had ulterior motives for devising the "special dispensation."[29] Indeed, by enticing these applicants to join their union through a modification of the audition, 310 staved off the possibility of an independent Black local in New York.

"Most of those present promptly joined," recalled Fletcher.[30] According to Jacob Goldberg, the New Amsterdam Musical Association, which today advertises itself as "the oldest African-American musical organization in the United States" and "the first black music union,"[31] had similarly agitated for a Black local in 1909 and met with the same offer from the board of Local 310.[32] The New York local managed to prevent permanently the formation of a competing Black local and it remained racially integrated throughout its history (even after its reincarnation as Local 802 in 1921).

Other large cities without separate Black units include Detroit and Newark. Bassist William ("Bill") May joined Local 16 in Newark in 1967 and eventually became its president.[33] He notes that although the Newark local was racially integrated, the jobs at the time he joined were not. There was de facto segregation in terms of employment, says May, and Black musicians rarely played in the largest union-controlled clubs. Because the jobs were segregated, May could circumvent Local 16's rules and play at times with nonunion performers. If the business manager of Local 16 showed up, he'd quickly disappear to avoid being fined. The nonunion personnel at the engagement would have to join the AFM on the spot.[34]

Black Locals and Black Political Activism

The emergence of so many Black locals in the period covered in Table 3.1 is hardly surprising in view of the dramatic rise in African American activism in the post–World War I era. Black soldiers returned home from the Great War with new determination to fight for their civil rights after demonstrating their bravery and loyalty to the country on the battlefield. One measure of this new determination is the growing membership in the NAACP. Founded in 1909 and at first "led by white do-gooders,"[35] the organization expanded rapidly, largely through the efforts of W. E. B. Du Bois, James Weldon Johnson, and Walter White. At the beginning of 1918 it had 9,200 members; by April 1919 membership had swelled to 51,023 and its journal, aptly named *The Crisis*, reached close to 100,000 readers.[36]

Unfortunately, there was equally strong pushback from racists fearing the end to white dominance in the country. The Ku Klux Klan, which had been suppressed through federal intervention in the early 1870s, saw a revival in 1915 in Atlanta. A spate of racist books also appeared in this period. In *Red Summer*, Cameron McWhirter highlights some of the most egregious: Robert Wilson Shufeldt's *The Negro, a Menace to American Civilization*, which asserted that Blacks had smaller brains than whites and were by nature savage, immoral, and barbarous (1907);[37] Charles H. McCord's *The American Negro as a Dependent, Defective and Delinquent* (1914); Cecil Chesterton's *A History of the United States* (1919); eugenics proponent Madison Grant's infamous *The Passing of the Great Race* (1916), which asserted Nordic superiority and even advocated selective breeding, for which stances it was warmly embraced by Hitler and the Nazi movement; and Lothrop Stoddard's *The Rising Tide of Color Against White World-Supremacy*, a bestseller that appeared in 1920 and predicted the collapse of white supremacy due to population growth among people of color. These books and others stoked fear among many whites. In addition, Oswald Spengler's *The Decline of the West* first appeared in English translation in 1919 while David Wark Griffith's racist film *The Birth of a Nation* (1915) was still packing the theaters. More than seventy Blacks were lynched in the first year after the war.[38]

The "Red Summer" of 1919, a term coined by James Weldon Johnson, "ushered in the greatest period of interracial strife the nation has ever witnessed," wrote John Hope Franklin in 1967. Jobs were less plentiful than during the war years, he notes, and rents climbed in segregated areas. "When it became clear that many whites were seeking to deprive them of some of the gains they had made during the war, Negroes bristled into action and showed a willingness to defend themselves that they had not shown before."[39] Indeed, McWhirter discusses violent race riots—which in fact amounted to anti-Black rampages—in twenty-five U.S. cities between April and November 1919. Black reaction was not to retreat but rather to endorse energetic and outspoken struggle. "While economic and political forces sparked a great spasm of white mob violence in 1919," writes McWhirter, "those same forces also awakened black resistance."

> By midyear, African Americans started to organize themselves with an energy and in numbers not witnessed since Reconstruction. Black groups had struggled for civil rights through decades of Jim Crow, but black political activism did not become a substantial force in American politics until the Red Summer. . . . Black reaction to the violence, the return of legions of soldiers, an increase in earnings for many black

workers, the migration of tens of thousands of blacks to the North, and an emboldened black press all combined in 1919 to create an unprecedented political awakening.[40]

A poem by Claude McKay, which became a rallying cry for African Americans seeking racial justice, appeared in the July 1919 issue of the socialist magazine *The Liberator* and captured the new spirit of resistance in the face of racial hatred.

> If we must die, let it not be like hogs
> Hunted and penned in an inglorious spot,
> While round us bark the mad and hungry dogs,
> Making their mock at our accursed lot.
> If we must die, let it not be like hogs
> So that our precious blood may not be shed
> In vain; then even the monsters we defy
> Shall be constrained to honor us, though dead!
> Oh, kinsman! We must meet the common foe;
> Though far outnumbered, let us still be brave,
> And for their thousand blows deal one deathblow!
> What though before us lies the open grave?
> Like men we'll face the murderous, cowardly pack
> Pressed to the wall, dying, but—fighting back!

Ten years later, V. F. Calverton (aka George Goetz) wrote in his introductory essay to the *Anthology of American Negro Literature*, that "the submissive acquiescences of the Booker T. Washington attitude and era have now become contemptuously anachronistic."

> The sentimental cry of a nineteenth century poet such as Corrothers ... has been superseded by the charging defiance of a twentieth century poet such as McKay.... The admission of inferiority which was implicit in so much of the earlier verse, the supplicatory note which ran like a lugubrious echo through so many of its stanzas, has been supplanted by an attitude of superiority and independence.[41]

The first appearance of McKay's poem in a socialist publication also exemplified the concern of some Black leaders that African Americans were increasingly vilified as radicals, socialists, and communists, adding to the racist propaganda of the era. In the middle of 1919, A. Philip Randolph and Chandler Owen published an editorial in the Black-run political and literary magazine, *The Messenger*. "The American Federation of Labor," they wrote, "has either ignored or opposed Negro workers.... No systematic effort has been made to arouse the interest and enlist the support of the Negro . . . with the exception, only recently, of the socialist Party of New York."

> Negroes must learn to differentiate between white capitalists and white workers; as yet they only see white men against black men. . . . Inasmuch as he thinks that all white men are his enemies, he is inclined to direct his hate at white employers as he is to direct it at white workers.
>
> Hence the editors of the Messenger sound this note of warning to the white ruling and working-class in America of a gathering race storm which can only be averted by more sober, enlightened and dispassionate studying of the problem, with the purpose of removing the cause of an impending explosion.
>
> Organized labor must harness the discontent of Negroes and direct it into working-class channels for working-class emancipation.[42]

In this charged climate, the formation of so many Black locals in the AFM takes on sharper focus. It was but one manifestation of the increasing activism by Black citizens—one of many efforts by African Americans to claim their civil and legal rights—in this case, in the area of equal employment opportunities, equal wages, and equal working conditions for the country's musicians.

CHAPTER 4

Early Black Locals
Three Case Studies

This chapter details the early history of three Black locals whose formation reflects the range of issues prompting African American musicians to form segregated units. In Chicago, overt racism blocked the entry of Blacks into the influential Local 10, prompting the formation of Local 208. San Francisco's Local 6, on the other hand, admitted some Black members from its inception, but other musicians failed the audition requirement, thereby barring them from working in the city. When Black musicians proposed forming their own local, Local 6 succeeded in preventing that action for seven years. In Seattle, a Black local did form despite evidence of racist attitudes by white unionists, but conflicts with the white local arose over pay scales and work rules.

In part these differing histories resulted from different demographics—the absolute number of Black musicians in the city, but more critically, the degree of geographical separation in housing and in the entertainment scene. As we will see, Chicago Blacks were able to forge a successful work culture due to their large numbers in the community and the active club culture that developed in the extensive, but confined south part of the city. These clubs welcomed patrons of both races but Black performers could not, for the most part, penetrate the venues in the northern white areas. In San Francisco and Seattle, on the other hand, the number of African American musicians was small enough, and the housing and club scene was dispersed enough, that Black and white musicians found themselves in direct competition for the same jobs. Ironically, the more open cities were to racially integrated housing areas, the greater was the competition for jobs and the more difficulties Black musicians faced in securing satisfying work.

These case studies exemplify the advantages and problems inherent in the dual-union structure and the resistance on the part of the white locals to the competition posed by Black organizations. The formation of Black unions, as noted previously, depended on acquiescence from white locals; once formed, however, these Black locals offered notable advantages to their members for a number of years. Eventually, however, conflicts overwhelmed this inherently unstable structure and a difficult transition to amalgamation ensued that absorbed the federation's attention for nearly two decades. The ramifications of this policy, which initially seemed to be helpful to African Americans, still resound today.

Chicago

Most writings on the AFM state (erroneously) that Chicago's Local 208 was the federation's first Black unit. As we have seen, Local 44 in St. Louis claims this honor, predating the Chicago union by five years after the AFM issued its formal charter in 1897. Nevertheless, because the St. Louis group had existed as an affiliate of the AFL prior to the AFM's formation, Chicago's 208, chartered in 1902, holds the distinction of being the first Black organization authorized directly by the federation after its formation. Due to its pioneering history and its dominance as the largest Black local in the federation, Chicago's 208 has attracted greater attention from researchers than any other African American local.[1]

Local 208 arose through the efforts of two musicians from the Eighth Illinois National Guard Regimental Band: the director, Alexander Armant (who became the local's first president) and solo cornetist George Edmund Dulf. In an interview in 1939, Dulf recalled that Armant's band had thirty-four members and achieved notable success, touring to Milwaukee, Indianapolis, Columbus, Detroit, Lexington, St. Louis, Peoria, Springfield, and other cities, where it performed concerts, dances, and parades. "Armant's Band played all dances of any consequence, both colored and white," said Dulf, echoing the reports of the high demand for Black musicians we already noted in New York. "As a matter of fact, they played so many white engagements that President Thomas Kennedy of Local 10, A. F. of M., came to one of the rehearsals in the fall of 1901 and asked the band to join his union."[2] Kennedy's request kicked off a controversy within Local 10 that led to a rejection of the Black musicians. A 1902 article in *The Presto* quotes Kennedy on the objections that prompted the establishment of a separate Black local:

> President Thomas F. Kennedy says: "Many of the members object to playing with a colored orchestra or band, but the chief objection is to

the appearance of a musical body [i.e., a union local] composed of black and white musicians. To obviate the necessity for continual rulings it was decided to separate the two bodies and give the colored union a charter."[3]

Dulf was neither surprised nor discouraged by the negative reaction on the part Local 10's members. From the start he was suspicious of Kennedy's motives and those of the faction favoring admission. Dulf saw their goal as politically self-serving.

> I readily observed that a factional dispute existed within Local 10. Naturally one faction was stronger than the other, and the stronger faction would have taken us in to gain the upper hand, later finding some plausible excuse to eradicate us. In other words, I had every reason to doubt their sincerity.[4]

Therefore, after a meeting with Local 10 members attended by several hundred musicians, Dulf requested permission to establish a separate Black local. On July 4, 1902, the AFM issued a charter to "Local 208 (colored), Chicago." According to *The Presto*, Local 208 had a hundred members.[5]

Dulf's brief recollections illuminate the dilemma faced by Black musicians, even in cases where the entrance audition posed no barrier. Local 10 did not assert that the Black musicians were unqualified; in fact, their credentials were impeccable.[6] Furthermore, on the surface the invitation from Local 10's president seemed genuine. Dulf and others, however, harbored a (justifiable) distrust of Kennedy's motivations, fearing that joining Local 10 would obligate the band's members to endorse his positions in internal disputes. Dulf had no interest in making the musicians into pawns in internecine struggles. He astutely judged that the well-being of Black musicians could best be served by an independent autonomous organization.

As with the outrage we noted in the discussion of Black strikebreakers in chapter 2, Dulf suspected that support for membership would come at a steep price and that Local 10 would be happy—indeed inclined—to get rid of the Black members when their support was no longer needed. We are reminded here of the warnings from W. E. B. Du Bois, Booker T. Washington, and A. Philip Randolph about the alienation of Black workers in general toward organized labor.

Indeed, the history of Chicago's white local itself gives credence to such concerns. AFM Local 10 was a descendant of the Chicago Musical Society (CMS), one of the founding affiliates of the NLM and later a part of the AFL. According to Sandy Mazzola, the CMS's 1880 charter stated that membership was open to "every *white male* person of good character and repute" (italics mine).[7]

In Chicago, the existence of separate Black and white locals—even with their official territorial overlaps—proved workable (if hardly ideal) because the large size of the Black population and the vitality of the club scene in the southern part of the city offered the opportunity for meaningful work venues separate from those that employed white ensembles. Thus, white and Black musicians could find employment without competing directly for the same jobs. Chicago's "black belt" area grew rapidly in the years after Local 208 formed—from 44,000 residents in 1910 to 80,000 in 1920 to 234,000 by 1930.[8] Local 208 at first experienced financial problems (Clark Halker says that Dulf "struggled to keep the local afloat and regularly covered its day-to-day operating expenses from his own pocket");[9] nevertheless, it quickly grew in size and influence. In 1910 it had only a single vote at the convention (and therefore a membership of fewer than 150). By 1920, it had three votes (329 members) and by 1929, it had six.[10] By 1954, Local 208 boasted 1,081 members (and therefore ten votes, the maximum permitted), considerably outpacing the next largest Black local, Philadelphia with 770 members.

At the same time, recalled Milt Hinton, many of the South Side clubs were owned by whites. Furthermore, he notes that white musicians would visit these clubs, but "we couldn't go where they were."[11] Indeed, the lucrative nightclub and hotel scenes in the northern part of the city were virtually closed off to Blacks, with the exception of nationally recognized stars such as Louis Armstrong. The white visitors to the South Side would copy the styles and techniques of the Black performers and even make recordings in their style, while Black musicians were kept out of the studios.[12] No African American obtained a broadcasting license until the late 1920s, although Amy Absher writes that "audiences did experience jazz and blues through late-night simulcasts from the 'black belt' clubs."[13] In November 1929, the white-owned radio station WSBC introduced a groundbreaking show, "The All-Negro Hour," hosted by Jack L. Cooper; it was the first radio program in the country to feature exclusively Black performers.[14]

"I can't blame [the white musicians]," said Hinton.

> I blame the establishment for holding me back and not letting me record . . . , and letting him come and hear me play, and let[ing] him partake of this and give a reasonable facsimile of it . . . and make money off it. . . . I studied with white and I studied with black ones, and I tried to take everything I possibly could from it. So it isn't a matter of taking. What I wanted . . . was equal opportunity for everyone.[15]

Even though the Black and white musicians in Chicago could work in musically satisfying venues in their respective areas of the city, they lived in a state of underlying tension. When one of the most violent race riots in the country broke out in Chicago in July 1919, following the murder of a young Black swimmer who inadvertently crossed into an unofficially segregated whites-only part of Lake Michigan, the five days of rioting and thirty-eight deaths that resulted represented the "tragic culmination" of a quarter century of racial conflict in the city's labor movement.[16]

Ultimately, the merger of Locals 10 and 208 in the mid-1960s proved to be extremely contentious. Because Local 208 had staked out fertile territory for the employment of its members, and because its officers had come to enjoy comfortable salaries and considerable prestige and power, the Black union resisted amalgamation for several years after hundreds of its members had left the organization and joined Local 10. Bitter accusations arose in both organizations and officials from the International had to broker an agreement. The details of the negotiating process, which found voice in dozens of articles in the local and national press, are the subject of discussion in chapter 8. The agreement that finally emerged set the model for many of the mergers that followed.

San Francisco

During the years following the establishment of Local 208 in Chicago, African American musicians in several large cities successfully established their own unions. Some, like New Orleans and East Liverpool, were short-lived, but quite a number functioned efficiently and successfully until the late 1950s or 1960s, for example Pittsburgh, Cleveland, Columbus, Springfield, Boston, Buffalo, and others.

In 1916, no doubt seeing the success of these Black locals in the Midwest and East, African American musicians in San Francisco approached Local 6 for permission to establish their own union. San Francisco, at the time, was the largest city west of St. Louis (Table 4.1) but unlike Chicago, the Black population was small: only 0.4 percent (Table 4.2). Oakland and Los Angeles had a larger percentage of African Americans (2 and 2.4 percent), but the total number of individuals was still small. The percentage of the population identified as African American in the 1910 census in Los Angeles and Oakland is actually comparable to that in Chicago, but the total number of individuals is not. There were about six times as many Blacks living in Chicago as in Los Angeles (which in turn had 4.5 times as many as did San Francisco). The importance of these statistics for our purposes is that the small Black population in San Francisco was not able to establish a sustainable racially separate club life. Unlike Chicago, where the two local unions

Table 4.1. Populations of the Largest U.S. Cities in 1910

Rank	City	Population
1	New York	4,766,883
2	Chicago	2,185,283
3	Philadelphia	1,549,008
4	St. Louis	687,029
5	Boston	670,585
6	Cleveland	560,663
7	Baltimore	558,485
8	Pittsburgh	533,905
9	Detroit	465,766
10	Buffalo	423,715
11	San Francisco	416,912
12	Milwaukee	373,857
13	Cincinnati	363,591
14	Newark	347,469
15	New Orleans	339,075
16	Washington, DC	331,069
17	Los Angeles	319,198

Table 4.2. Population Data by Ethnicity: San Francisco, Oakland, and Los Angeles, 1910–1920

Date	Area	Total Population	White	African American	Chinese American	Japanese American
1910	**San Francisco**	416,912	400,014 (95.9%)	1,642 (0.4%)	10,582 (2.5%)	4,518 (1.1%)
	Oakland	150,174	141,956 (94.5%)	3,055 (2%)	3,609 (2.4%)	1,520 (1%)
	Los Angeles	319,198	305,307 (95.6%)	7,599 (2.4%)	1,954 (0.6%)	4,238 (1.3%)
1920	**San Francisco**	506,676	486,114 (95.9%)	2,414 (0.5%)	7,744 (1.5%)	5,358 (1.1%)
	Oakland	216,261	202,726 (93.7%)	5,489 (2.5%)	3,821 (1.8%)	2,709 (1.3%)
	Los Angeles	576,673	517,107 (89.7%)	15,579 (2.7%)	2,062 (0.4%)	11,618 (2%)

could each secure rewarding work for their members, Black musicians in San Francisco found themselves competing for the same jobs as whites.

In December 1915 the board of Local 6 considered a request by a "Mr. Jackson, representing Colored Musicians, to be permitted to organize a local." Jackson and a colleague attended the regular union meeting the following month seeking "a permit for a strictly colored union, to operate indiscriminately within and without this jurisdiction." In January 1916 Local 6 denied permission.[17]

In this case, the issue prompting the request seems to have been the difficulty of the required audition, as suggested by a conflict that arose three months later. In April 1916 a member of a Black sextet—the So Different Orchestra, headed by pianist Sid LeProtti (see Figure 4.1)—approached Charles Swanberg, the (white) owner of the Portola Louvre Café, an establishment in an upscale area near Union Square. Swanberg was happy to hire the band, but as saxophonist Reb Spikes recalled, "Old man Swanberg had a Union place, so we had to be Union. We went down and took the Union examination, and they said three of us could read and the other three couldn't read.... If we'd taken the job that way, that would'a broken up our combination."[18]

The unpublished minutes of Local 6 support Spikes's recollection, although they differ in detail. On April 25, 1916, Spikes himself passed the audition, as did clarinetist Adam Mitchell and bassist Clarence Williams. But LeProtti failed, as did drummer Peter Stanley. Flutist Gerald Wells is not mentioned in the minutes and perhaps was already a union member. Indeed, Local 6 had a number of Black members by this time; for example, ten musicians from Ferdon's Quaker Medicine Show Band had joined in 1908–9.[19]

Eleven days later, Local 6 administered a second audition, but LeProtti and Stanley failed again. On May 9, 1916, a lawyer (Mr. Grasty) appeared before the board, whose members assured him that Local 6 "would not make any race discrimination and would give the applicants [the] privilege of taking a third examination." On May 16 the examination committee reported a third failure.[20] Swanberg called a friend in Los Angeles and the So Different Orchestra played at Levy's Tavern in that city for about six weeks until a strike by Local 6 beginning on August 1 allowed them to come north again and play in Swanberg's club as well as in other venues that were hiring nonunion personnel.[21]

On the same day that LeProtti and Stanley failed their third audition, the Portola Louvre Café hired two (white) musicians from Seattle. Local 6 conducted a thorough investigation of the situation on May 18, 1916, during

Figure 4.1. Sid LeProtti's So Different Orchestra at the Portola Louvre Café, 1915. Left to right: Clarence Williams, bass; Reb Spikes, saxophone; Adam "Slocum" Mitchell, clarinet; Sid LeProtti, piano and leader; and Gerald Wells, flute. The percussionist is not identified but judging by the date of the photo, it is probably Pete Stanley. (Courtesy of the San Francisco Traditional Jazz Foundation.)

which managers at the café reported that some of the hiring personnel had heard rumors regarding a "colored orchestra coming in" as well as instructions to "keep the colored men out if possible"; but they also noted that a Mr. Berger had told the amusement manager at the establishment that "if he could get a colored orchestra they would make a great hit, and business would pick up."[22]

Local 6 managed to prevent a Black union from forming in the city until 1923, when the board finally gave its authorization. After that time, Black Local 648 and white Local 6 seem to have operated with relative calm until the Depression, when the loss of jobs became so severe that the white union took drastic action to block Black musicians from work, leading to one of the most serious racial battles in the AFM's history. But that's a story for our next chapter.

The events of 1915–16 in San Francisco bring to light two important elements in the history of racially separated unions within the AFM. First, they accentuate the hurdle that auditions based on Western classical music, requiring sophisticated reading skills, posed for some African American applicants. Reb Spikes admitted to Tom Stoddard years later (in 1972) that he and Williams, two of the three who passed the audition, were not primarily improvisers. "I was never much of a jazzman," said Spikes. "I played a lot of counterpoint like cello parts." He claims that bassist Williams played "nearly all cello parts.... He'd play counter-melodies like I'd play on the saxophone."[23] On the other hand, LeProtti, the pianist who failed the audition three times, had less than a year of classical training and later told interviewers that his playing was mechanical until he took the advice of "Old Henry Stewart, an old singer with the minstrel show," to "get around some of them ear piano players and learn how to fill in and fake."[24] Improvisation was apparently not a skill tested by Local 6's audition.

On the competing side of the issue, however, is the important revelation that at least some white club managers assumed that a Black band would be popular with white customers and would increase business. As we noted in the discussion of New York, Black bands that provided attractive entertainment for white patrons made the potential competition from an independent Black local all the more threatening.

Seattle

If the Chicago story illustrates the role that overt racism and Black distrust of organized labor played in the formation of African American locals, and San Francisco shows the negative impact on Black musicians of entrance auditions based on Western classical music and sightreading, Seattle tells another equally common tale: the conflict between Black and white locals in terms of competing pay scales and work rules.

The first Black local in Seattle (Local 458) received its charter on October 1, 1918. Up to that time, Seattle musicians were represented only by Local 76, which had been in existence since March 1, 1898. Local 76 had one Black member: Powell Barnett, a tuba player who joined the union in 1913. Barnett remained a member of Local 76 throughout his life, even after he joined Local 458 as well.[25] He had tried without success to convince other African American musicians to join, but they balked. Local 76 would only admit Blacks on the condition that they would waive social rights, such as access

Figure 4.2. Powell Barnett in 1956, receiving an Annual Urban League award. (Photo by Gil Baker. Courtesy of the University of Washington Libraries, Special Collections SOC18056.)

to the union's clubhouse, notes historian David Keller.[26] We are reminded here of the defensive protestations of Terence Powderly and Samuel Gompers in advocating for work rights for African Americans but disclaiming any support for social equality. Black musicians in Seattle apparently did not agree to Local 76's restrictions and refused to affiliate with that body.

In August 1918 Local 76 acquiesced to the formation of a Black local providing its members agreed to abide by 76's price list (except when they played for Black audiences).[27] At this time, more than a hundred locals in various fields were members of Seattle's Central Labor Council; only nine of them admitted African American or Asian workers.[28]

Seattle's Black population had grown exponentially after 1900, in large part due to expansion of the shipbuilding industry. By the time Local 458 received its charter in 1918, Seattle had produced about a quarter "of all the tonnage manufactured for the government during the war."[29] Blacks at the time constituted about 0.9 percent of the population—somewhat larger than in San Francisco.[30] But like San Francisco, the number of African Americans in the city was not substantial enough to support a separate musical scene that would offer (like Chicago) plentiful jobs in segregated locations. After Prohibition (1920), however, the waterfront became "the focal point for a new jazz scene"[31] and the social spaces for Black music-making flourished. Times were good, and in the period 1918–21, relations between Locals 76 and 458 were, for the most part, peaceful.

Nevertheless, this period was marked by occasional accusations by the officers of Local 76 concerning Black musicians playing below the agreed-upon scale, and these accusations increased in the early 1920s. One example concerned two dance halls owned by the Gatt Brothers. Robert Pitts, who says that five Black musicians were playing at each establishment, dates the crisis to the spring of 1923 and reports that the city's licensing board refused to renew the Gatt brothers' licenses unless they hired white musicians.[32] The owners replaced the African Americans. According to Keller, the Black musicians were playing below scale.[33] Local 458 wanted to bring charges to the International against Local 76 but were unable to prove that the white local was behind the decision of the licensing board. Such conflicts were not restricted to musicians, of course, or even to African Americans. Dana Frank notes, for example, that Asian culinary workers accepted work at lower wages than whites and the union tried to impose boycotts to pressure white employers to fire them.[34]

Another report of racist behavior on the part of city officials involved the denial of a permit for the Tenth Division (Black) Band to play park concerts. According to Pitts, the Park Board rebuffed the band several times, and then allowed a trial for one season, at the end of which they denied the band a contract on the grounds of "inefficiency." Continued efforts by the band to play in the parks led to a trial concert, resulting in another denial. Pitts reports, without citing a source, that no members of the Park Board were present at the concert. Eventually the Board reversed its decision and allowed five paid appearances.[35]

Such racism was commonplace in the city. Local 76's newsletter ran a "continuing series of derogatory jokes and remarks stereotyping Japanese, Chinese, and African Americans," and Keller documents several incidents of Blacks being squeezed out of jobs in white-dominated territory.[36] Local 458's complaints to Local 76, however, fell on deaf ears.

By 1924 Local 458 faced a crisis. It was divided into competing factions, the secretary's position was contested, and the conflicts with Local

76 continued. Early in the year, one faction of the membership wrote to the International to dispute alleged infractions and to question Local 76's authority; an opposing faction then tried to mollify Local 76 by writing that the complaint did not represent the majority view within 458.[37] Local 76 was not appeased, however, and its officers submitted an appeal to the IEB to revoke 458's charter on the grounds of an illegal election in 1921 and other abuses (for example, violating the wage scale and the prescribed length of the work week).

A case brought before the Seattle Labor Council by Local 76 in February 1924 provides a small window on the types of disputes that affected the two locals.[38] The Strand Dance Hall had hired a white band from Local 76 but then replaced it with a band that the white union asserted to be nonunion. Local 76 appealed to the Labor Council to reinstate its band or place the establishment on the "unfair" list. However, Powell Barnett and another member of Local 458 explained to Council that the new band was part of their Black local and that therefore the Strand was in compliance with rules requiring the hiring of union musicians. (Race is not mentioned in the Council's minutes.) The Council decided—again for reasons not specified—to wire the International to ascertain whether Local 458 was "in good standing." If they were not, then the Council would require the Strand to reinstate the Local 76 band. The International responded that Local 458 was indeed a legitimate, functioning, constituent member of the AFM and therefore, on March 26, the Council dropped the case. The Council's minutes offer no insight on why the band from Local 76 was dismissed in the first place, but as we've noted, dance halls could presumably hire very popular union-affiliated Black bands at more competitive prices than white bands demanded. Nor do the minutes explain why the Council needed to take the extraordinary step of sending a telegram to the national AFM office to determine whether Local 458 was in good standing. We must assume that Local 76, which had brought the charge (like many others) to the Council, had asserted that 458 was *not* an authorized representative union body.

As a member of both Local 76 and Local 458, Powell Barnett pleaded with Local 76's board to reconsider its request to the IEB to cancel 458's charter. His appeal, however, proved ineffective. On April 22, 1924, only a month after the interaction with the Labor Council over the Strand Dance Hall band, and despite the assertion by the International that 458 was in good standing, AFM president Joseph Weber sustained the complaint of Local 76 and two days later the IEB revoked its charter.[39]

For the remainder of 1924, Black musicians in Seattle had no union representation. They repeatedly appealed to the International to reinstate the charter, but Local 76 managed to block their efforts. Finally on December 9, the IEB approved a charter for a new Black local with a new number, Local 493, following approval in October by Local 76. Powell Barnett had spearheaded the approval process. This new local was small; in the late 1920s, it had about fifty members. The much more powerful Local 76, in contrast, had about 1,200. Reflecting the problems inherent in the segregated union structure, the IEB authorized the formation of Local 493 only on the condition of tight controls. For instance, a member of Local 76 was to be present at all of the Black local's meetings and would supervise all trials for infractions of union rules.

To be clear, the new local was not a subsidiary. It was nominally independent with full rights and representation at the national conventions. At the same time, however, AFM president Joseph Weber and the IEB considered Local 493 to be under the watch of Local 76. In 1928 Local 76's board, seeking confirmation of their supervisory role, asked Weber to "define the position of Local 493 and its relation to this local." Weber replied that "in all affairs of Local 493, white Local 76 had complete supervision."[40] His response not only reveals the inherent weakness of the segregated union structure, but also sets the scene for the implementation of subsidiary status in some cities during the following decade, a move that would punish select Black locals who became too much of an irritant to their white counterparts. Seattle's Black musicians did not suffer that demeaning fate, but twelve other subsidiaries would form by mandate of the AFM.

A case brought to the Seattle Labor Council in 1926, two years before Local 76's inquiry to Weber, substantiates the white union's supervisory role. In this instance, Local 493 wanted to place the Elks Lodge on the unfair list due to violations of certain working conditions. They could only bring the case to the Council, however, by "request of the Musicians Union #76 on behalf of Local #493."[41]

* * *

The case studies detailed in this chapter illustrate both the incentives and the impediments to the formation of Black locals in the early years of the century—as well as the inevitable conflicts that resulted from chartering dual locals in the same territory. In Chicago, racist attitudes blocked the admission of African Americans even when some white musicians seemed to offer support. As we have seen, however, Blacks suspected ulterior motives—namely, bolstering the self-interest of selected factions within the white local, just as Black workers in labor unions nationwide were welcomed into overwhelmingly white organizations only when their presence was judged advantageous (and were often dismissed later when their support was no longer needed). In San Francisco, the barrier seems to have been primarily the audition specifications, which emphasized musical literacy and failed to recognize improvisation skills, although as we have noted, racist attitudes (which the Local 6 officers were quick to deny) may have played a part in the formulation of the audition process, the judgment that the applicants did not meet the local's standards, or both. The New York local, as we saw in the previous chapter, took another approach to combatting pressure for a separate Black local by modifying its entrance requirements and thus luring the improvisers into their organization. Even when the white locals did agree to the formation of a competing Black local, as in Seattle, conflicts inevitably emerged, especially over pay scales and work rules.

Despite the resistance of many white unions, the number of Black locals grew exponentially, as shown in Table 3.1, and the resulting dual unions managed, for the most part, to maintain relatively cordial relationships during the 1920s. The economy was strong and work was plentiful enough to offer adequate opportunities for members of both locals (even though Black musicians were typically forced to accept lower wages). That cordiality, however, would soon disappear as musicians not only confronted the economic crisis of 1929 and beyond, but also found themselves waging a losing battle against a new threat: the advent of sound films, which would deprive them of some of their highest-paying work. The disastrous economic position of musicians throughout the country in the 1930s and its impact on the AFM's segregated unions is the subject of our next chapter.

CHAPTER 5

From the Glories of the '20s to the Despair of the '30s

Music and the Movies

The 1920s were a heady time for the country's musicians. Despite the passage of Prohibition in 1920, some speakeasies and many dance halls continued to offer live music; and new opportunities arose in radio and movie theaters. Following the advent of silent film at the beginning of the century, theaters sprang up rapidly throughout the country and became fixtures of popular culture. These movie houses featured live performers, from solo artists to orchestras, to accompany the visual images. By 1926, at least twenty thousand musicians nationwide were playing regularly in theaters, which ranged from small neighborhood venues to combination motion picture and vaudeville establishments to deluxe downtown movie palaces.[1] The small theaters might employ a single pianist or organist, or even a three- or four-member combo. The larger venues, however, could feature ensembles of as many as thirty-five players and the first-run theaters might boast of even larger orchestras—occasionally up to eighty, wrote Hugo Riesenfeld in 1926. Riesenfeld was the Managing Director of the Rivoli, Rialto, and Criterion Theaters in New York.[2] Black musicians could find work in the small establishments, but the larger venues were typically restricted to whites. Saxophonist and flutist Lloyd Smith, for example, recalled playing regularly in small bands in Black neighborhood theaters in St. Louis; the larger venues, he said, had twelve- to fifteen-piece (white) bands.[3] Some Black artists, notably Fats Waller and Count Basie, honed their keyboard skills playing the organ in silent movie houses, experiences that in part shaped their later creative output.[4]

These jobs were extremely lucrative. Riesenfeld wrote that the minimum salary in the larger theaters in New York was $83 weekly. First stand players, he reports, could earn $7,000–$10,000 a year, equivalent to approximately $116,000–$166,00 in 2022.[5] The AFM, whose membership peaked in 1929 at 146,326 (before again exceeding that number in 1944)[6] was aggressive in securing good terms for its members. To cite but one example, by the late 1920s Local 77 (the white local in Philadelphia) had contracts with 133 theaters employing 486 musicians. These contracts specified not only wage scales, but also the required number of players, the length of the season, and the duration of individual performances.[7] Indeed, reporter Maurice Mermey complained in 1929 that the theater musician had become a "virtual dictator."[8] Thus, the development of effective sound-on-film technology and its commercialization in the late 1920s through "talkies" (motion pictures with synchronized sound) understandably alarmed musicians and their union representatives throughout the country.[9]

By 1929, about a thousand theaters nationwide had been equipped for sound and that number was increasing by 150 per month.[10] As theaters began to dispense with orchestras, musicians in many cities went on strike and convinced projectionists, janitors, and stagehands to walk out in sympathy—actions that were later banned by the 1947 Taft-Hartley Act. Philadelphia musicians, for example, struck local theaters twice: in fall 1930 and again in fall 1931.[11] They worked out compromises with management in both instances, but it was clear that the movie house musicians' days were numbered.

Violence erupted in some cities. In San Francisco, for example, Local 6 initiated a lawsuit in 1929 against Nasser Brothers, operators of twenty-five theaters in the Bay Area, aiming to hold the theaters to their signed two-year contracts. The theater operators claimed they were paying the musicians to play cards.[12] The case eventually reached the California Supreme Court, but by the time the court ruled, the contract had expired. Meanwhile, on June 1, 1930, a bomb placed on the roof of the Royal Theater exploded, "tearing a four-foot hole in the roof, damaging the projection room and wrecking windows in nearby apartment houses." Fortunately, no one was hurt, as the last performance had ended two hours earlier.[13]

By 1933, the number of theaters with sound projection had risen to thirteen thousand and musicians throughout the country found themselves unemployed. The problem of automation, of course, affected not only jobs in theaters, but also those in radio and in other areas where mechanized sound threatened to replace live performance—areas of employment dominated by whites. Sound films, however, dramatically (and quite abruptly) propelled the downward trajectory, plunging musicians during the Great Depression into even more dire straits than those of other workers.

Chicago became a major battleground, pitting James Petrillo, president of Local 10 against the major movie houses in the city.[14] (In 1940 Petrillo would become the controversial and combative national president of the AFM.) Two thousand musicians had worked in Chicago theaters prior to 1927; by the mid-1930s, only 125 jobs remained.[15] As musicians in both white Local 10 and Black Local 208 suffered from the nation's financial crisis, union membership declined precipitously. To support its members, Local 208 held Thursday night dances, at which players would make $3–4, out of which the local could deduct a small amount for dues.[16]

In 1954, *Business Week* reported that while most occupations had expanded since 1930, work for musicians had contracted by a staggering 40 percent. Tracing the historical trend, the article noted that in 1930, 71 percent of AFM members enjoyed full-time employment; by 1940, that number had dipped to 59 percent; and by 1954 it stood at a dismal 23 percent.[17] Overall, the AFM's membership itself declined by 31 percent between 1928 and 1934.[18]

As jobs for white musicians began to disappear, these now-unemployed artists began to encroach on venues dominated by Blacks, thus fueling conflicts between racially separated locals. As we have seen in discussions of New York, Seattle, and San Francisco, club and dance hall managers in the teens and twenties were particularly enamored by Black talent, which was not only musically inspiring but could also be secured at an attractive price. In St. Louis whites also tried to displace popular Black performers on riverboats. As the panic of unemployment grew, officials in many white union locals began to adopt increasingly aggressive tactics to wrest jobs from African Americans.

In major cities throughout the country, night clubs and dance halls closed, throwing musicians of all races out of jobs. In New York, for example, the city's licensing bureau estimated that between 1929 and 1930, 105 dance halls went out of business.[19] I. A. Hirschmann wrote in *The Nation* in November 1933 that 12,000 members of New York's racially integrated Local 802 were out of work.[20] In this year—prior to the establishment of the Federal Music Project in 1935—relief efforts proved dismally inadequate. According to Hirschmann, Local 802 had dispensed, during the previous three years, $150,000 in outright grants to indigent members and was experimenting with imposing a 1 percent tax on earnings. Private entities in the city, such as the Musicians' Emergency Fund, and locally organized benefit concerts provided help, but the aid was not nearly enough to meet the need.

The AFM responded aggressively to these developments. In 1930 the federation launched the Music Defense League, which eventually spent $550,000 to run ads promoting "Live Music." The ads repeatedly featured images of robots to represent recorded sound, thus setting up a dichotomy of live versus dead, human versus mechanical.[21] Noting that by 1928 the number of AFM members employed in theaters throughout the United States and Canada had reached about thirty thousand, President Joseph Weber launched an even more aggressive program in 1931: Living Music Days (LMD). Each local would designate a particular date on which bands and orchestras would play (with no admission charge) in local stores. Newspapers issued widespread publicity and ran ads highlighting both the musical organizations involved and the participating stores. Beginning in San Francisco, LMDs spread to cities across the country and were often highly successful. Stores were packed and some of them contracted with the musical ensembles to present additional free concerts. In October 1931, for example, the secretary of Local 30 in St. Paul wrote to President Weber that one store had been employing orchestras regularly since their LMD two months earlier, and that it was so crowded that patrons had to make reservations to eat in its tearoom.[22] By February 1932, 150 newspapers throughout the country had agreed to participate.[23]

Weber argued that music's "expression is bound up in the soul and temperament, with the genius of its exponent."

> It does not lend itself to mechanization; its loftiness, its spirit and soul-inspiring qualities preclude this. Through mechanization it is reduced to emotionless, rasping sound, standing in even less valuable artistic relationship to real music than a cheap chromo of one of Raphael's masterpieces stands in relation to the original.[24]

Indeed, the poor fidelity of early recordings lent support to Weber's position: these imperfect audio reproductions could hardly substitute for the vibrant sound of live performance. But of course, the trend was not reversible—not only in regard to the demise of silent film, which was obvious at the time, but also in view of the increasingly realistic sound quality of recorded music that was to come, a development that Weber could hardly have foreseen.

Thus, the country's musicians, hard-hit by the combination of the 1929 crash, the closure of clubs due to Prohibition, and most crucially, the end of lucrative theater jobs, suffered disproportionately during the 1930s. White locals, whose members faced massive unemployment, fought back in desperation and sometimes targeted the Black locals in their jurisdictions in an attempt to wrest jobs from their members. In several cases, the increased tension between the Black and white locals led to the revocation of the Black locals' charters and the relegation of its members to a nefarious subsidiary status. We will examine two such cases in detail below: St. Louis and San Francisco.

Even when subsidiary status was not forced on African American musicians, however, the impact on Black locals was notable. In 1932 alone, six of them lost their charters.[25] Five more disappeared in the following two years.[26] To be fair, many white locals suffered as well. In 1934, for example, no fewer than fourteen locals went under (two of them Black).

Early Attempts at Amalgamation

Meanwhile, some of the segregated locals explored merger possibilities, which were uniformly rejected, in some cases by the white locals and in other cases by the Black locals. In Chicago, for example, the officers and board of Local 208 presented a proposed merger plan to Local 10's officials in March 1931. After a lengthy discussion, the Local 10 board deferred for a month, then met without any representation from Local 208 and rejected the proposal. Local 10's minutes report a motion passed at the meeting stating that merger was not in "the best interests of either organization, and . . . that the present arrangement of the two separate organizations . . . [should] be continued."[27] (Ironically, when merger negotiations began in earnest in the 1960s, it was Local 208 rather than Local 10 that mounted the fiercest resistance.)

In Seattle, Powell Barnett (the African American member of both 76 and 493) began an effort at amalgamation locally and nationally in the early 1930s. His first step was a proposition presented to (white) Local 76 in 1931, which resulted in a promise of a report that never materialized.[28] The following year Barnett pursued the matter at the national convention in Los Angeles. In his role as a representative of Local 493, Barnett pressed other Black delegates to support mergers.[29] According to an unpublished account reported by David Keller, Barnett stated that his colleagues characterized their relationship with their white counterparts as being "like two doves in the same nest." Barnett found their protestations disingenuous and feared that their opposition might reflect the officers' current "access to the gravy."[30] Significantly, the gravy might have included not only the officers' salaries, but also their easy access to jobs; local officials, in many cases, were also bandleaders and contractors and were therefore positioned to take on work for themselves and their groups when clients called.[31] Barnett's suspicions unfortunately foreshadow similar accusations that would erupt in Chicago thirty years later, when some Black musicians favoring amalgamation lashed out against the entrenched leadership of Local 208 (see chapter 8).

At the Los Angeles convention, Barnett did manage to meet with the International Executive Board.

> I asked them that we be realistic. Whenever dual locals were going to be established we should see that there was eventually going to be trouble. We should discourage the establishment of dual locals and persuade the musicians to join into one union. We should see that these dual locals would not be set up any more. After establishing that policy we should attempt to eliminate those dual locals that exist.[32]

Although Barnett was not successful in convincing the IEB to change course, his actions reminded the board of the inevitable difficulties posed by the AFM's segregated structure and, however slowly, helped to press the case toward amalgamation.

In the meantime, Barnett had established a connection to Ray Jackson, the secretary of Black Local 533 in Buffalo, New York, who had organized a subgroup of African American AFM delegates at the 1927 convention.[33] On February 28, 1932, members of the Buffalo local discussed a letter they had received from Seattle that advocated mergers. This time the rejection came not from the white local but from the Black local, anticipating the type of heated debates that would take place much later in the 1960s and '70s. The consensus of 533's board was that a merger with Buffalo's (white) Local 43 would be of no benefit "and would also tend to cut down our representation in national conventions."[34] At the 1934 convention, Jackson proposed appointing "a national investigator and representative for the Black locals." Two years later, the federation appointed him to that position.[35] In this capacity Jackson traveled throughout the country investigating conditions for Black musicians and recruiting members to join the union.

These actions and others document the mounting pressure on federation officials to address the increasingly troublesome situation of racially separated locals with overlapping jurisdictions. At a minimum, urged Black delegates, the AFM must do away with the powerless subsidiaries that had formed in several cities over the previous few years. In 1937 the president of Buffalo's Local 533, Lloyd Plummer, along with representatives from Black Locals 587 (Milwaukee) and 471 (Pittsburgh), introduced a strong resolution to abolish them.[36]

Whereas, There is no provision for, or mention of Subsidiary Locals in the Constitution and By-Laws of the A. F. of M.; and

Whereas, The very foundation of these United States was laid on the fact that "Taxation Without Representation" is tyranny; and

Whereas, This form of organization is a subterfuge to evade the organic law of the A. F. of M.;

Therefore, Be It Hereby Resolved, that beginning immediately no further Subsidiary Locals shall be organized; that the Subsidiary Locals now in existence shall be either absorbed by the parent body giving said members the same voice and vote; or given a full and separate charter; and that from this day forward no Local shall be given supervision over another.[37]

The Board, however, decided that "the present system works out satisfactorily" and therefore no change was needed. It would be another seven years before the IEB would change its tune.

Subsidiary Locals: Two Case Studies

St. Louis: Locals 2 and 44

On February 18, 1932, the AFM officially revoked the charter of its oldest Black union: Local 44 in St. Louis. The IEB had actually made the decision more than a month earlier, but the specific rationale for their action remains to this day buried in obscurity. The published minutes record only the following:

> January 6: "Charges are considered against the Colored Local 44 in St. Louis, Mo. All the documents in the case are read. Laid over for further consideration";

> January 7: "Further consideration is given to the charges against Local 44, St. Louis, Mo. (colored). On motion the Local is found guilty and its charter is revoked, the President of the A. F. of M. being directed to carry out the purport of this action and make such arrangements in the St. Louis jurisdiction as shall appear to best meet the interests of the A. F. of M. and which may include the reorganization of the colored musicians."[38]

About a month later, on February 16, AFM president Joseph Weber sent a letter to (white) Local 2. "This is to advise you," wrote Weber, "that Local No. 44 has been found guilty as charged by your local and as a result its charter has been revoked." He attached a lengthy document specifying how "colored musicians may maintain a local in a city wherein a white local is also maintained."³⁹ The enclosure specified rules regarding subsidiaries, whose members paid dues to the white local in the area but were severely constrained in their rights. Notably, the restrictions applied not only to business matters but also to professional collaborations, evoking memories of the early protestations of Powderly and Gompers regarding "social equality." To summarize: in addition to the lack of voting rights, access to facilities, and representation at national conferences, the members of the subsidiary had to agree to the following policies:

- The subsidiary must adhere to the rules and regulations of the parent local.
- Members of the subsidiary pay a two-dollar charter fee to the parent local.
- The white local defrays expenses of the subsidiary as long as these costs do not exceed the total amount the subsidiary pays to the parent local.
- The white local appoints three members of the subsidiary to handle its business. One acts as chair at meetings, one acts as secretary, and the third acts as business agent.
- Decisions made by the subsidiary apply only to its members and must not be opposed to the interests of the white local. The subsidiary may hold social functions and retain monies accrued through them; the subsidiary can assess members for death benefits.
- Charges for violations by subsidiary members are to be tried by the white local. The subsidiary may send three representatives to the trial and they shall have a voice and vote.
- The white local's business agents may also officiate for the subsidiary local.
- And finally: "The members of the subsidiary local and the white local can only intermingle for professional purposes with the consent of both locals."

Presumably this last rule was intended to curtail the establishment of interracial bands by requiring prior union approval from both Blacks and whites.

Local 44 was taken by surprise. According to later reports by several of its members, the local had no warning, much less any opportunity to refute the charges—which, in any case, were not detailed. In numerous oral histories, former members of Subsidiary Local 2 comment that Local 44 could never determine the nature of (white) Local 2's complaints. According to Eddie McKinney, secretary of Local 44 at the time of the charter revocation, officers wrote directly to the office of the AFM president for an explanation, "but only received communications that because of the report of irregularities, the charter of Local No. 44 was revoked."⁴⁰

Black musicians found themselves in a no-win situation. On the one hand, they were understandably insulted by the removal of their charter without warning and by the president's proposal for demeaning subsidiary status; on the other hand, they needed union affiliation to work both locally and in other cities. If any of the Black musicians wished to play out-of-town engagements, for example, union membership was required to obtain a traveling card. On the local scene, pianist and bandleader Fate Marable, whose Black bands were a fixture on the extremely popular Streckfus Line Steamers, needed a union card to retain his prestigious job on the company's largest and most popular boat, the *St. Paul*.[41] Indeed, the Streckfus company, whose headquarters were in St. Louis, provided steady income for numerous musicians in the city—both Blacks and whites. The company ran morning and evening cruises that offered sightseeing at various ports, but more importantly, gave the passengers the joy of dancing to big bands. The evening cruises started at sundown and typically ended at midnight, offering many hours of drinking, socializing, and dancing. The *St. Paul*'s enormous dance floor could accommodate 1,500 couples at a time.[42] Marable played on the Streckfus Steamers from 1907 to the beginning of the Second World War. He wrote to the federation offering to organize a new Black local and said he had commitments from fifteen musicians, the minimum number required,[43] but no such local materialized.

Therefore, with a good deal of reluctance, the Black musicians of St. Louis agreed, in the middle of 1932, to the establishment of Subsidiary Local 2. The first president was trumpeter Dewey Jackson, followed in 1933 by drummer Elijah "Lige" Shaw.[44] The last meeting of the legendary Local 44—which had predated the establishment of the AFM itself—took place on December 6, 1932.[45]

As president of the subsidiary, Shaw showed the tenacity of a bulldog in his efforts to regain an independent charter for St. Louis Blacks. In two interviews in 1971 and 1972,[46] he told Irene Cortinovis that he appeared before the IEB repeatedly at national conventions to request reinstatement of a Black local. Indeed, Shaw proved to be a force to be reckoned with. The AFM *Official Proceedings* show that he spoke to the IEB three times: in 1935, 1937, and 1939. In the first instance, his request was denied; in the second, it was "laid over for further consideration"; and the third time, it was referred to the President's office "for the purpose of having an officer assigned to St. Louis to try and iron out the situation."[47] Because Shaw was not an official delegate (subsidiaries were not entitled to representation), he often had to pay his own way.[48] Even if he didn't succeed in establishing a new local during the 1930s, Shaw nevertheless made the federation increasingly uncomfortable with its subsidiary policy.

Figure 5.1. St. Louis drummer Elijah ("Lige") Shaw, performing on a riverboat in 1959. (Courtesy of the State Historical Society of Missouri Photograph Collection, Arthur Witman Photograph Collection S0836, 770.)

Supplementing Shaw's personal campaign, Subsidiary Local 2's officers also repeatedly pressured the International. On June 20, 1934, for example, the IEB denied "a request of the subsidiary Local of Local 2 . . . for equal representation on the Executive Board of that Local."[49] Two years later the group again forced the executive board to confront the issue of subsidiaries: on June 28, 1936, the IEB reaffirmed "its position that a subsidiary Local is not entitled to representation of its own at a Convention, being represented by the Local of which it is a subsidiary."[50] The next year, the *Official Proceedings* record still another appeal to the IEB: Subsidiary Local 2 requests "full autonomy," state the minutes from the meeting of June 21. The Board denied the request when it rejected the resolution introduced by Plummer and others to eliminate all subsidiaries.

This new subsidiary policy represents an unfortunate degeneration of the IEB's long-running efforts to deal with the very real problems posed by segregated locals. We have already seen in the discussion of Seattle's locals that the IEB drew a clear line of responsibility: in all cases, the decisions of the white local were preeminent. Now, however, the AFM had created an official *category* of local in which Black musicians paid dues without gaining the privileges of full representation. "What is a subsidiary local . . . ? How does it differ from the jim-crow [sic] on railroads?" asked St. Louis *Argus* columnist Frank Mitchell in an imaginary dialogue between Mr. A and Mr. B. Mr. B responds: "No difference whatever, since there are unequal accommodations in both and the money all goes to one central point."[51]

At the same time, Local 2 did not prevent the Black musicians from working. Saxophonist and band leader Hayes Pillars recalled: "They wouldn't take your money. . . . It was just the idea that they were over you. . . . So we were second class members. . . . Which was unfair."[52]

Later in 1932, the federation revoked the charter of the Kansas City Black local. The *Argus* columnist reported that "the Kansas City musicians have taken a stand unanimously against being forced into a subsidiary local with duties to collect funds and turn [them] over to the white local who in turn tells them who their officers shall be."[53] The Kansas City Black local won its charter back in 1933.

In later years, Black musicians in St. Louis continued to speculate on the nature of Local 2's accusations. John Cotter, in his comprehensive thesis from 1959, could only report generalities, including "working under the scale price" and suspected laxities among the officers.[54] Years later Lige Shaw did provide some concrete information about the conflict. In a 1971 interview, Shaw told Irene Cortinovis that the revocation originated from a request by Joseph Streckfus that the unions consent to a "concession price" on his huge excursion boats. When Local 2 refused, said Shaw, Streckfus replaced his lineup of three white bands and one Black band with four Black ensembles, which prompted Local 2 to form a committee that, according to Shaw, managed to bring about the revocation of Local 44's charter.[55]

In addition to this specific incident, several oral histories point more generally to the advent of talkies as the stimulus for Local 2 to attack its Black

Figure 5.2. Eddie Randle and his Blue Devils, 1936 (Courtesy of the Eddie Randle Collection, National Ragtime & Jazz Archive, Southern Illinois University at Edwardsville.) Eddie Randle, trumpeter, stands in the center of the back row. Also pictured is Lloyd Smith (flutist and saxophonist), cited previously in this chapter (back row, second from the right).

counterpart. During the 1920s work was plentiful for Black musicians in St. Louis. As in other cities, they "more or less controlled" the dance halls and night clubs, and some bands even played regularly on local radio stations.[56] In St. Louis, however, Black musicians also had the opportunity of satisfying work on the riverboats. Whites, as elsewhere, controlled the lucrative large silent movie houses; when sound film deprived them of work, says Shaw, they tried to push their way into areas controlled by Blacks.[57] Lloyd Smith was particularly emphatic on this point. Prior to the talkies, he says, white musicians played in the large theaters, but didn't play jazz. Once their jobs began to dry up, they began to "hang around" the Black musicians to learn to imitate them, with the aim of taking over their jobs.[58]

Nevertheless, to have the federation revoke 44's charter required proof of "irregularities." In a 1982 interview, Eddie Randle, leader of the Blue Devils, recalled flaunting union rules not by playing under scale, but rather by working for a percentage of the gate, which he knew was against union rules.[59] He recounts two specific instances in which he arranged to take a percentage of the income, but he made sure that all band members were paid what they were owed. "When it becomes necessary that you make a living," Randle reflected, "you'll find a new way to do anything."[60] The normal response of the union in such cases would be to discipline the individual. How, then, could such infractions lead to the revocation of the entire charter? Some insight is provided by Cotter, stemming from his interviews with Eddie McKinney and Shaw. Apparently, the leadership of Local 44 was not inclined to discipline such individuals, and, in fact, 44's president might himself have been playing under scale. "It was reported," says Cotter in a footnote, "that the officers were not reprimanding their members for working under the scale price."[61]

San Francisco: Locals 6 and 648

In contrast to St. Louis, the events leading to the revocation of the charter of Black Local 648 in San Francisco are crystal clear.[62] In this case, aggressive actions on the part of (white) Local 6 closed off jobs to African Americans, who then filed a lawsuit in Superior Court. The judge seemed inclined to rule in favor of the Black musicians, but they abruptly withdrew their suit and Local 648 lost its charter.

In San Francisco, as elsewhere in the country, the employment situation for musicians had grown bleak by 1934. On January 19 of that year, (white) Local 6's president Walter Weber wrote to AFM president Joseph Weber (the two men were not related) that 40 percent of the local's 2,500 members could find no work.[63] The annual payroll for theater musicians was running at about $250,000, compared to $1.5 million in 1928.

The San Francisco Symphony was also experiencing hard times. Its 1932–34 seasons included only seven subscription performances, five municipal programs, and a severely curtailed summer series. In 1928, in contrast, the orchestra had presented thirteen subscription concerts, eleven pops concerts, run-outs to other Bay Area cities, a ten-concert summer season, and five high profile programs sponsored by the city.[64] Matters became so severe that the symphony canceled its entire 1934–35 season. Only a "Save

Our Symphony" (S.O.S.) campaign that culminated in a voter-approved city property tax kept the orchestra alive.[65]

If economic conditions for whites were dismal, those for blacks were worse. A 1934 study by the Joint Committee on National Recovery reported that Black workers in five metropolitan areas had lost their jobs at twice the rate of whites.[66] In San Francisco alone, three times as many African Americans were unemployed in 1937 as in 1930.[67] In the debate on the National Industrial Recovery Act of 1933, Congress heard arguments favoring a lower wage scale for Blacks than whites. Proponents claimed that Black workers were less efficient than whites and only obtained work through their willingness to accept lower pay; therefore, mandating equal wages would actually exacerbate Black unemployment. Ultimately Congress refused to accede to these racist arguments, but did allow some loopholes such as granting companies the right to classify types of work, "thus completely exempting some blacks from coverage while placing the remainder in the lowest possible classification."[68]

The unemployment woes were not limited to musicians, of course, and on the West Coast the labor situation reached a crisis. In May 1934 longshoremen along the entire Pacific Coast walked off their jobs, demanding higher wages, improved working conditions, and a closed shop. Sympathetic strikes by seamen and teamsters brought the shipping industry to a virtual standstill, and the companies (typically) hired African American strikebreakers. In early July, attempts to forcibly open San Francisco's ports led to rioting and two deaths. A funeral parade on July 9 attracted 40,000 marchers, and on July 16, 127,000 workers stayed home, marking the beginning of a three-day general strike.[69] The AFM's Local 6 acted in consort with its labor colleagues. Members were ordered off the job at the end of their engagements on July 15 and were prohibited from accepting any work except religious services for the duration of the strike. Five members of Local 6 attended all sessions of the General Strike Committee. One of them was secretary Eddie B. Love, who became a member of its executive committee.[70] Love would ultimately spearhead the attack on the members of Black Local 648, leading to the court action.

On a more positive note, Local 6 saw the repeal of Prohibition in 1933 as a new opportunity for work in night clubs. Even before the state approval process to ratify the Twenty-First Amendment was completed on December 5, 1933, the local's board of directors engaged in lengthy discussions about prices and classification.[71] A committee headed by Eddie Love took on the job of enforcing the new wages in the hundreds of clubs springing up in the city. Love reflected later that "when . . . the repeal of the Eighteenth

Amendment began to appear as a reality, a tremendous task confronted your [Local 6] officers."[72] His committee attacked this job with gusto; in Love's words, they "slept, drank and ate Night Clubs and Speaks for . . . eighteen months." Their contention was that since these establishments were now legitimate businesses, they "must be prepared to recognize legitimate competition, be content with legitimate profits, operate along legitimate lines, [and] pay their employees legitimate wages."[73]

The club owners didn't necessarily agree, of course, and when they "went up in arms and threatened wholesale reprisals," Local 6 sent a telegram to the AFM's national office "requesting forbidden territory for . . . all first and second-class clubs of any consequence."[74] AFM president Joseph Weber granted their request. The forbidden territory designation targeted employers who undercut union scale. Establishments were required to hire only members of the local union; those who violated this restriction faced boycotts not only from the musicians' union, but also from other sympathetic labor organizations, thus threatening their ability to stay in business. Designating establishments that violated union rules as "forbidden territory" aimed to preserve union jobs. The problem, of course, was that the San Francisco area had *two* local unions—6 and 648—with jurisdiction over the same establishments.

Normally the AFM imposed forbidden territory restrictions on a case-by-case basis. Had Local 6 used this approach, the conflict with Local 648 might not have escalated into full-scale war. But the AFM president's ruling not only set up Local 6 as the predominant union in the area, but also cast a blanket restriction over the entire region. Beginning in February 1934, the following announcement appeared every month in Local 6's magazine, *The Musical News*:

> Forbidden Territory List: All speakeasies and night clubs in the jurisdiction of Local No. 6, San Francisco, Calif., are declared Forbidden Territory to all members of the A. F. of M. other than members of Local No. 6. [Signed]: Jos. N. Weber, President, A. F. of M.[75]

Unsurprisingly, serious confrontations soon erupted between Locals 6 and 648 from this overriding restriction that reserved the entire Bay Area club scene exclusively for Local 6. For example, in December 1933, Local 6's board brought charges against 648's secretary Charles W. Strather "for working with non-members at the California Tavern in Oakland." And, as evidence of the high public demand for Black musicians, Local 6's board considered a request by one of its members in April 1934 to play at a reduced scale at the Alameda Walk-A-Way Derby in the East Bay; otherwise, he warned, the "operators will put in a colored orchestra."[76]

Employers, for their part, naturally wanted to keep entertainment costs down; and Black bands were not only economical, but also wildly popular. In the classical music field as well, African American artists performed in the city for enthusiastic, predominantly white audiences. On March 5, 1933, for example, tenor George Garner received a warm welcome by a large audience at the Community Playhouse;[77] and on December 29 of the same year, three thousand fans braved the pouring rain to hear tenor Roland Hayes sing at the recently opened War Memorial Opera House with the San Francisco Symphony, prompting an outstanding review from the often acerbic critic Alfred Metzger.[78] In 1937 contralto Marian Anderson made her San Francisco debut in solo recitals, as well as performances with Pierre Monteux and the Symphony in the 3,200-seat opera house. The *San Francisco Chronicle* published ten preview and review articles about her concerts and noted that at her appearance with the symphony she "electrified a capacity audience."[79] Anderson returned to San Francisco annually for several years. Although the AFM was an organization of instrumentalists only, the battles that these and other Black vocalists fought against racial prejudice were hardly less serious than those of AFM members. That Garner, Hayes, and Anderson were welcomed so enthusiastically in San Francisco and that they were featured in such high-profile venues suggests that the general population greeted talented Black singers with the same enthusiasm that Black bands experienced in night clubs.

Before World War II and the accompanying dramatic influx of Africans Americans to San Francisco, there was no segregated Black district in the city. (The African American population of the city mushroomed during the war years, increasing from 4,846 in 1940 to 43,502 in 1950.) Those Black residents who had moved to San Francisco before 1930 "scattered over a wide area,"[80] but many members of this tightly knit minority lived in the Western Addition, a multiethnic region composed mostly of working-class families. Jazz drummer Earl Watkins, who grew up in this district, remembers the city of the 1930s as lively and open. "We'd ride the Muni [street cars] up and down Market Street, enjoying shopping in all the stores," he recalled. The proud and confident Black population was careful to maintain an image of respectability. "We had to behave," says Watkins. "Because anywhere we went, there were members of our community; and if we acted up, our parents soon knew about it!"[81] To a significant extent, then, the small size of San Francisco's African American community and the relative lack of racial barriers in the city in this period actually exacerbated the union conflict in the 1930s by bringing Black musicians into direct competition with whites.

Local 648 didn't take the actions of Eddie Love's Night Club Committee lying down. It appealed repeatedly to the AFM's New York office. John

Figure 5.3. San Francisco drummer Earl Watkins (1920–2007) in 1952. (Courtesy of Earl Watkins. Photographer unknown.)

Terrell, Local 648's secretary, told San Francisco's Black newspaper *The Spokesman* that he had written "at least a dozen letters" and received no answer.[82] In September 1934, the *Chicago Defender*, which had picked up the story, reported that 648's "repeated wires and letters to national headquarters have been met with either a reference to Local 6 or with stony silence."[83] In contrast, when Local 6 charged Local 648 with "inept maintenance," it received word from the AFM that the "matter will be immediately taken up by Federation."[84]

Figure 5.4. Wilbert Baranco's band, 1938–39. Left to right: Vernon Alley, Bob Barfield, Wilbert Baranco. (Photo courtesy of Earl Watkins. Photographer unknown.)

Love's committee proved to be even more bellicose than might have been anticipated. Two incidents in the late summer of 1934 illustrate its hard-hitting tactics, which led directly to the lawsuit. In the first case, Bud Fisher, owner of the Tip Top Club, located near Union Square, was featuring a Black band from Local 648 led by Wilbert Baranco (see Figure 5.4). Fisher had reputedly lost $4,200 with the "Nordic" bands he previously employed.[85]

One night in mid-August, Baranco's band showed up for work to find police at the door. They were told their services were no longer needed. Indeed, Local 6 had registered a protest with the national office, and AFM President Weber had responded by "advising that members of Local No. 648 who accepted engagement at the Tip Top Club have terminated their membership in the Federation by doing so and requesting list of members involved."[86] Eddie Love admitted to a reporter from *The Spokesman* that he and his committee were instrumental in having the group discharged. Fisher was forced to vacate his lease and by September 1934 the Tip Top

Club was under new management and featured a band from Local 6.[87] Byron "Speed" Reilly, who wrote a weekly "Star Stuff" column in *The Spokesman*, fumed that members of Local 6 "are said to have approached the owner and when he refused to discharge the sepia ork . . . , he was warned that he would 'make a change or else.'"[88]

Soon a similar situation arose at the Liberty Theater, located on the edge of Chinatown. In this case, the theater management dismissed a band led by Wade Whaley (a board member of Local 648) four days after the group began work; union rules required two weeks' notice. *The Spokesman*'s reporter wrote that "the manager of the theater was very indignant and . . . that persons affiliated with the white union told him, 'Get those N——s out of here or your place will be closed.'"[89]

The dismissal of Whaley's band pushed the growing conflict into pitched battle. On August 24, 1934, Lester Robinson (a member of the band) and three other musicians from Local 648 filed for an injunction against Local 6 in the San Francisco Superior Court. Five days later a summons was served on Local 6's officers and an Order to Show Cause was filed requesting interim relief. The plaintiffs demanded that Local 6 cease "interfering with [their] performances."[90]

Unfortunately, San Francisco's Superior Court has destroyed the transcripts of all cases from this period; but the Record of Action survives and is shown in Figure 5.5.[91] Together with reports in the Black press, we can reconstruct the legal battle. The plaintiffs secured the services of a well-respected attorney, Alexander Mooslin.[92] Local 6 pulled out the big guns, hiring the firm of Dunne and Dunne, one of whose named partners, Harvard-educated Arthur B. Dunne, later became president of the San Francisco Bar Association.[93]

On August 28 Local 6's board discussed the "action brought by members of the Colored Local in the Superior Court," which specifically named its officers as defendants: Walter Weber (president), Karl Dietrich (business agent), Jack Haywood (vice president), Clarence King (treasurer), and Eddie Love (secretary); see Figure 5.5, lines 2–4. Dietrich contacted AFM president Joseph Weber, who in turn warned Local 648's secretary that if the court case proceeded before all internal remedies were exhausted, the members involved would be expelled from the union and the Black local risked losing its charter. Local 648's members, however, voted to proceed despite these threats. Meanwhile, Local 6's board instructed Eddie Love to file a formal grievance with the International.[94]

Judge Louis Ward, however, proved receptive to the arguments of the plaintiffs. He allowed time for an amended complaint but, according to *The*

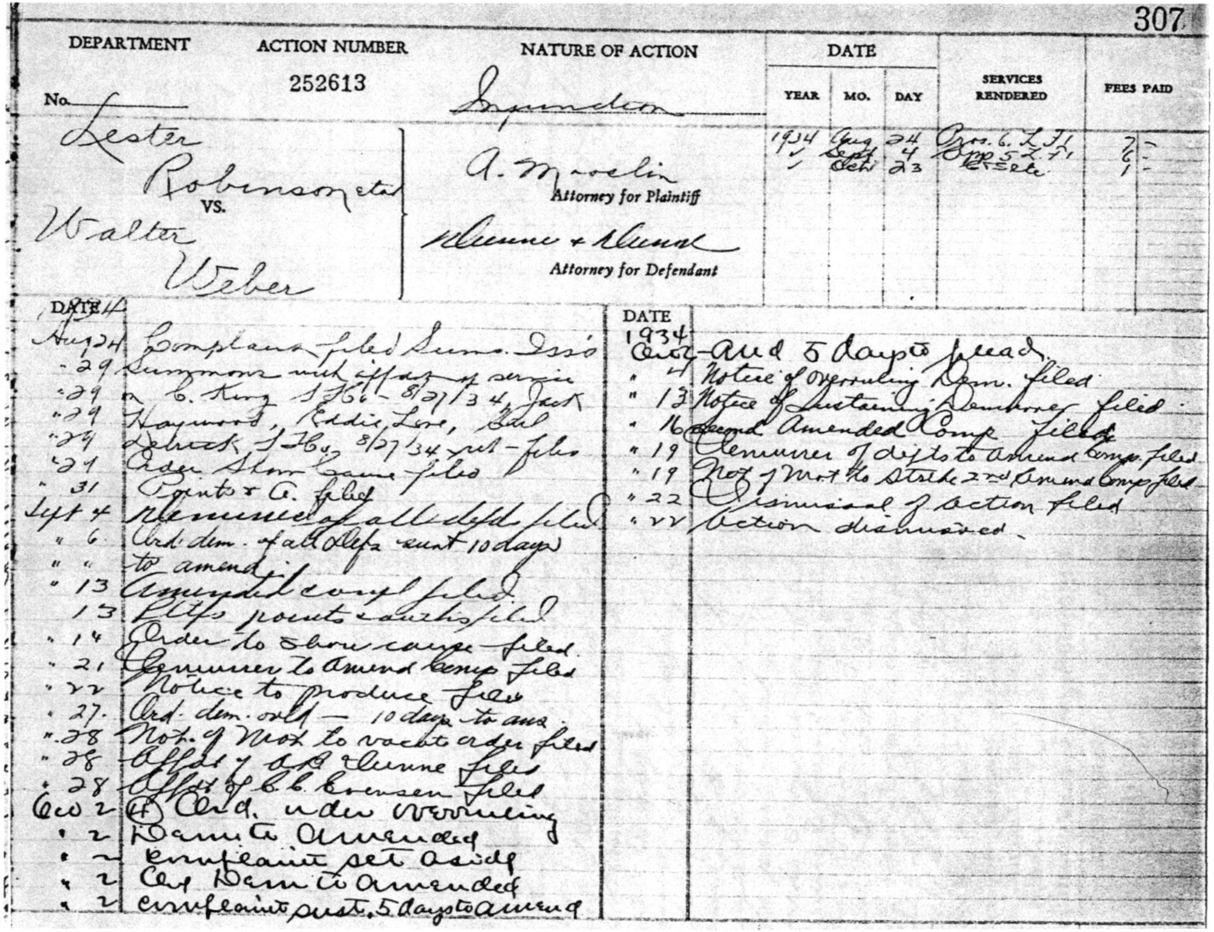

307

DEPARTMENT | ACTION NUMBER 252613 | NATURE OF ACTION Injunction | DATE: YEAR, MO., DAY | SERVICES RENDERED | FEES PAID

No. Lester Robinson et al vs. Walter Weber

A. Mocelin, Attorney for Plaintiff

Dunne & Dunne, Attorney for Defendant

1934 Aug 24 — 7.-
Sept 4 — 6.-
Oct 23 — 1.-

DATE 1934
Aug 24 Complaint filed Sum. Iss'd
" 29 Summons with affdt of service
" 29 on C. King 8/27/34, Jack
" 29 Haywood, Eddie Lee, Carl
" 29 Petrock 8/27/34 ret-filed
" 29 Order Show Cause filed
" 31 Points & A. filed
Sept 4 Demurrer of all defts filed
" 6 Ord. dem. of all defts sust 10 days
" " to amend
" 13 Amended compl filed
13 Pltfs points & auths filed
" 14 Order to show cause filed
" 21 Demurrer to Amend Comp filed
" 22 Notice to produce filed
" 27 Ord. dem. ovrl — 10 days to ans.
" 28 Not. of Mot to vacate order filed
" 28 Affdt of Dunne filed
" 28 Affdt of C. C. Evensen filed
Oct 2 (4) Ord. order overruling
" 2 Dem to Amended
" 2 complaint set aside
" 2 Ord Dem to amended
" 2 complaint sust. 5 days to amend

DATE 1934
Oct — and 5 days to plead
" 4 Notice of Overruling Dem. filed
" 13 Notice of Sustaining Demurrer filed
" 16 Second Amended Comp filed
" 19 Demurrer of defts to Amend Comp. filed
" 19 Not. of Mot to Strike 2nd Amend Comp filed
" 22 Dismissal of action filed
" 22 Action dismissed.

Figure 5.5. San Francisco Superior Court Record of Action, case no. 252613, 1934.

Spokesman, told the white union that "unless they proved, when the case is heard again . . . , that they have not interfered illegally with the hiring of Negro musicians in the Bay district, he will issue a court order COMPEL-LING them to keep hands off managers of theaters, restaurants, hotels, and nite spots using Negro orchestras."[95] The court took testimony from John Casey of the Liberty Theater, who said he was threatened that his stage hands, projectionists, and other union employees would walk out unless he fired Whaley's band; and from Mimi Imperato, a flamboyant impresario and restaurant owner who said that he was forced to fire the band Ennis and his Gang.

The case made headlines in Black papers elsewhere, including *The Chicago Defender* and the *California Eagle* in Los Angeles.[96] The *Defender* highlighted Local 6's success in enlisting the help of the police:

> It is also currently reported that . . . the white local is using its purposed [*sic*; purported?] influence with the police department by having the local police harass such places whose operators cannot entirely stand before the law or whose places are a trifle shady. . . . The business agent of Local 6 called and informed the operators [of the Tip Top Club] they would have to get rid of the Negro musicians. The operators demurred, as they were having good crowds and making money, whereupon, it is reported, the police became suddenly active and began to crack down on the place, imposing such restrictions as to make it impossible for the club to continue.[97]

The defense alleged that Local 648 was under the "watch care" of Local 6,[98] an argument reminiscent of Weber's 1928 ruling regarding the supervisory privileges of (white) Local 76 in Seattle. Nevertheless, on Thursday, September 27, Judge Ward ruled in favor of the plaintiffs, giving Local 6's lawyers ten days to answer. Dunne and Dunne immediately submitted a motion to vacate.

On October 1, 1934, just after the lawsuit reached this stage, the American Federation of Labor opened its fifty-fourth convention in San Francisco. A. Philip Randolph mounted his annual protestations concerning the AFL's record of (not) dealing with its overtly racist unions. With support from the NAACP and local Black attorneys, San Franciscans organized a picket line: "Neatly-dressed young Negro men and women paraded back and forth before the Whitcomb Hotel," where the delegates were housed, and at the doors of the civic auditorium, where 2,000 attendees "were applauding idealistic utterances."[99] The picketing seems to have been invisible to the white press, but *The Spokesman* heralded it as "one of the Aframerican's boldest and most dramatic strokes for economic equality in American history."[100] Members of Local 648 were not present, apparently exercising "excessive caution" lest they jeopardize their recent advances in court.[101] In the convention hall, Randolph introduced five resolutions dealing with Black workers, again demanding, as he had many times in the past, the expulsion of unions with "whites only" clauses in their constitutions or rituals, as well as the appointment of a committee to study the plight of African American union workers.[102] Once again, the AFL rejected the expulsion demand (the familiar argument: the federation could not interfere with the inner workings of its member unions), but the convention supported the appointment of an investigative committee to report back in 1935. AFL president William Green eventually appointed a Committee of Five—all whites—which issued a report urging immediate action. This report never reached the delegates, however. Instead, the 1935 delegates saw a substitute version prepared by George M. Harrison, president of the historically racist Brotherhood of Railway Clerks. The same 1935 convention witnessed a physical confrontation between John L. Lewis, head of the United Mine Workers, and William Hutcheson, head of the carpenters' union, over the issue of industrial versus craft organization. The AFL delegates voted to continue their craft structure, thereby effectively expelling those unions interested in industrial organization. The rebels, led by Lewis, formed the rival CIO, which courted Black workers.[103]

Meanwhile, actions in the Superior Court continued apace and the judge continued to indicate his sympathy with the plaintiffs. Then, however, the situation took a surprising turn: the Black musicians withdrew their action and on October 22, 1934, the case was dismissed with no ruling (see Figure 5.5). We can only speculate on what occasioned this unexpected move. AFM president Joseph Weber was one of eight vice presidents of the AFL and he attended the San Francisco convention. He might well have applied pressure on the Local 648 officers in phone conversations or personal meetings. Local 6's minutes are not enlightening; they simply report a communication from Dunne and Dunne "advising plaintiff had dismissed the case."[104] *The Spokesman*'s reporter speculated that Local 648 withdrew its suit because members feared the loss of the union's charter.[105]

A week later, Local 648's secretary Terrell—in an apparent attempt to make peace—appeared at the Local 6 board meeting "re supervising all steady engagements where their members play."[106] But a more insidious action was simultaneously underway. On November 13, Local 6's minutes report a communication from the AFM's secretary, William J. Kerngood: "The International Executive Board has found Local 648 . . . guilty of the complaint of this Local [6] and its charter has been revoked."[107] Local 6's board contended that the revocation was not based on the lawsuit, but rather on the fact "that conditions of working, rates of pay, and punishment of its members for infractions of rules by Local 648 are not in accordance with union orders."[108] Local 648 filed a response, "but no reply was received other than the demand for their charter."[109]

In retrospect, it appears likely that officials from the International persuaded the Local 648 plaintiffs to drop their suit, perhaps under the threat of losing their charter or through false assurances of an equitable resolution of the conflict (or both). The negative effect of a revoked charter, however, was in fact minimal because the Black musicians were already barred from work by the Forbidden Territory ruling that reserved all jobs in Bay Area clubs for Local 6—the focus of the lawsuit in the first place. Even if the plaintiffs had won in court—which seemed likely based on the judge's rulings—and even if they could prevail in any appeal process, they would stand to lose in the long run.

Despite the revocation of their union's charter, African American musicians continued to play in Bay Area clubs. Baranco, notes an article in *The Spokesman*, was "heading a six piece orchestra at the Dawn night club," only a few blocks from the Tip Top Club.[110] Local 6's minutes confirm that the Dawn Club had "gone non-union" and that the place was "100 per cent colored throughout." Dawn Club owner H. LaFerne ran several cafes in San Francisco that were repeatedly picketed by various white unions. The success and expansion of his businesses, claimed *The Spokesman*, "has been possible only through the savings made by hiring Negro workers."[111]

On January 7, 1935, the IEB considered an application by the Black musicians in the Bay Area for a new charter. It referred the matter to AFM President Weber, who in turn sent it to Local 6 for comment.[112] Local 6's new president, Albert Greenbaum, told fifty musicians of the former 648 that current AFM policy prohibited a new charter, but the AFM could offer subsidiary status, which *The Spokesman* described as an "olive twig."[113] The obvious alternative—simply admitting the musicians of Local 648 to Local 6 as regular dues-paying members—was apparently never considered. Instead, as in St. Louis, the Black musicians faced two undesirable alternatives: fighting continual turf battles with Local 6 as nonunion employees, or accepting far less than equal union status. The subsidiary option, though demeaning, at least offered the prospect of steady employment and peace within the union ranks. *The Spokesman*, despite its strong advocacy for African American rights, advised the musicians to hold their noses, accept the offer, and work for change from the inside.[114] It would be nine years before such a change took place and then only with considerable reluctance on the part of Local 6.

The AFM established "Subsidiary Local 6" on April 15, 1935.[115] Black musicians didn't see immediate improvements in employment, however. As usual they were caught in a no-win situation: if they accepted rates below the white scale, they faced discipline from Local 6; if they charged equal rates, employers hired white bands instead. At the Dawn Club, for instance, owner LaFerne fired Baranco's band as soon as he discovered he'd have to pay them at the Local 6 rate. Despite his impassioned (and seemingly genuine) professions of support, LaFerne hired a white group in their place.[116]

CHAPTER 6

The 1940s
Change Is in the Wind

The July 1944 issue of the *International Musician* featured a welcome announcement on page 1, highlighted in box. "The colored delegates to the Chicago Convention," read the blurb, "appointed the following delegation to represent them before the International Executive Board, requesting that the Board consider granting the subsidiary colored locals full autonomy and that subsidiary locals be abolished."[1] There followed a list of seven representatives from Black locals, including Lloyd Plummer from Buffalo, who had introduced the failed resolution to abolish subsidiaries seven years earlier; representatives from some of the largest and most influential Black unions (Cleveland, Atlanta, Chicago, Los Angeles, and Washington, DC); and traveling representative Ray Jackson, longtime agitator for Black local independence (mentioned in chapter 5). "After due consideration," the announcement continued, "the International Executive Board by unanimous vote has abolished subsidiary charters in connection with colored locals. There were twelve locals operating as subsidiaries.... These former subsidiary locals will receive a charter of their own ... and will govern themselves in the same manner as any other local." The announcement is signed by AFM President James C. Petrillo, who had succeeded Joseph Weber in 1940 (see Figure 6.1).

Thirteen years later Petrillo boasted to *Downbeat Magazine* that he was personally responsible for this long overdue change. "One of my first acts when I became president," he asserted, "was to insist on the abolition of the 'subsidiary' local status for negro locals."[2] This self-serving statement, however, may have inflated to a certain degree Petrillo's personal role in fighting racism. Since 1922 he had been (and continued to be, even while

> ## Subsidiary Locals Granted Autonomy
>
> The colored delegates to the Chicago Convention appointed the following delegation to represent them before the International Executive Board, requesting that the Board consider granting the subsidiary colored locals full autonomy and that subsidiary locals be abolished:
>
> R. L. Goodwin................Local 550, Cleveland, Ohio
> P. S. Cooke......................Local 462, Atlanta, Georgia
> Harry W. Gray................Local 208, Chicago, Illinois
> L. V. Plummer................Local 533, Buffalo, New York
> Edward Bailey......Local 767, Los Angeles, California
> William H. Bailey......Local 710, Washington, D. C.
> Traveling Representative Jackson
>
> After due consideration, the International Executive Board by unanimous vote has abolished subsidiary charters in connection with colored locals. There were twelve locals operating as subsidiaries under control of the white locals in their respective jurisdictions. This means that these former subsidiary locals will receive a charter of their own from the American Federation of Musicians and will govern themselves in the same manner as any other local.
>
> JAMES C. PETRILLO, President.

Figure 6.1. *International Musician*, July 1944. Announcement of the abolition of the twelve subsidiary locals.

he served as AFM president) the head of the huge Local 10 in Chicago, which on several occasions had declined to admit African Americans. (Local 10 had nearly ten thousand members in the year in which subsidiaries were eliminated.)[3] The decision to abolish the subsidiaries came not as one of Petrillo's first acts, but four years after his election as president. Furthermore, it was not simply a directive from the president, but rather an IEB decision, prompted by urgings from Black delegates. Although the IEB vote was unanimous, the committee doesn't seem to have prioritized the matter on its long agenda. The board had met regularly during the six days of the 1944 convention, but this issue came up only at the eleventh hour—in a late-night session the day after the convention ended. An obscure item buried in the annual *Official Proceedings* records the minutes of that June 11 meeting: "The question of eliminating subsidiary charters is considered. On motion passed, it is decided that subsidiary locals be given separate charters on condition that they are bound by the price list of the principal local for the class of business done by such local."[4]

The specification that new independent Black locals would only be authorized "on condition that they are bound by the price list of the principal local" not only confirms that the IEB considered the white locals to be preeminent ("principal") over their Black counterparts, but also suggests that Black musicians working below the white local's scale had been a major cause for creating subsidiaries in the first place. In principle, the (non-subsidiary) Black locals enjoyed the same rights and privileges as any other local in the federation, which included, of course, determining their own price lists; but if they were not authorized to set their own wages, were they truly independent? Or were they in fact operating under the authority of their white counterparts?

The minutes of the IEB say nothing about any urging from President Petrillo, although he certainly would have been instrumental in approving the delegation shown in Figure 6.1. That delegation had met with the IEB the evening before the vote "to discuss various phases of the situation and ask that subsidiary locals be granted independent charters."[5] Nevertheless (and despite the late timing of the IEB vote), Petrillo must have had confidence in the board's decision when the convention began. Lige Shaw from St. Louis later recalled that when he "walked into the Sherman Hotel in Chicago," he ran into Petrillo who said to him, "You won't have to fight for your charter this time; we're going to give it back to you and Local number 2 has agreed to it."[6]

An unrelated action by Petrillo two years earlier offers a somewhat different perspective on his own attitudes. Shortly after he became president of the AFM, he chose to honor none other than Eddie Love, the brash Local 6 secretary from San Francisco who had spearheaded the belligerent actions that led to the 1934 lawsuit described in chapter 5. Petrillo appointed Love as one of his assistants and brought him to New York. We must assume that he was unaware, however, of the unsavory revelations (unrelated to the lawsuit) that would soon emerge about his new employee. Shortly after Love left San Francisco, Local 6's treasurer, Clarence King, began discovering financial irregularities. A five-month investigation brought to light the history of Love's dishonesty: between 1936 and 1942 he had embezzled $8,228.30 from the Local 6 treasury (equivalent to more than $145,000 in 2022). The bulk of the money came from required standby fees paid by radio stations. Love's scheme was not terribly sophisticated. He simply failed to report these fees and deposited the money in his personal bank account. Because King's office handled "close to a half million dollars a year and fifty thousand transactions," Love avoided detection until he left the area.[7]

Upon King's discovery of the embezzlement, Local 6 officers brought Love back from New York and charged him with fraud. At a meeting on May 7, 1943, he pleaded guilty. Despite his entreaties for leniency based on his long service record, members presented a petition with fifty-four signatures, urging the board to press criminal charges.[8] Instead, the administration settled for repayment. Love paid off part of the debt in cash, handed over a car, and agreed to monthly payments of fifty dollars. He lost his job in New York, was expelled from the AFM, and went to work in the shipyards. By August 1945 he was unemployed. Two months later he applied for a booker's license; Local 6's board recommended against issuing it.[9] Despite his Herculean efforts in uncovering the details of Love's offenses, treasurer King also took a fall; after twenty-nine years of service, he was defeated by James Voss in the election of December 1943.[10]

The AFM's 1944 national convention took place in Chicago, home not only to the enormous (white) Local 10, but also to the federation's largest Black local (No. 208). Although membership throughout the federation had shrunk considerably since the late 1920s, Local 208 still topped the Black local roster with 677 members.[11] The next closest was Los Angeles with 481.

African American musicians, including many representatives from Local 208, occupied a place of honor during the convention's activities. The meeting opened, for example, with a lengthy concert by the Chicago Symphony featuring renowned African American contralto Marian Anderson, who performed both opera arias and spirituals (as was her custom).[12] In addition, a concert band conducted by the Black music educator Walter Dyett entertained the delegates on four separate occasions, preceding the morning and afternoon sessions on June 7 and June 10. At the end of the sessions on June 9, William Everett Samuels, secretary of Local 208, invited the delegates to a jam session at the prestigious Club DeLisa, where Red Saunders led the house band. In the 1960s Saunders would spearhead and guide the complex and contentious amalgamation efforts between Locals 208 and 10. Bands from Local 10 also performed prior to morning and afternoon sessions on June 8 and June 9.

Soon after the IEB's vote, new charters began to be issued to members of the now-defunct subsidiaries. Table 6.1 shows the twelve subsidiaries and their status after June 1944.

Most of the new Black locals were small, typically with fewer than a hundred members. The largest was St. Louis's Local 197, with 226 members in 1946, followed by San Francisco's Local 669 at 183. As Table 6.1 shows, it took two years to resolve the situation in some cities. San Francisco offers a particularly curious—and quite revealing—case. In June 1945 the board of Subsidiary Local 6 wrote to the IEB asking to *remain* a subsidiary.[13] This surprising request may have been designed to convince the IEB of the good working relations the subsidiary had forged (or attempted to forge) with

Table 6.1. The twelve subsidiaries in existence in 1944 and their status after subsidiaries were abolished at the June convention.

City	Affiliation of Black Musicians after the June 1944 Abolition of Subsidiaries	Date of New Action	Subsequent History
Tulsa, OK	New Black local: No. 808	1944, July 24	1965: merged w Local 94
St. Louis, MO	New Black local: No. 197	1944, Oct. 27	1971: merged w Local 2
Fort Worth, TX	New Black local: No. 392	1944, Nov. 1	1966: merged w Local 72
Steubenville, OH	Action unclear; "charter abandoned"; subsidiary members possibly absorbed into white local 223	1945, Jan. 31	
Atlantic City, NJ	New Black local: No. 708	1945, Apr. 16	1969: merged w Local 661
Richmond, VA	New Black local: No. 695	1945, Apr. 17	1963: disbanded
San Francisco, CA	New Black local: No. 669	1946, Mar. 7	1960: merged w Local 6
Lexington, KY	New Black local: No. 635	1946, Apr. 1	1967: merged w Local 554
Galveston, TX	New Black local: No. 699	1946, Aug. 12	1947: charter revoked
Little Rock, AR	Membership absorbed by (white) local 266		
Columbia, SC	No record after 1944		
Anaconda, MT	No record after 1944		

white Local 6, in the hopes that admission to Local 6 as regular members would follow. Indeed, the minutes of Local 6 over the years preceding the abolition of subsidiaries imply peaceful interactions between the two groups. Figure 6.2, for instance, shows a paid holiday ad from the subsidiary that appeared in Local 6's newsletter in January 1944. Despite its gracious tone, one must question whether the expressed good wishes and thanks to Local 6's officers and members were really a sign of the subsidiary members' satisfaction with their disenfranchised status. Instead, the ad may well have represented an attempt to reassure the Local 6 board of the cooperation they could expect by admitting the subsidiary's members to full membership. The officers of the subsidiary might also have learned about the resolution of the situation in Little Rock, where subsidiary members were absorbed into the white local (shown in Table 6.1). In any case, at the end of September 1945, Alex Forbes, secretary of San Francisco's subsidiary, presented a petition to the board of Local 6 requesting that the Black musicians be made regular members of the white local.[14] The matter never came up for a vote by the Local 6 board, however. Instead, a delegation from both Local 6 and its subsidiary met with the IEB on January 17, 1946, and the next day

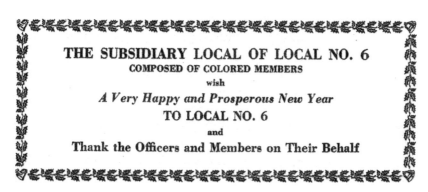

Figure 6.2. Paid ad in Local 6's monthly newsletter, *The Musical News*, January 1944, 23.

the IEB determined that a new Black local should be formed. Local 669 received its official charter on March 7, 1946.

Although the Black musicians of San Francisco did not achieve their goal, their actions are revealing in terms of later efforts at amalgamation. Unlike African Americans in most other cities, the San Francisco group clearly wanted to be part of the white local, even though they would constitute only about 4.5 percent of a merged membership: in 1946, Local 6 had twenty-two times as many members as the new Local 669.[15] Given these figures, it seems rather mean-spirited of Local 6 to have refused to grant its Black subsidiary members full rights. White musicians would hardly have noticed the change, much less been disadvantaged by providing membership with complete rights to the Black musicians. When mergers began to take place in earnest beginning in the late 1950s, Local 669 would again campaign for amalgamation but Local 6 would again resist. In contrast, in most other cities the Black locals were the ones that opposed merger.

Pressure Increases to End Segregation

Calls for the amalgamation of Black and white locals increased dramatically during the 1940s. A revealing article, headlined "Must There Be Segregation in the Union?" appeared in *Music and Rhythm* in 1942.[16] Brief responses from twenty-nine leaders in the popular music field follow. Despite Black locals having organized originally at the behest of Black musicians—albeit in response to overt prejudice or intentional (or unintentional) barriers erected by the white locals—the implicit assumption of most respondents was that the AFM currently mandated segregation. Many of the responses highlighted the hypocrisy of fighting Nazi racism and antisemitism abroad while tolerating racism at home. "When we are fighting Hitler because he insists on racial prejudice, it is time that our country showed its democratic hand by everyone cooperating in the fight against any evidence of prejudice," said Glenn Miller. "Keeping the colored artists out of the same union as white musicians throughout the nation is definitely a form of bias." The majority of the twenty-nine respondents urged merger. "Abolishing colored locals would be a great step toward breaking down and eliminating race prejudice," said Count Basie. Zutty Singleton suggested that amalgamation "would encourage good fellowship." "Hotels and ballrooms who now must deal with a white local exclusively would hire Negro artists," said Milton Ebbins. "Colored musicians . . . could receive more money for their work." A few respondents, however, expressed caution that mergers might in fact disadvantage Blacks—an argument that numerous African American locals would voice in the decades to come. Citing the situation in Kansas City, for example, songwriter Bob Strong worried that "if the locals were combined and the scales increased, wouldn't a lot of small night spots playing colored talent fold up?" While many of the respondents praised New York's Local 802 for its integrated membership (apparently unaware of its predecessor's early moves to prevent a Black local from forming), pianist and arranger Billy Moore asked, "Why is the New York Roseland Ballroom scale $55 a man and the Savoy scale $38?"

Indeed, the situation of dual locals was rapidly becoming untenable. The AFM might argue that Black musicians had requested their own unions, but the issue was now crystallizing into a condemnation of unjustifiable racial segregation. The war also hastened efforts throughout the country to eliminate segregation in whatever guises it had assumed. The reality of Black soldiers defending the United States with their lives against authoritarianism and the horrors of genocide was hardly lost on the proponents of integration. For the federation to refuse to recognize the poisonous implications of racial discrimination in the country is "like an ostrich sticking his head into the ground," reflected Sonny Burke. "Segregation is most un-American."[17]

At the same time, the elimination of subsidiaries in 1944 seems to have brought about improved feelings for the AFM on the part of Black musicians. For example, at the 1946 convention in St. Petersburg, Florida, the Black delegates introduced a "resolution of thanks" to Petrillo, the IEB, and the "entire convention" for canceling a picnic on June 4 because Black delegates would have been prohibited from riding on integrated buses. Petrillo terminated the event and turned over the $3,500 designated for refreshments to a local charity. He later claimed that he took this action "in the face of vicious criticism by the local press and officials, and threats of criminal prosecution under a local ordinance."[18] A unanimous decision by the IEB led to the cancellation.[19] The entire group of Black delegates to the convention signed the resolution of thanks, including forty-one members, representing 5.5 percent of the total number of attendees. Among them are some familiar names: Elijah Shaw, now representing Local 197 (St. Louis), Harry Gray from Local 208, Alex Forbes from Local 669 in San Francisco, and members of the 1944 delegation that had spearheaded the abolition of subsidiaries (Edward Bailey, William Bailey, P. S. Cooke, and Gray).

At the same time, it would be naive to suggest that the strain over segregated locals had ended. *Downbeat* issued a steady stream of articles reporting on racial tension in the union. One example was a disturbing series of events in Miami in 1949 that evokes memories of the conflict in San Francisco fifteen years earlier, though without such drastic repercussions.[20] Bill Preyer, operator of the Sky Club, had hired Earl Hodges, leader of a (white) jazz trio, both to perform and to book other ensembles. The concerts proved highly popular, attracting sold-out crowds. After the fifth performance, Hodges, who was a member of New York's Local 802 performing in Miami as a traveling musician, arranged for a Black trio to appear on the series. He soon received a telegram from the president of Miami's white Local 655 telling him he was only authorized to hire members of that union. Black Local 690 countered that its charter allowed its members to play anywhere in the city. (Local 690, by the way, did not have much presence on the national scene. This Black union did not send any delegates to the annual convention from its chartering in 1946 through its dissolution in 1957.)[21]

At the next concert Hodges read the telegram from Local 655 to the audience, prompting the white local to mount competing events at two other venues. Club operator Preyer reported that a member of the liquor board visited him and insisted he discontinue using the "n—— musicians." Preyer also asserted that for the next two weeks, when the Black trio performed, union representatives from 655 showed up right before the show and began very slowly checking union cards, thereby delaying the performance for an hour. These actions caused the cancellation of the entire series of concerts at all of the venues involved. Local 655 asked that the AFM place the Sky Club on the Forbidden Territory list; they tried Hodges in absentia and levied fines of $400 on him and $200 each on his colleagues. The alleged offenses involved playing under scale and intimidating the club manager. Hodges retorted that the first offense stemmed from one instance of running a few minutes past 7 p.m., when the scale went up, and advertising the concerts under his name instead of Preyer's. Preyer was understandably disgruntled.

"I told them what to do with their local," he said. "I'd still be hiring 10 or 15 of their men a week if it hadn't been for their Jim Crow policy."

In Kansas City, Black local 627 had thrived, even during the Great Depression when others were suffering. Journalist Dave Dexter reported that between 1930 and 1935, membership had increased tenfold, from about forty to about four hundred.[22] But in the late 1940s bitter conflicts developed with the police concerning popular Sunday afternoon interracial events at the Hot Club.[23] In Detroit, racially integrated Local 5 allegedly began cracking down on jam sessions in 1947, assessing fines for "under-scale pay . . . , too many on the stand at a time," and other offenses. "Charges have been made," asserted *Downbeat*'s reporter, Lou Cramton, "that the union has frowned on mixed sessions."[24]

Since the mid-1930s (and the publicity generated when Teddy Wilson began performing with Benny Goodman), interracial bands had become increasingly common. *Downbeat* tracked the trend in a series of articles beginning in August 1939: "Goodman Adds Noted Negro Pianist" [Fletcher Henderson], followed the next month by a front-cover headline "Can Goodman Erase Color Line?" and an internal article noting that "Goodman Plans to Add More Negroes to Band." Other articles appeared over the next decade, for instance, "[Juan] Tizol [trombonist with Ellington] Sees Mixed Bands for Future" and "First Mixed Group Hits Pittsburgh." The magazine's editors reflected on the simultaneous decrease in popularity of all-Black bands. One columnist asked provocatively, "Are Colored Bands Doomed as Big Money Makers? Negro Leaders Could Make More Money Running a Rib Joint," and then followed up two weeks later with a hypothesis on the cause: most of the white bands were "stealing ideas from the Negro" by using Black talent and Black arrangers, thereby making all-Black bands less distinctive.[25]

The anachronistic AFM organizational structure made travel by racially integrated bands both cumbersome and increasingly senseless. When such bands moved from city to city, Black members had to register with one local while whites registered with another. Adding to the restrictions imposed on African Americans by hotel and restaurant constraints, outrage began to mount in the face of the dual local processes, as did pressure for merger.

As usual, developments in the AFM mirrored those in the society at large. Progress in dismantling segregation both in the union and in the country was slow, but at the same time a series of laws and court rulings during the 1940s began to pave the way for more substantial progress in the next two decades. For example, in June 1941 FDR, alarmed by the scheduling of a March on Washington on July 1, signed Executive Order 8802, the Fair Employment Act, mandating that "there shall be no discrimination in the employment of workers in defense industries or government because of race, creed, color, or national origin." A. Philip Randolph, who had organized the march, canceled it in response, but established the March on Washington Movement (MOWM) to maintain pressure on Roosevelt and the federal government in general to discontinue segregationist policies.[26] Although the act set a precedent for anti-racist legislation and established the Fair Employment Practices Committee (FEPC), it contained no provisions to ensure enforcement. The FEPC was quite ineffective until FDR's Executive Order 9346 (1943), which established the President's Committee on Fair Employment Practice. In regard to labor in particular, Order 9346 forbade unions from discriminating by race, creed, or sex. The FEPC conducted investigations into the shipbuilding and railroad industries,[27] where explicit whites-only constitutional restrictions were still in effect. Bolstered by activism on the part of the MOWM, the NAACP, the National Negro Congress (founded in 1936), and other organizations, Black workers began to make slow progress toward dismantling segregation. They also began to seek redress from the courts and, as we will see, won some favorable rulings in 1944. Among the other developments during this decade, we might note the establishment by the CIO of a Committee to Abolish Racial Discrimination (1943) and Harry Truman's Executive Order 9981, mandating desegregation of the military (1948).

James v. Marinship: A Landmark Anti-Segregation Victory

An important step forward in California came about through the efforts of a San Francisco–based singer who was also an expert welder. A native of South Carolina, Joseph James had studied at Boston University, sung in the Hall Johnson Choir in a production of *Green Pastures*, worked as a pickup actor in Hollywood films in typically racist roles ("mostly running around as a savage in a G-string, feeling pretty silly"),[28] and sung with the Eva Jessye Choir in the original 1935 Boston/New York production of *Porgy and Bess*. Three years later he came to Los Angeles for the revival of *Porgy*, again as a member of the chorus. The troupe then moved to San Francisco, where, in February–March 1938, it presented the show in a three-week run at the 1,800-seat Curran Theater.[29] Thereafter, James stayed in northern California.

In the San Francisco area, James joined the (segregated) East Bay chorus organized under the WPA's Federal Music Project and conducted by Elmer Keeton.[30] The chorus had developed an outstanding reputation throughout the Bay Area for its technical expertise and passionate interpretation, and in June 1939 Keeton's group mounted a show, *Swing Mikado*, at the Golden Gate International Exposition on Treasure Island. (The production was a remake of Gilbert and Sullivan's 1885 *Mikado*, now set on a South Seas island; it used Arthur Sullivan's music but added a half dozen interpolated swing numbers.)[31] James sang the role of Pooh-Bah.

To earn a living, James had gone to work as a welder for Marinship, one of the many shipyards created by the U.S. Maritime Commission during the Second World War. Nearly 70 percent of the workers in Bay Area shipyards were represented by the Boilermakers' Union, which relegated Blacks to "auxiliary" units, similar to the subsidiary locals in the AFM.[32] The Boilermakers, who had excluded Black workers entirely prior to 1937, established these auxiliaries beginning in the Southern states, but the practice soon spread throughout the country and by 1944 there were forty-four such units with 13,678 members.[33] The first Black auxiliary in the Bay Area started in 1942. Black workers paid dues to the national, but had no independent grievance procedure, no right to hire their own business agents, no vote on local matters, no apprenticeships, no representation at national conventions, reduced insurance benefits, and limited opportunities for career advancement. In 1943, testifying at a hearing by the President's Committee on Fair Employment Practice, Herbert Northrup spelled out these and other restrictions on Black workers, noting that "the only similarity between a white local and a negro auxiliary [in the Boilermakers' union] was that the dues paid by each were the same."[34]

James, who was a member of the "Flying Squadron" of expert welders, had achieved recognition at the company for providing extracurricular vocal entertainment. "As a concert baritone," reported an article in the company's magazine in August 1943, "Mr. James is known to musical circles from coast to coast.... He has been heard often at yard programs and at launchings, where he is a popular favorite."[35] (See Figure 6.3.)

James might have been a favorite with his coworkers, but he became a thorn in the side of Marinship's management when he decided to challenge the Boilermakers' segregationist policies. He became, in the words of the *Labor Citizen*, the "sparkplug" in the fight,[36] encouraging his colleagues to battle the separatist requirements of the union. After about half of the 1,100 African American boilermakers in the San Francisco area refused to join the union's Black auxiliary, Marinship began to dismiss them. By the end of November 1943, 160 Black workers—James among them—had been fired. Under the auspices of the San Francisco Committee Against Segregation and Discrimination, James then spearheaded a lawsuit (*James v. Marinship*) that sought reinstatement by the company and monetary damages from the

Figure 6.3. Joseph James sings at a Marinship launch, ca. 1943. (Courtesy of the San Francisco Maritime National Historical Park, P82-021.1n SAFR19067.)

Boilermakers. The Marin Superior Court ruled in favor of the plaintiffs and, on appeal, the California Supreme Court upheld the decision in a landmark ruling issued on January 2, 1945.[37] The court prohibited the union from requiring African Americans to join auxiliary units as a condition of employment and by 1948 all of the union's locals in the Bay Area were integrated.

Indeed, many unions had made significant strides toward racial integration. In 1950 Fred Stripp published an article on "The Treatment of Negro-American Workers by the AFL and the CIO in the San Francisco

Bay Area." He reported that the Hotel and Restaurant Workers, Commercial Telegraphers, Blacksmiths, Railway Clerks, and Railway Carmen had all "removed the color bar from their membership requirements."[38] There remained, he noted, five large exclusionary white unions in San Francisco. One of them was the AFM's Local 6. That situation—not just in San Francisco, but throughout the musical federation—was about to change, however. And, as we will see in the next chapter, Los Angeles would lead the way.

CHAPTER 7

Leading the Pack
The 1953 Los Angeles Merger

Like Chicago, Los Angeles by the 1940s had developed a lively, innovative, but racially segregated Black music scene, in this case focused in a four-square-mile area in the South Central part of the city. The locus was Central Avenue—by day a bustling thoroughfare of shops, banks, groceries, hair salons, department stores, cafes, and other businesses, and at night a lively jumble of clubs and dance halls emitting a cacophony of musical styles and packed with patrons of all races and economic strata.[1]

Los Angeles had grown rapidly since the 1920s, far overtaking San Francisco (which was geographically restricted by water on three sides) and sprawling outward in a series of interlinked suburbs. Immigrants were attracted to the City of Angels by its warm climate, its relatively affordable housing market, and its expanding economy. By 1950 L.A. had grown into the fourth largest city in the country, with a population of 1,970,358.[2] The city became a mecca for artists in all fields, including, of course, musicians, who were attracted to the potential for fame (or just jobs) in the fast-growing metropolis.[3]

The Black population of the city grew even faster than the city itself in every decade from 1900 to 1950. As Table 7.1 shows, Los Angeles's overall growth slowed during the period 1930–1950 compared to the first three decades of the century; the city grew by only 53 percent during these two decades. In the same period, however, the African American population exploded by 232 percent. As in San Francisco, the spectacular increase between 1940 and 1950 reflected new job opportunities in the defense industries (particularly in shipbuilding) during the Second World War; more than 100,000 African Americans moved to the city in that decade. With this

Table 7.1. Los Angeles Population Statistics, 1900–1950

Date	Total Population	Growth Per Decade in the Total Population	Black Population	Growth Per Decade in the Black Population	Percentage of Blacks in the Total Population
1900	102,479		2,131		2.1%
1910	319,198	211%	7,599	257%	2.4%
1920	576,673	81%	15,579	105%	2.7%
1930	1,238,048	115%	38,894	150%	3.1%
1940	1,504,277	22%	63,774	64%	4.2%
1950	1,970,358	31%	171,209	168%	8.7%

influx came a commensurate growth and increased diversity in the city's musical life. Due to draconian restrictions on housing from redlining covenants, most of the Black newcomers settled in the crowded South Central district. By 1940, reports Steven Isoardi, 70 percent of African Americans in Los Angeles resided in the Central Avenue corridor.[4] Housing might have become scarce, but the Central Avenue musical scene blossomed, fueled by the density of clubs and the people frequenting them.

To Black Los Angeles musicians, Central Avenue was much more than a place to work. Those who were active during its lively heyday in the 1940s and 1950s remember it romantically as a magic kingdom. Central Avenue "was a spirit," reflected the renowned trumpeter Clora Bryant.[5] "There was an aura. There was a feeling." "Glamorous," said jazz woodwind player Jackie Kelso (Jack Kelson). "It's like putting makeup on. When the sun goes down, all of the flaws and imperfections [are disguised]. Suddenly there's an aura of mysterious wonderfulness. . . . There's a new special magic. . . . It's almost as if special spirits of joy and abundance bring special gifts at night that are not available in the sunshine." And flaws there were, noted these same musicians. Many of the area's residents were poor, buildings were in dire need of maintenance, and the city in general was plagued by throat-clogging smog in this era prior to catalytic converters and the emission control regulations that began in the 1960s. The headquarters of Black Local 767, chartered in 1920, were modest and the upkeep lax. At the same time, however, this local was a powerful force in the AFM, as was its white counterpart, Local 47. By 1952, the year in which the merger terms were worked out, Local 767 ranked second among the African American locals, with a membership of 597 (trailing only Chicago's Local 208 at 991). Local 47 was the second largest union in the federation overall, with 13,769 members; only New York had more (and considerably more, at 30,746).[6]

Local 767's headquarters provided a social space, a rehearsal space, a clearing house, a place for the young to learn from the seasoned, a place to jam, a welcoming venue where one could participate without fear of making mistakes, and a source of local pride.

As in Chicago and New York, whites also enjoyed the lively Black entertainment in the Central Avenue clubs. Audiences included not only casual auditors and musicians wanting to hear the latest styles, but also stars of radio and screen who delighted in visiting the area's dynamic venues such as the Club Alabam or The Downbeat, where music could be enjoyed well into the wee hours of the night.[7] "Central was a showcase for talent," recalled William "Brother" Woodman Jr., "a place of entertainment . . . a melting pot for all races."[8]

Nevertheless, as in the Windy City, local Black musicians could rarely find meaningful or well-paying work outside the Central Avenue area. Nationally recognized Black artists could perform in these parts of the city. Nat "King" Cole's trio was the first in L.A., appearing in the cocktail room at the Trocadero on the Sunset Strip in June 1944, followed by appearances by Duke Ellington at Ciro's and the Benny Carter Orchestra at the Trocadero a year later,[9] but, for the most part, local Black artists could not break into these or similar venues.

A case from 1943[10] involving drummer Lee Young (brother of saxophonist Lester Young) illustrates the formidable racial impediments that Black musicians faced in Hollywood. Young was hired on short notice by a contractor from Local 47 to play in the NBC radio musical variety show *Camel Caravan*. At the end of the show, the conductor told Young he had the job for thirteen weeks, but when Young appeared the following week, a white drummer was set up to play in his place. The contractor dismissed Young, saying "he had been requested" to hire another player. Young took the matter first to Local 767 and then, after not receiving a satisfactory resolution, he filed charges with the International's office in New York. At the hearing, the committee called the conductor, who confirmed Young's account. "When they hung up they said I won the case. They paid me, but they didn't give me the gig," Young recalled in a later interview.[11] *Downbeat*'s (unidentified) reporter took up the cudgel, fuming about the situation in the paper's lead story under a five-column headline on May 1, 1943: "Color Loses Lee Young's Job." "The first Negro musician ever engaged to play with a white orchestra on a network program originating in Hollywood played one show and was dropped without notice due to a 'request' issued from some undisclosed source," read the paper's opening paragraph.[12] The radio representative for Local 47 said the contractor had called him in the first place to get permission to hire Young, once again reflecting the assumed oversight role enjoyed by white locals. The reporter asks, parenthetically but in bold type: "Why did the contractor have to call the 'white' union to get permission to use a Negro musician?" Edward Bailey, president of Local 767, told the magazine that "not one Local 767 musician has ever been given a job on any of the commercial programs originating in Hollywood and not one has secured employment in the staff orchestras maintained here by the networks." His statement summarizes, in a nutshell, the complaints and frustrations of Black musicians in Los Angeles that led directly to calls for amalgamation.

As we have seen in other cities (such as the Miami conflict described in chapter 6 and the court battle that erupted in San Francisco in 1934), the overlapping jurisdictions of the white and Black locals inevitably led to employment conflicts. Even in metropolitan areas where the white and Black music scenes were geographically separated, it was often impossible to avoid these disputes. In Los Angeles, in particular, the disenfranchisement of Blacks was noticeable in their exclusion from high-paying jobs in the entertainment industry. As usual, the white local assumed that it had priority—as did the contractors, as Young's tale illustrates—and Local 47's denial of membership for Blacks kept the conflicts boiling. For example, *Downbeat* reported that in 1942 Barney Bigard, clarinetist with King Oliver, Duke Ellington, and others, "was promised a job on a network radio show on the condition that he be accepted for membership in Local 47," which he could not obtain. His membership in Local 767 would not suffice.[13]

The Main Players

The Los Angeles merger resulted from a confluence of economic forces, the activism of musicians in the Black local, and support by an outspoken group in the white local. In the African American community, two figures stand out as central to the effort: multi-instrumentalist Buddy Collette and pianist and arranger Marl Young. Both of them have recounted the history of the merger in detail.[14]

Buddy Collette

Collette's recollections of the merger process appear in at least four separate accounts over fifteen years—all virtually identical, though with greater or lesser detail.[15] Significantly, the process originated with interracial music-making. Collette credits Charles Mingus, whom he had known and played with since before the Second World War, as the initial catalyst. He recalls that Mingus was playing in an orchestra at L.A.'s Million Dollar Theater under Billy Eckstine and was the only African American member of the group.[16] "He was always a fighter," says Collette. "We used to talk about studio work for black musicians. We knew that it was going on and that we weren't a part of it."[17] Mingus pressed the orchestra's leaders to hire his friend, and finally arranged for Collette, who had studied flute for only two years, to have a sight-reading session of duets with the ensemble's flutist, Julie Kinsler. (Collette modestly jokes that the duets Kinsler chose—by Friedrich Kuhlau—were ones he had previously explored on his own, and therefore his presumed sight-reading was actually practiced.) Collette and Kinsler began to discuss the merging of the two locals and approached the band's drummer Milt Holland to join in the dialogue.

The result of this musical meeting was not only the initial discussion of merger, but also, and perhaps even more significantly, the formation of the Community Symphony Orchestra (whose name later changed to the Humanist Symphony). The ensemble was a rehearsal orchestra that met on Monday nights at Humanist Hall. Its purpose, in Collette's words, was to serve as a "training ground" for Black musicians, who were primarily experienced in improvisatory performance and who tended to be unfamiliar with much of the standard classical repertoire.[18] With active recruitment on both sides, the interracial group eventually grew to sixty-five members. Furthermore, the collaboration proved to be so productive that the group added Sunday afternoon jazz sessions, in which the classical (white) players learned techniques of improvisation from the Black musicians.

In none of his several accounts does Collette specify a date for the formation of the orchestra, but it is possible to fix the time based on events he recounts. He states, for example, that the "first night we had a conductor who was world renown—Eisler (*recte*: Izler) Solomon," who "happened to be in town for a week or so."[19] Indeed, Solomon came to Los Angeles in March 1950 to provide expert advice to high school students in a chamber music festival at Occidental College sponsored by the Los Angeles Junior Chamber of Commerce and the city's Board of Education.[20]

Through the Humanist Symphony, Collette secured a job on the Groucho Marx show when Jerry Fielding, who was later blacklisted by the House Un-American Activities Committee, heard him at one of their rehearsals. Collette's success is notable in itself, of course, as is the productive musical collaboration among the orchestra members, which paved the way for labor unity. However, the event Collette singles out as most influential was the appearance at one of their Sunday afternoon rehearsals of African American entertainer and civil rights activist Josephine Baker. She pulled no punches, outspokenly lobbying the orchestra members and the large audience to pursue the merger of Locals 47 and 767. Baker graphically illustrated the rewards of racial harmony by calling to the stage two little girls—one white, one Black. After whispering to them, the girls "grabbed each other, hugged and wouldn't let go," recalls Collette. "Josephine looked at the audience and winked, 'These kids will show you how to do it,' and [she] walked out."[21] Again, Collette gives no date, but again, newspaper reports pinpoint her appearance: Baker performed in Los Angeles for the first time on July 4, 1951—her first visit to the West Coast.[22] From that time forward, informal talks ensued among the members of both locals.[23]

Marl Young

Meanwhile, in 1947 Marl Young had moved to Los Angeles, where he became a leader in the pro-amalgamation forces within Local 767. Young was not only a musician, but also a lawyer and he would later draft the merger proposal that was eventually accepted by both unions. Prior to moving to the West Coast from Chicago, Young had already demonstrated his perseverance in fighting for his rights, as well as his fearlessness at confronting union authorities. When the manager of Lionel Hampton's band refused to pay Young $15 for his arrangement of "Step Up and Meet the People," but used the piece anyway at Chicago's Grand Terrace Cafe, Young complained to Harry Gray, president of (Chicago's) Local 208. Gray advised him not to return to the job, but Young ignored the advice, for which Local 208 fined him $25. He then appealed to the national AFM, won his case, and approached Gray to refund his fine. Relations between the two men were thereafter strained and Young reflected later that "I know Harry Gray was glad when I left [Chicago]."[24]

Young was not the only member of Local 208 to bump heads with Gray. As we will see in the next chapter, Red Saunders, the spark for starting merger negotiations in Chicago, also had serious conflicts with him. In Los Angeles, however, Young's negotiating skills, his determination, and his forcefulness were exactly what was needed. Soon after his relocation to the West Coast, he met Estelle Edson, who, he says, was working on a Master's thesis, "The Negro in Radio," at UCLA. Not surprisingly, Edson found few Blacks employed in the broadcast industry. She soon joined Young in working for the amalgamation of Locals 47 and 767.

The Process

Both locals were divided between pro- and anti-merger forces. The first official move arose from within 767, when a group of amalgamation proponents came to a general meeting of the Black local in 1951 to introduce a resolution to instigate merger talks. Trumpeter Gerald Wilson recalls standing up and making a motion "that a special meeting will be called for the specific purpose of discussing the amalgamation of Local 767 and Local 47." Drummer Bill Douglass's memory is slightly different: he remembers being the one designated to make the motion. In either case, the leadership of 767 seemed decidedly uninterested. "We were gaveled down," says Douglass. "We were 'out of order.'"[25]

Nevertheless, the issue became the most prominent one at the Black local's meetings. "By mid-summer of 1951," wrote Marl Young, "amalgamation was the number one issue at the monthly Local 767 meetings, and there was always a quorum."[26]

The Local 767 elections of December 1951 resulted in split leadership, with the pro-merger forces holding a slim 5–4 edge. Collette lost in his bid for the presidency, as did David Bryant for treasurer and Estelle Edson for secretary. But Bill Douglass captured the vice-presidency, Marl Young and Benny Carter won seats as trustees, and Russell McDavid and John Anderson became members of the board of directors. The anti-merger officers included president Leo Davis, secretary Florence Cadrez, treasurer Paul Howard, and trustee Harvey Brooks.[27]

Collette later recalled this election and the opposition to amalgamation by officers of Local 767. His reflections also serve to counteract, to a degree, the utopian images of Central Avenue voiced by some Black musicians quoted at the beginning of this chapter:

> I ran for president of Local 767. You see, we had all the publicity and people were doing fine, but we didn't know how to pull [the merger] off. So the next thing would be, "Maybe we'll have to be officers so we can move it from that standpoint." Because our officers at the black local didn't want it. Our place was not a great union. The building was kind of tearing down and the pianos were terrible. We really didn't have that much. But, the way they thought, at least it was still ours. So we set up a whole slate and we ran. The incumbent guy beat me by about twenty votes out of about four hundred. We did win a couple of seats on the board of directors.... But we still didn't have enough power.[28]

Despite their slim majority, the pro-merger forces acted expeditiously to further their cause. At the regular meeting in January 1952, members approved a resolution to begin talks with Local 47 and appointed a committee of seven—Young, Edson, Collette, Douglass, and Carter (on the pro side) as well as Davis and Howard (on the anti side).[29] On February 7, 1952, this committee appeared at a board meeting of Local 47, where Carter, the appointed head of the committee, read a formal statement noting that Local 767's members "have officially gone on record as favoring the establishment of one local for all musicians in the Los Angeles area," and requesting a statement of 47's "disposition toward the matter of amalgamation."[30] In executive session after this appearance, the 47 board members unanimously passed a resolution stating that if Local 767 would dissolve, Local 47 "will be pleased to accept Local 767 members on the same terms as any other members of the Federation." Recognizing that this solution would probably be rejected by the Black local, however, the resolution left the door open for continued dialogue: "In the event that this proposal is unacceptable to the Committee representing Local 767, then it is suggested that the Committee confer, and come back at a later date with concrete proposals based on the fact that the problems involved are many, complex and in the main, financial."

Although Local 47's response might sound reasonable on the surface, serious difficulties (and disadvantages for the Black musicians) would result, including, among others:

- To dissolve Local 767 would require the written approval of 90 percent of its membership, not a realistic possibility;
- Black musicians would have to pay a $100 initiation fee to Local 47 (equivalent to more than $1,100 in 2022);
- Life members of Local 767 would lose all seniority; and
- Local 767 members over the age of forty would lose their death benefits.

Within Local 47, however, was an enthusiastic group favoring merger, and they pressured their own leadership to find a solution. The May issue of the local's monthly newsletter, *The Overture,* contained a lengthy article by secretary Maury Paul,[31] in which he included a letter dated April 10, 1952, signed by three members—Alexander Koltun, Seymour Sheklow, and Robert Konrad—that urged unification. The three signatories were at the same time circulating the letter to the entire Local 47 membership, and according to Marl Young, 350 members eventually affixed their signatures to it.[32] "We propose," the letter concludes, "that an amalgamation be quickly consummated on the following basis: 1) Financial resources of Local 767 to be merged with those of Local 47; [and] 2) Immediately full membership to occur upon completion of amalgamation, subject to the constitution and by-laws of Local 47." Paul commented that although Local 47's board was "opposed to racial discrimination," the issues were far more complex than the letter's authors recognized. In terms of the death benefit, for example, Local 47's fund was currently secure, due to an annual contribution by members of eight dollars a year. The board of directors feared that the addition of nearly six hundred new members might potentially incur a liability of six hundred thousand dollars. An additional complication was that Local 47's death benefit was $1,000 and Local 767's was only $400; who would receive the larger amount? Paul noted that Local 47's board awaited a new proposal from Local 767.

That proposal arrived in the form of a detailed document written by Marl Young (but signed by Benny Carter, head of 767's amalgamation committee) and sent to Local 47 on May 13, 1952. Young proposed a sensible settlement of the death benefit matter: During the first year after merger, death benefits for Local 767 members would remain at $400 and would be covered by an amount set aside from 767's assets (the remainder of which would be transferred to Local 47). After one year, 767 members under forty would be covered by 47's $1,000 allotment, whereas those over forty would continue to be eligible only for the former $400 benefit. Members of 767 would retain within the merged local whatever status they had previously enjoyed in 767.[33]

On July 8, 1952, Local 47's board voted to respond to Local 767 with another counterproposal, specifying again that 767 dissolve before any merger could take place.[34] They did allow that the former 767 members could join 47 for an initiation fee of $50 (instead of the current $100); that those under forty years of age would be entitled to 47's (larger) death benefit; and that 767's members could join 47's Musicians Club for $1. (The Musicians Club is a legal entity established to purchase property and improvements for Local 47. Because unions were not legally permitted to own property in many states, they established such "clubs." Local 767 had an equivalent entity called the Rhythm Club.)[35] But the Local 47 board refused to recognize the Life Membership status of the Black local members or to accept any of its assets until the local's charter was relinquished (by whatever procedure was in accordance with the constitutions of 767 and the AFM). The reasoning came primarily from legal counsel, who advised that accepting 767's assets opened the door to lawsuits by its members due to their property rights in their own building. At the same time, the minutes state that "it is the feeling of our Board of Directors that there is a certain amount of merit in the argument that members of Local 767 have been resident in the Los Angeles area, and therefore, should be entitled to preferential treatment."

The preferential treatment Local 47's board was willing to grant, however, was simply to treat Local 767 members the same way as they treated AFM members "who had transfers on deposit prior to November 28, 1951, when the initiation fees of Local 47 were raised."

If the AFM had hitherto been able to negotiate temporary (if, at times, unjust) solutions to the vexing problems created by racially separated dual locals, it appeared now that such solutions were no longer viable and the era of ignoring or patching over the inevitable conflicts was rapidly coming to an end. Even though segregation in the AFM had originated from the requests for independence and fair play by Black musicians, the resulting separate structure had actually created unequal rights and unequal employment opportunities for them. Yet the dual structure, with its problems and inequities, was becoming increasingly hard to undo. Property rights, seniority benefits, death payments, differential initiation fees, and membership fees stood in the way of a simple merger of two locals that, though ostensibly equal in the eyes of the national organization, were anything but.

The response of Local 767 was, unsurprisingly, a rejection of the 47 board's new response, accompanied this time by a request that its proposal be placed on the white local's ballot at its election on December 15, 1952. Meanwhile, an increasingly outspoken contingent of Local 47 members intensified their campaign for amalgamation. On August 5, thirty-five members of Local 47 appeared before its board and requested permission to use the local's mailing list to present their views to the membership at large.[36] In the face of this mailing, which many members assumed to reflect the local's official position, the Board of Local 47 agreed, on August 26, to submit Local 767's proposal to a vote of the rank and file.[37] *The Overture* of September 1952 contains an extended history of the merger negotiations, the proposal from Local 767, and the unanimously approved resolution to place the matter on the general Local 47 ballot. At the same time, however, it also included an explanation of why Local 47's board could not endorse it. Among the reasons, explained the notice, were that

> Local 47 and the Musicians Club of Los Angeles, Incorporated, to which all members of Local 47 must belong, have a combined net worth . . . well in excess of $8,000,000. These properties belong to the membership of the two organizations and represent an accumulation of more than 56 years of initiation fees, dues and dues taxes paid by the 13,500 members of the two organizations. The Board of Directors does not feel that it can recommend a proposition to take in approximately 550 [*recte:* 597] members with the payment of no initiation fee whatsoever except the assets of Local 767, which would pay only a small portion of the initiation fees.[38]

Furthermore, the explanation included warnings about possible lawsuits:

> Just as the members of Local 47 and the Musicians Club enjoy property rights in the assets of the two organizations, so do the members of 767 enjoy property rights in the assets of that organization. Therefore, any member of Local 767 who disagreed with the proposition of turning Local 767's assets over to Local 47 could file suit against Local 47 for recovery of his or her share of those assets.[39]

Within Local 767, the sentiment regarding merger was likewise far from unanimous. The internal disagreements pitted many of the younger musicians who favored merger against the older ones, who were more entrenched in the history of the distinctive Black organization and fearful of the negative effects of the change. The local abolished the Amalgamation Committee, and the election of December 2, 1952 resulted in a realignment of forces: the slim majority of 5–4 now rested with the anti-merger proponents, although the pro-merger forces retained a majority on the Board of Directors. Arguments in favor of amalgamation included the current isolation of Black musicians; their exclusion from jobs in white areas and in stage, radio, and screen ensembles; the declining effectiveness of Local 767, which was suffering from financial woes; the fact that 767 had already adopted the pay scale and most of the bylaws of 47 anyway; and the reality that contractors rarely approached Local 767 for jobs both because they assumed (without cause) that the Black musicians did not read music fluently and because of the overriding domination of the enormous Local 47. Arguing the opposing position, some members feared that once amalgamation took place, job requests would not be directed toward the minority of Black union members; that the combined local would have very few African Americans in positions of authority; that Blacks would lose an organization that had fought vigorously for their rights; and that they would forfeit all of their property. In short, segregation could be eliminated, but racial prejudice could not.[40] Unfortunately, many of these fears would prove true not only in Los Angeles but also elsewhere in the country, and the AFM would scramble to find remedies.

The October 1952 issue of *The Overture* contained extensive coverage of the situation, as well as an invitation for Local 47 members to attend an in-person discussion of the pros and cons on October 27. That October issue also contained a lengthy explanation by the "Musicians for Amalgamation"—the group that had sent out the flyer advocating for merger—in which they combatted arguments by the anti-merger contingent, including the fear of lawsuits. Local 767, they argued, need not dissolve, but could simply resign its charter, which would "be an adequate legal and proper procedure to enable Local 767 to then merge with Local 47." Directly addressing the potential legal pitfalls, the statement continued: "Article II of Local 767's Constitution states that the object of the Association . . . is to unite the instrumental musicians of Los Angeles and vicinity for the better protection of their interests," which the merger clearly would accomplish. "The turning over of Local 767's assets to Local 47 . . . would be part of the process of the merger, which act would be legally sound under Local 767's Constitution. In view of this, no member of Local 767 would have legal cause to sue Local 47."[41]

Because members of Local 47 had to appear in person at the union headquarters to cast their ballots, the pro-merger forces in both unions engaged in extraordinary publicity to alert members to vote.[42] In the November issue of *The Overture*, Maury Paul highlighted the election but, to the relief of the pro-merger forces, remained neutral about how to vote.[43] The steering committee of Local 47's "Committee for Amalgamation" (fourteen members) ran a two-page endorsement of the merger that resembled the presentation style typical of state ballot propositions—filled with upper-case type, bullet points, and exclamation points—making the matter jump out as urgent to members of the local.[44] The ad made the following important points:

- Amalgamation would be financially beneficial to Local 47, increasing its assets by $19,000–$25,000 and its annual income by $10,000–$12,000 through the addition of six hundred new members and the acquisition of assets from Local 767.
- Local 767's members are already AFM members and have paid initiation fees to their local. "They are not new [AFM] members. They have been working here for many years."
- Merger would enable "professional contact with many musicians who have earned the highest respect in the musical world through their great talents, in spite of the terrific odds against them."
- This move would "bring added respect and prestige to Local 47 from other unions and the public at large by ending segregation and discrimination."

Local 47 musicians indeed turned out in large numbers for the December 15 election. The ballot proposal won by a substantial 233-vote majority (1,608–1,375). In a special election in January 1953, Local 767 approved the proposal by more than a two-thirds margin.

What remained now was to iron out details, effected through a committee from the national federation in dialogue with members of the two locals.[45] In January 1953 Marl Young attended a meeting with AFM officials in

Figure 7.1. Marl Young (second from the left), appearing with Maury Paul (left), NAACP Secretary Lester Bailey (standing) and Estelle Edson (right), signs the final document transferring Local 767's assets to Local 47 in March of 1953, marking the final step in the amalgamation of the two locals. (Photo courtesy of AFM Local 47's *Overture* archives.)

New York during which, he asserts, IEB member C. L. Bagley, in coordination with Local 47's president John Te Groen in Los Angeles, attempted to derail the merger.[46] The meeting became extremely contentious. Petrillo later wrote to George Meany, president of the AFL, that Young, who was understandably frustrated, "became so belligerent I was constrained to ask him to leave."[47] Indeed, Bagley had expressed his opposition to the merger a month earlier, noting that he "had assisted in the formation of the separate AFM local, for Negroes only, in 1920, that it was the desire of the Negro musicians at that time to have their own union, and that what was satisfactory to all concerned 32 years ago ought to be all right now."[48]

Despite this initial animosity, the merger did take place and Local 767 members began joining Local 47 on April 1, 1953. Three months later, on June 25, the IEB passed the following resolution:

Leading the Pack   109

Whereas, on April 1, 1953, Locals 767 and 47 of the American Federation of Musicians, with the approval and consent of their respective memberships, consolidated their two locals under the name of Local 47 American Federation of Musicians; and

Whereas, all of the assets, real and personal and wheresoever situate, of Local 767 have been transferred to Local 47;

Now, therefore be it resolved, that the said merger of the said locals is hereby approved, consented to, and in all matters ratified.[49]

Three years later Marl Young won an elected seat on Local 47's board of directors.

Looking Ahead

As we will see in our concluding chapter, some of the fears of the anti-merger forces in Los Angeles unfortunately came to pass—the loss of the fellowship offered in the Black union's headquarters, the dispersal of its close-knit Black musical community, disadvantages suffered by the older members of 767 (who didn't benefit from the increased death benefits), and the distance to, and anonymization of, the merged union's physical headquarters.

In point of fact, however, the merger might only have accelerated trends that were already in the making. The Central Avenue residential community was dispersing regardless of the actions of the American Federation of Musicians. The outlawing of restrictive housing covenants by the landmark 1948 Supreme Court ruling *Shelley v. Kraemer* provided the opportunities for Blacks to leave the crowded area and spread throughout the city.

Nor did the merger end racism within the local. In 1958, for example, some of the Black members of Local 47 noted that their race was being identified in union records. Carter, Collette, Douglass, and Harper Cosby appeared at a board of directors meeting, where the practice was soundly condemned and immediately terminated.[50] Los Angeles was not the only place where such subtle discriminatory actions were practiced, of course. As late as 1986, for example, staff at Local 5 in Detroit were apparently tracking voting records by race by placing a small x in the upper left corner of the secret ballots submitted by Black members, according to its president at the time, Gordon Stump.[51] He firmly put an end to the practice.

The Los Angeles merger paved the way for the rest of the more than fifty segregated locals in the country to combine forces during the following eighteen years. The issues that the two locals in Los Angeles negotiated were financial, but those in other cities included representation and personnel matters as well—in particular, the loss of delegates to the national convention and the disempowering of the officers of the Black locals, who had worked so diligently for racial employment equity.

Four years after amalgamation, the Los Angeles delegates to the national convention introduced a resolution that would have mandated the elimination of membership restrictions based on race throughout the federation, and would have empowered the IEB to pursue amalgamation efforts. The resolution was shelved after strenuous objections from sixty delegates, the vast majority of them from Black locals. As we will see in our next chapters, undoing the now-entrenched segregation in so many cities would indeed prove to be a formidable task.

CHAPTER 8

Mergers from 1954 through 1966

State Labor Laws and the Battle of Chicago

In 1954, the year after the Los Angeles locals merged, the *Official Proceedings* of the Convention recorded fifty-three surviving Black unions, shown in Tables 8.1a and 8.1b. The largest of these locals was, of course, Chicago, with more than a thousand members, followed by Philadelphia (770), New Orleans (355), St Louis (351), and San Francisco (346). The majority of them eventually merged with the white locals in the same jurisdiction. Table 8.1a shows the official merger years as recorded in the AFM's *Charter Book*. Table 8.1b presents a list of locals for which no merger information appears in this source. However, in a 1958 letter to AFL-CIO president George Meany, James Petrillo stated that mergers had actually taken place in some of those cities, or at least that "integration has been accomplished," which seems to indicate that Black musicians simply joined the white local without any formal merger agreement.[1] Information from Petrillo's letter appears in the last column of Table 8.1b. What happened to the assets of these Black locals is not clear. Data is lacking for Hartford and Richmond, for which the AFM *Charter Book* lists charter revocations but does not record any merger. Members of these Black locals might have joined the white local without any formal union merger, but as the revocation date for their charters postdates Petrillo's letter, they are obviously not mentioned in that document.[2] Finally, as noted previously, Cincinnati's Local 814 and Philadelphia's Local 274 resisted all attempts by the federation to negotiate mergers with their (mostly) white counterparts. After talks reached a stalemate, the International unilaterally canceled their charters in 1970 and 1971.

1957: Los Angeles Presses for Mergers, but Black Locals Object

Local 47 in Los Angeles was apparently very pleased with the outcome of its amalgamation process in 1953 because four years later, its delegation introduced at the convention a resolution calling for mergers throughout the federation. Resolution 34[3] included six "Whereas" statements, which can be summarized as follows:

- The constitution of the (now combined) AFL-CIO[4] states that the organization's purpose is "to extend the benefits and privileges of union membership and protection to all working people, regardless of race, color, creed, religion or place of national origin";
- Several U.S. Supreme Court cases have confirmed the federal government's policy of eliminating "all distinctions, discrimination, and segregation" based on the same criteria;
- The maintenance of dual locals separated according to race "is contrary to our good morals, and tends to degrade all members of our Federation";
- The AFM desires "to bring dignity and respect equally" to all of its members;
- Article 7 of the AFM Constitution prohibits the jurisdiction of any local from extending "into the municipal lines of a town or city in which another local union is chartered"; and
- In many instances, two locals exercise jurisdiction in the same town or city (contrary to the prohibition stated in the previous point).

Therefore, the resolution called for:

- The convention to publicly announce opposition to maintaining segregated locals;
- The members of such locals to be urged to take immediate steps to eliminate restrictions based on race, color, and so on;
- Segregated locals to take steps to merge immediately "on an equitable basis";
- The IEB to be empowered to outlaw segregated locals, to direct locals to amalgamate, or both.

Following this resolution in the convention report is a petition signed by sixty delegates urging that it be *rejected* (see Figure 8.1). Fifty-six of the sixty signatories represented Black locals. Among the unions listed in Table 8.1, almost all the delegates signed the petition. Of those locals that

Table 8.1a. This table shows Black locals listed in the *Official Proceedings* of 1954 and merger dates with white locals as recorded in the AFM's *Charter Book*. As shown, the first merger, in Los Angeles, took place the previous year. Membership numbers are given in parentheses.

Official Merger Year*	City	Black Local (no. members in 1954 unless otherwise indicated)	White Local (no. members in 1954 unless otherwise indicated)
(1953)	(Los Angeles)	767 (597 in 1952)**	47 (13,769 in 1952)**
1958	Seattle, WA	493 (103)	76 (2,040)
1960	San Francisco, CA	669 (346)	6 (5,185)
	Columbus, OH	589 (162)	103 (838)
	Denver, CO	623 (91)	20 (1,092)
	Sioux City, IA	743 (25)	254 (c. 200; 213 in 1952)
1962	Cleveland, OH	550 (274)	4 (2,612)
1965	Dallas, TX	168 (53)	147 (980)
	Parkersburg, WV	185 (24)	259 (87)
	Pensacola, FL	548 (23)	283 (130)
	San Antonio, TX	658 (69)	23 (589)
	Tulsa, OK	808 (53)	94 (673)
	Oklahoma City, OK	703 (56)	375 (599)
	Fort Worth, TX	392 (48)	72 (446)
1966	Chicago, IL	208 (1,081)	10 (11,355)
	Pittsburgh, PA	471 (99)	60 (2,231)
	New Haven, CT	486 (25)	234 (628)
	Baltimore, MD	543 (278)	40 (1,218)
	Milwaukee, WI	587 (108)	8 (2,580)
	Springfield, IL	675 (75)	19 (306)
	Norfolk, VA	702 (c. 100)	125 (352)
	Houston, TX	699 (204)	65 (903)
	Newport News, VA	722 (88)	199 (118)

Table 8.1a. (continued)

1967	Omaha, NE	558 (73)	70 (631)
	Lexington, KY	635 (40?)	554 (254)
	Washington, DC	710 (173)	161 (1,578)
	Louisville, KY	637 (96)	11 (645)
1968	Atlanta, GA	462 (161)	148 (408)
	Bridgeport, CT	549 (43)	63 (401)
	Mobile, AL	613 (75)	407 (114)
	Topeka, KS	665 (38)	36 (266)
	Montgomery, AL	718 (63)	479 (82)
1969	Wilmington, DE	641 (78)	311 (293)
	Birmingham, AL	733 (173)	256 (315)
	Youngstown, OH	242 (24)	86 (646)
	Buffalo, NY	533 (135) becomes 92 post-merger	43 (1,177)
	Atlantic City, NJ	708 (49)	661 (425)
	New Orleans, LA	496 (355)	174 (801)
1970	Toledo, OH	286 (55)	15 (463)
	Dayton, OH	473 (84)	101 (588)
	Boston, MA	535 (153)	9 (2,382)
	Kansas City, MO	627 (215)	34 (1,335)
1971	St. Louis, MO	197 (351)	2 (1,478)

* Often the merger agreement took place unofficially in the previous year and Black musicians began to join the previously white locals, but the finalization of the merger depended on the legal transfer of property and the resolution of financial issues.

** Because the Los Angeles locals merged in 1953, membership numbers are given for 1952 instead of 1954.

Membership numbers come from the convention delegate listing in the *Official Proceedings*. When data are not available for 1954, I have found the membership numbers for the closest prior year and indicated the year in parentheses. One additional Black local (no. 704) was chartered in 1955 in Savannah, GA.

Table 8.1b. This table shows Black locals listed in the *Official Proceedings* of 1954 for which the AFM's *Charter Book* shows no merger. In most of these cases, however, James Petrillo, in a 1958 letter to George Meany, reported that mergers either had taken place or "integration" had "been accomplished" (listed in alphabetical order).

City	Black Local No.	No. of Members in 1954	Notation in the AFM's Charter Book	Information from Petrillo's 1958 Letter
Asheville, NC	698	28	1957: Charter revoked	"Merged its members with various white locals in that area"
Cincinnati, OH	814	128	1970: Charter canceled on Nov. 27. (Black local resisted attempts by the IEB to force a merger with Local 1; IEB canceled the charter)	
Des Moines, IA	740	35	1956: Charter revoked	"Integration...accomplished" with Local 75
Gary, IN	622	85	1956: Charter revoked	Merged with Local 203 in Hammond, IN
Hartford, CT	335	68	1961: Charter revoked	
Jacksonville, FL	632	61	1959: Charter canceled	"Members have joined" Local 444
Miami, FL	690	?*	1957: Charter revoked	"Integration...accomplished" with Local 655
Philadelphia, PA	274	770	1971: Charter canceled on Mar. 31. (Black local resisted attempts by the IEB to force a merger with Local 77; IEB canceled charter. See the description of the process in chapter 1.)	
Richmond, VA	695	(56 in 1951)	1959: Charter canceled	
Uniontown, PA	455	(20 in 1951)	1955: Charter revoked	Merged with Local 417 in Connellsville, PA
Wichita, KS	701	35	1956: Charter revoked	"Integration...accomplished" with Local 297

* Local 690 did not send any delegates to the national convention from 1946, when it was chartered, until its charter revocation in 1957.

The following petition, signed by many of the colored delegates, was submitted to the Law Committee in connection with Resolution 34:

We, the undersigned, being duly elected delegates to this Sixtieth Annual Convention of the American Federation of Musicians, wish to go on record as being opposed to Resolution No. 34, presented by Local 47, A. F. of M.

The subject matter contained in Resolution No. 34 should not be acted upon at this time because of the financial aspect involved with some of the larger colored locals, who have spent many years of hard work to attain their present status in the Federation.

The subject matter can best be resolved by its various locals involved, who are better informed as to the advantages or disadvantages of a merger. Under no circumstances should a merger be forced upon us, but should rather be accomplished by mutual agreement between parties concerned.

HARRY W GRAY,
WM. EVERETT SAMUELS,
EDWARD J. McCANTS,
Local 208.
W. L. SMITH,
Local 635.
JAMES SHORTER, SR.,
CHARLES GAINES,
Local 274.
JOHNNIE WARREN,
Local 548.
SAMMY HARRIS,
Local 702.
BARON McCLOUD,
Local 632.

FRANK M. JONES,
Local 392.
CLEMON E. JACKSON,
WILLIAM W. GOODING,
Local 535.
LEONARD N. REED,
Local 486.
JESSE HICKS,
Local 185.
VELMER MASON,
Local 286.
CHARLES H. LOTT,
Local 613.
ROBERT W. EASLEY,
Local 115.
CAMPBELL A. TOLBERT,
CONRAD O. JOHNSON,
Local 699.
JOHN T. WHATLEY,
NEWMAN J. TERRELL,
Local 733.
P. S. COOKE,
Local 462.
LOUIS COTTRELL,
SEYMOUR ALCORN,
SIDNEY CATES, JR.,
Local 496.
DONALD W. FIELDS,
EDWARD J. WHARTON,
HOWARD ROLLINS,
Local 543.
CHARLES W. CARTER,
Local 675.
CHARLES S. EXUM,
Local 242.
GRADY JONES,
Local 168.
GEORGE W. CHILDRESS,
RUBY L. YOUNG,
CARL N. ARTER,
Local 471.
C. RAYMOND ELLIS,
Local 549.

C. RAYMOND ELLIS,
Local 549.
GEORGE W. ABERNATHY,
Local 587.
JOHN C. COTTER,
GEORGE L. SMITH,
ELIZABETH YOUNG,
Local 197.
WEBSTER RUCKER,
Local 623.
JOSEPH E. THOMAS,
Local 462.
HENRY P. BUTLER,
Local 703.
R. H. COLEMAN,
Local 627.
DELBERT L. SIMPERS,
Local 641.
LOUIS R. SCHVOM,
ROMEO CELLA,
JAMES P. PERRI,
Local 77.
JAMES R. BACOTE,
Local 335.
ARTIE JONES,
Local 637.
GLADYS I. MOORE,
LOUIS H. AIKENS,
GEORGE F. ROBINSON,
Local 710.
W. FRANKLIN SYMPSON,
HEZEKIAH OLDWINE,
C. C. GARDNER,
Local 550.
CARL P. WRIGHT,
Local 704.
EDWARD E. BEARD,
CLEVE GOOD,
Local 589.
PERRY GRAY,
Local 533.
GEORGE F. ALLEN,
Local 708.

Figure 8.1. Petition opposing Resolution 34 (taken from the *Official Proceedings* of the AFM convention of 1957). Resolution 34, submitted by Local 47 in Los Angeles, would have paved the way for mandatory mergers of Black and white locals throughout the country. (C. Raymond Ellis is listed twice.)

are not represented, only three had memberships of more than a hundred: Seattle, San Francisco, and Cincinnati.[5] Seattle's locals had already voted to merge the previous year and the process would be finalized after the sale of property in January 1958.[6] San Francisco's Local 669, in contrast to most of the other Black locals, had been asking for merger with Local 6 ever since the 1930s, but white Local 6 had continually refused. The absence of signatures from the delegates of Cincinnati's Local 814, who were present at the convention and whose officers would resist merger to the end of the amalgamation process, seems curious, but Petrillo later wrote to Meany that "later eight delegates voiced their agreement with the petition in writing inasmuch as they could not be found at the time the petition was circulated."[7] Of the four delegates from white locals who affixed their names to the petition, one was from the small city of Olean in southwestern New York state, and the other three came from Philadelphia's (white) Local 77;

therefore, both the Black and the white locals in Philadelphia are on record opposing the call for merger.

The stated reasoning behind the negative petition was financial: "Some of the larger colored locals," wrote the petitioners, "have spent many years of hard work to attain their present status in the Federation." They requested that the question of merger be handled on a case-by-case basis; "under no circumstances" should it be imposed by the federation, but rather should "be accomplished by mutual agreement between the parties concerned." As we will see, that path was the one ultimately followed by the AFM. Each pair of locals would carry on its own negotiations, but with significant input from national officers, not only requiring time-consuming discussions and expensive travel, but also leading to quite different agreement terms.

Belying the explanation given in the 1957 petition, most of its signatories were not from "large unions." Furthermore, the highlighting of financial concerns seems to be a bit of a red herring. Although financial arrangements could certainly complicate the merger process, the Los Angeles model demonstrated that locals could agree on acceptable terms. Thus, it is incumbent on us to probe more deeply the underlying reasons why most of the Black locals opposed amalgamation, just as in chapter 3 we analyzed the motivations that had driven them to form in the first place.

On the purely emotional level, the potential loss of communal identity, neighborhood audiences and interactions, and a supportive local club environment created strong disincentives to become a small minority in a large, anonymous interracial union. Melting into the mainstream threatened the creative, tight-knit, and vibrant Black musical communities. The characteristic distinctiveness of Black ensembles was, in the view of many of the signatories, under attack. It is helpful here to quote at some length the assessment with which C. Vann Woodward, in his progressive persona as the champion of civil rights prior to his decisive swing to the Right beginning in the 1960s, concludes his influential book on Jim Crow. Citing "two historic instances" in which "Negro Americans have been beneficiaries—as well as the victims—of the national compulsion to level or blur distinctions," namely, the legal end of slavery and the legal end of segregation (with the *Brown v. Board of Education* ruling in 1954), Woodward writes:

> Both abolitions left the beneficiaries still suffering under handicaps inflicted by the system abolished. The emancipators made abortive and unsuccessful efforts to remove the handicaps and then proclaimed the emancipated equal. After the legal end of Jim Crow, the emancipated were expected to shed not only such distinctions as they abhorred but

those distinctions they cherished as essential to their identity. They found they were unable to rid themselves fully of the former and unable wholly to abandon the latter. Under these circumstances, the promise of integration took on a different aspect. So long as it had been truculently withheld, it seemed infinitely more desirable than when it was grudgingly proffered at prices that seemed too high.[8]

Aside from such generalized concerns, mergers also posed practical disadvantages. Black musicians in the AFM rightly feared that becoming a small minority in a large white pool of workers would result in being passed over for meaningful work when contractors called. They also recognized that they were likely to lose vital representation on the national level (a concern that indeed proved prescient). Another motivation—never stated explicitly, but cited by some young musicians in the Black locals—was the preservation of power (and salaries) by entrenched older union officials. Such sub-rosa accusations date back at least as far as 1932 when Powell Barnett, campaigning for the end of dual locals at the Los Angeles convention, encountered opposition from his colleagues and speculated that they feared the impending loss of their positions of authority (chapter 5). After all, the delegates to the conventions (and thus the signers of the 1957 petition) were most often salaried officers in their local unions.

The committee of the AFM reviewing Resolution 34 recommended referring it to the office of the President, an action that the *New York Times* characterized as in effect choosing the path of continued segregation.[9] Petrillo defended the decision by warning that the small Black locals would likely be swallowed up by the large white ones.

The Los Angeles proponents of the resolution did not let the matter drop, however. A group from Local 47 calling itself the "Musician's [sic] Committee for Integration" (MCI) wrote to Petrillo three times after the June convention: on October 3, November 23, and December 5, 1957. By the following spring the group had still received no reply and so they wrote directly to AFL-CIO president Meany on March 17, 1958.[10] The MCI consisted of eighteen members of Los Angeles's Local 47 and included not only the expected names (Benny Carter, Buddy Collette, Bill Douglass, Red Callender, Marl Young), but also—giving additional prestige to their missive—Nat "King" Cole. One important new point they raised was that Black musicians in integrated locals were required, when traveling to cities with dual locals, to register with racially segregated ones. It is "inconceivable," the MCI members said, that a union can allow locals to practice membership restrictions and tolerate segregation while professing support for FEPC legislation and giving "lip service to democracy." Furthermore, said the writers, "it is inconceivable to us how unions can ask Negroes to vote against right to work legislation when, by practicing race discrimination based on race, they themselves deny Negroes the right to work."[11]

These were powerful words and Meany acted expeditiously. Nine days later he wrote to Petrillo asking for a response. Petrillo answered with a seven-page letter on April 8 in which he reported that following the 1957 convention he had written to all of the Black locals and asked them to assess the opinion of their members regarding the Los Angeles resolution.[12] At this point, there were forty-seven Black locals remaining and Petrillo told Meany that a "cursory examination" of their responses showed that the overwhelming majority opposed the resolution. (Ray Marshall provides exact numbers; in 1966 he wrote that forty locals voted against the Los Angeles merger resolution, five supported it, and two did not respond.)[13] Petrillo emphasized that he opposed "any trace of race inequality in our union . . . but it is not our purpose undemocratically to impose an unfair, unwanted result upon the very members we are determined to help."

The AFL-CIO took the matter under consideration. The head of its Department of Civil Rights, Boris Shiskin, wrote to secretary-treasurer William F. Schnitzler that he hoped the organization's executive council would "encourage President Petrillo to expedite action in bringing about early elimination of segregated locals" and that he trusted that segregated locals could be eliminated by the AFM's June 1958 convention.[14] Unfortunately, it took another thirteen years to effect that goal.

On the public front, Petrillo emphasized to the *New York Times* reporter that "he was personally opposed to segregation" and warned white locals that "if a colored local wants to join you, you had better take them in. Because if you don't we're going to force you to."[15] Petrillo named no specific locals, but the warning was obviously directed at San Francisco.

Seattle, San Francisco, Cincinnati, and the Effects of Fair Employment Legislation

Meanwhile, in Seattle, both Local 76 and Local 493 officials had set up committees to negotiate possible terms of merger and by 1954 they had achieved substantial agreement.[16] Powell Barnett, who was a key player in the process, describes a succession of three committees—the first advisory only, the second reviewing and endorsing the recommendations of the first one, and the third finalizing the terms that were ultimately put to a vote by the membership.[17] Barnett characterized the dialogue as taking place in "a fine spirit of cooperation," with "intelligent consideration ... given to every item presented." Even in this case, however, some members of Black Local 493 opposed the action, fearing that amalgamation would disadvantage them. Nevertheless, the votes at the end of 1956 by both unions endorsed the merger: Local 493's response was unanimous; that of Local 76 was 232 in favor, 128 opposed.[18]

The path in San Francisco proved considerably more treacherous. Relations between Locals 6 and 669 seemed, on the surface, friendly and cooperative. Local 669 rented two rooms on the third floor of Local 6's building; its constitution, bylaws, and pay scale were identical to those of Local 6. At the same time, there was resentment and even, at times, animosity, according to drummer Earl Watkins. "It was all about employment and jealousy. You see, so many of the white musicians weren't very good at improvising; and if you had a jazz club and were a Caucasian owner, and a hot black band came in, you'd want to hire them."[19]

In June 1955, Local 669's president Elma Graves appeared before the IEB at the national convention regarding amalgamation, but "due to certain complex circumstances" (undefined), the matter was referred to Petrillo.[20] The following year Graves took up the issue directly with Local 6. In August 1956 he officially requested that Local 6 place a merger proposal on its December ballot—the same procedure that the Los Angeles and Seattle locals had used. The terms were quite unfavorable to Local 669, but its officers had agreed to them nonetheless: all physical equipment and funds of the Black local would become property of Local 6, and no member of Local 669 would hold an appointive office in the merged union.[21] The only possible cost to Local 6 came in the form of death benefits, and even in this case, the larger benefit offered by Local 6 would only kick in gradually over a period of two years.

Earl Watkins recalled that as the December 1956 vote approached, some members of Local 6 visited clubs to lobby against the proposition. Indeed, despite the highly favorable terms for Local 6, the naysayers triumphed: the proposition was defeated, 554 yes to 786 no. Only 25 percent of Local 6's membership (now standing at 5,400) had cast ballots, allowing the energetic opposition to exert outsized influence. Ralph Gleason scolded Local 6 in the *San Francisco Chronicle*. Noting that racially integrated bands were now common, he wrote: "It hardly seems necessary to point out how utterly out of step with history this [vote] was.... Unless musicians open their eyes as well as their ears, music will lose its place as a force for human rights."[22]

Pressed by the news media, Local 669's officers showed remarkable restraint. "You can't force things . . . ," said 669's new president, Sammy Simpson. "We'll just wait it out."[23]

Although the AFM couldn't (or wouldn't) "force things," the state of California could. On April 16, 1959, Governor Pat Brown signed into law a Fair Employment Practices Act that specified that labor organizations could not refuse membership on the basis of race, creed, color, national origin, or ancestry. It also prohibited segregated locals.

On October 19, 1959, while discussions were underway as to how to implement the new law, Black guitarist and folk singer Walter Browne decided to join the union.[24] He went to the Local 6 and 669 offices on Jones Street and mounted the stairs to Local 669's headquarters. The secretary was late and Browne's parking meter was running out. He went down to feed it, and on his way back he ran into Charles ("Pop") Kennedy, president of Local 6, who told him there were two unions and he could join either one. Not realizing that he was making history, Browne decided to join Local 6. On October 20, 1959, he became Local 6's first Black member since the early 1920s. By contrast, Local 669 at this time was interracial. As in other cities, its membership included a number of whites and Asian Americans.

In a series of meetings in February 1960, the boards of Locals 6 and 669 hammered out the details of the merger, assisted by officers from the International. The arrangements proved considerably more favorable to 669 than the 1956 proposal. Local 669's secretary-treasurer Curtis Lowe and business agent Samuel Landers would join the Local 6 staff as coordinators. A third member (Simpson) would serve on the executive board until the election of December 1960. In addition, "all Local 669 members who are in good standing as of March 31, 1960, will enjoy the same conditions and privileges as applicable to Local 6 members." The official merger of the 390-member Local 669 and the 5,528-member Local 6 took place on April 1.[25]

In a foreshadowing of the difficulties that would later arise in other cities, Lowe felt compelled to write a justification to the members of 669.[26] "I am well aware of the many sacrifices made by the members and officials of Local No. 669 for many years to build the organization into the thriving local which it became," he wrote. "One cannot help but feel a deep sense of loss that this organization as such, no longer exists. Rest assured, the American Federation of Musicians' Charter of Local No. 669 was not revoked for failure to properly conduct its affairs, but was retired . . . because there no longer was a necessity for two . . . Locals in the San Francisco jurisdiction."

In the election of 1963, Black bassist Vernon Alley, a former member of Local 669, won a seat on the Local 6 board and in the next two elections he received more votes than any other candidate. Ironically, Alley had been one of the members of the Baranco band that had been dismissed from work at the Tip Top Club back in 1934 (see chapter 5).

California was not the only state to institute a Fair Labor Practices Act. Ohio, for example, enacted a similar statute in 1959.[27] Part of that act established a Civil Rights Commission, which in 1962, on its own initiative, instituted a complaint against the two Cincinnati AFM locals: no. 1 (white) and no. 814 (Black). These racially separate locals were now illegal under Ohio law, stated the complaint, as they violated the Revised Code section 4112.02(C)(1), which "prohibits labor organizations from limiting or classifying their membership on the basis of race or color."[28] The problem facing the commission, however, was that Black Local 814, which now included five white members, did not care to merge with Local 1 even though Local 1 had reputedly expressed willingness to do so. This refusal "placed the Commission in an awkward position," states the report. "Merger would entail forcing members of a minority group to accept integration against their wishes." The trial examiner recommended that the complaint be dismissed because there was no evidence of deliberate illegal discrimination. (As we have seen, Local 814 resisted amalgamation to the very end of the process, forcing the IEB to cancel its charter in 1970.) The Ohio Civil Rights Commission upheld the recommendation of the trial examiner, in effect requiring a dispute before granting relief, but it noted that "the separate facilities are contrary to the purposes of the Ohio act." Significantly, the report noted that "it would be illegal to call a musicians' local and ask for a white or a Negro band," but the union separation allowed employers to do just that; they could choose the race of the band merely by selecting which local to call.[29]

This case exposes the very real dilemma the AFM would soon face in forcing amalgamation of locals against the wishes of Black musicians. As Table 8.1 above shows, the federation did manage to effect agreements in all cases but two (Cincinnati and Philadelphia), but it did so with difficulty, through stressful negotiations, sometimes with rancor, and even, in the end, by compulsion.

An important voice in this new controversy was that of A. Philip Randolph, who by this time had risen to the position of a vice president in the AFL-CIO, but was still battling that umbrella organization—as he had since before 1920—in his continued efforts to expel railroad unions stubbornly maintaining whites-only clauses in their constitutions. At the AFL-CIO's annual convention in 1959, Randolph found himself in a loud angry verbal jousting match with president George Meany not only over exclusionary Jim Crow rules, but also on the topic of segregated unions in which Black members resisted mergers.[30] Randolph, the most influential Black voice in organized labor, which now included 1.5 million African American workers, introduced two resolutions. The first demanded the ouster of the Brotherhood of Railroad Trainmen and the Brotherhood of Locomotive Firemen and Enginemen unless they acted within six months to eliminate constitutional barriers barring Black members. The second called for the "liquidation and elimination" of segregated locals in all unions. On the first resolution, the federation—as it had for decades—substituted a watered-down version calling for fulfillment of a pledge the railroad unions had made two years earlier to eliminate the color line, but for the umpteenth time, it refused to impose any required time frame. The second resolution provoked an angry outburst from Meany and objections from the bricklayers, who, like the musicians, maintained separate Black locals. Randolph insisted that the federation "should not tolerate long-established segregated locals, even where Negro members wanted to keep them." Meany retorted that he was in favor of "the democratic rights of Negro members to maintain the unions they want." Randolph, who was now an iconic and celebrated spokesman for Black workers, concluded that "to allow unions to maintain Jim Crow locals 'merely because the members want it . . . ' would be to say that it would equally be permissible to have Communist-dominated unions or unions under gangster influence if the members wanted such unions." The conflicting viewpoints found public exposure in the press and the battle lines were thus drawn for the fight over merger within the AFM.

Chicago: Setting a Model for the Future

The stakes for amalgamation were perhaps highest with the federation's largest Black local, no. 208 in Chicago. As in Los Angeles, the impetus for merger arose from the activism of individual Black musicians, but the path in the Windy City proved far more contentious than it had in L.A.

Chicago's motivating force was drummer Red Saunders, leader of the house band at the prestigious Club DeLisa from the late 1930s until its closure in 1958. The Chicago merger began to take shape in 1963, but Saunders had already had a major run-in with his own local's leadership. Coincidentally, Josephine Baker was once again in a front-and-center role. In 1960 Saunders was hired to assemble an orchestra for Baker's appearance at the Regal Theater. In addition to those instrumentalists he could enlist from Local 208, Baker required accordionists, for which he needed to turn to (white) Local 10. Although the pay scales of the two locals were ostensibly equal, Saunders discovered that he'd have to pay more for Local

Figure 8.2 Drummer "Red" Saunders and his band at the Club DeLisa, Chicago.

10's musicians, which he agreed to do. The action constituted a violation of union rules, for which he was reprimanded and fined by Local 208. Saunders says that the issue was not "the integrating of the band so much as it was for me pulling the cover off of Local 208 as to what they were doing"—namely undercutting the pay scale of Local 10.[31]

How significant this event was in pushing Saunders into the lead role in the merger process is not clear, but it reveals the types of tense relations that existed at the time between members and officers within Local 208—tensions that would burst out publicly in ugly conflicts a few years later. By the end of 1962, informal secret talks about amalgamating with Local 10, the third largest local in the AFM, had begun at Saunders's house. He enlisted the members of his orchestra and other bandleaders who were frustrated by racial exclusion in the Chicago job market and disgruntled by what they saw as a lack of support from their own union.

While they pondered their next steps, an incident in the affluent suburb of Oak Park lit a racial spark that reverberated far beyond Chicago and might well have played a part in bringing the union conflict to a head.[32]

On December 4, 1962 Carol Anderson—a 23-year-old Black violinist who had graduated the previous year from the Boston Conservatory—played a rehearsal with the amateur Oak Park & River Forest Symphony conducted by Milton Preves. Preves, the principal violist with the Chicago Symphony, knew Anderson's skills because she played in the North Side Symphony, which he also conducted. He later explained that in preparation for the Oak Park orchestra's concert on February 17, 1963, he needed Anderson to strengthen the second violin section.[33] Soon after that first rehearsal on December 4, Anderson received a call from Marie Dock Palmer, chair of the symphony board, who told Anderson that she needn't return; the board had decided she could not play. Anderson recounted the phone call at the time: "Mrs. Palmer told me she was sorry, of course, and that she was sure I was a nice girl, but that if I stayed it would mean that the community would withdraw its support of the orchestra. She said that I would understand that, as a Negro, I would not be acceptable as a member of the orchestra in this community."[34]

If Palmer expected her call and the board's decision to be well received by the community, she was mistaken. The outburst that ensued led not only to an apology from Palmer and the orchestra management, but also to a major shake-up in the symphony. The Oak Park Village board met in executive session on February 11 and issued a statement deploring Palmer's comments and the symphony's actions.[35] Conductor Preves submitted his resignation, noting both the affront to Anderson and Palmer's anti-Semitic comment that he should be "grateful" as a Jew to be conducting in Oak Park.[36] A group of sixty-one "friends of the Catholic Interracial Council" supported his decision to resign.[37] Furthermore, an interfaith group of twenty-five local clergy members demanded that Anderson play or they would withdraw their support of the orchestra.[38] And perhaps most seriously in the short run, the Oak Park School Board retracted its permission for the orchestra to use the town's high school auditorium for the concert unless Anderson was among the orchestra members.[39]

Ultimately Anderson agreed to play, and Preves agreed to conduct, but only for this single performance. As Preves walked on stage, the audience applauded for nearly a minute, and when he shook hands with Anderson at the end of the performance the attendees expressed their enthusiastic acclamation.[40] Among the audience members was Anderson's father, Leon Anderson, a physician from Wilmington, Delaware.[41] In the aftermath, the orchestra lost Preves and Anderson, and twenty-five orchestra members threatened to resign in protest.[42] Palmer, who was also the orchestra's first cellist, never played with the group again. She died in 1967.[43] During the controversy, H. B. "Bob" Law, president of the Chicago Urban League, commented in an editorial in the *Chicago Tribune*: "The orchestra's board does deserve a public service medal—for forcing racism out from under its log into the sunlight, and for giving decent people a chance to show where they stand."[44]

One month later—on March 20, 1963—a large group of Local 208 members, estimated at the time at nearly two hundred, took overt action against union segregation.[45] Led by Saunders, and calling themselves the Chicago Musicians for Harmonious Integration (CMHI), they marched to Local 10's headquarters and demanded membership. On the advice of counsel (and to the surprise of the Black musicians themselves), Local 10 welcomed them. In a front-page article in *The Defender* under a screaming banner headline, Bob Hunter explained CMHI's motivations—some of them specific to Chicago and others more broadly characteristic of cities elsewhere in the country.[46] "A merger would eliminate what is now known as 'white territory' and 'Negro territory,'" he wrote. Up to this point, Blacks have been unable to play "plush dates" in North Side venues. He quoted drummer Lester Walton as saying: "We feel that we can get more work by joining Local 10. For instance, the studios downtown don't hire us." Additional advantages to joining the white local included lower quarterly dues and reduced taxes on earnings, as well as death benefits that were double those in Local 208.[47]

Subsequent reports differ about how many Local 208 musicians were involved. The initial reports of two hundred were drastically reduced, and ultimately reporters seemed to have agreed on about a hundred. Whatever the specific number, it was enough to alarm the officials of Local 208. Particularly outspoken in his criticism was 208's president, Harry Gray, who, claimed the rebel musicians, was in danger of losing his "high position."[48] Gray reportedly earned an annual salary of $14,000 (equivalent to about $135,000 in 2022).[49]

On the advice of Local 10 officials, the CMHI musicians did not relinquish their memberships in 208, but rather maintained affiliation with both unions, thereby stoking fears by Local 208 officials that these members would exercise undue influence in the Black local on behalf of the white group.[50] Gray and his colleagues in the leadership of Local 208 decided to fight back. In July 1963 he and Local 208's secretary, William Everett Samuels, sent letters to the "rebels," instructing them that they needed to choose one local or the other.[51]

The president of Local 10 at this point was Barney Richards, who had just assumed that post after the defeat of James Petrillo in the local's election of December 1962. Four years earlier Petrillo had stepped down from the presidency of the AFM after eighteen years in office and been replaced by Herman Kenin; but he had retained the presidency of Local 10, which he had held continuously since 1922—even while he was national president. According to Sam Denov, percussionist with the Chicago Symphony and a member of the steering committee of the Chicago Musicians for Union Democracy—the faction of Local 10 aiming to oust Petrillo—opposition to his continued role as president mobilized after Petrillo requested that Local 10 "vote him a life pension equal to his salary as president."[52] Prior to 1962, said Denov, Local 10 had never held an election by secret ballot, but they were required to do so at least once every three years by the 1959 Landrum-Griffin Act. Previously, he claims, members were afraid to stand up to their powerful president. In 1962 they relieved him of his controlling role in the Chicago local.

In his new position, Richards almost immediately had to confront the crisis of the dual unions in Chicago. He responded to Gray and Samuels by noting that AFM rules allowed membership in more than one local as long as members paid dues and work taxes. (Readers will recall that Powell Barnett in Seattle, for one, was a member of both the white and Black locals.) In August 1963, a month after Gray and Samuels sent their warning letter to the Local 208 musicians who had joined Local 10, AFM president Kenin issued a statement agreeing with Richards, and rejected a request from 208 that those who had joined 10 be forced to return to the Black local. By this time the number of African American members of Local 10 had swollen to nearly three hundred, according to a press report at the time.[53] Kenin's decision was consistent with a new, more aggressive move on the part of the International to increase pressure on locals to merge. Six months earlier he had publicly announced that he would be "pressing a drive to eliminate segregated locals."[54]

Meanwhile, meetings between the Chicago locals in April and June 1963 had proven fruitless.[55] Both the federation and the local negotiators realized that the ramifications of any agreement they reached would resonate throughout the AFM. Because Local 10, with 11,731 members, trailed only New York and Los Angeles in size,[56] and 208 was the largest Black local in the country (its membership in 1963 was 1,280), terms of their merger would set a model for the remaining dual locals. Gray and colleagues responded to the actions of the rebel contingent by accelerating their aggressive tactics; they began to deny continued membership in Local 208 not only to those who had joined Local 10, but also to their family members. Third-quarter dues payments submitted by the rebel faction and their relatives in September 1963 were simply returned.[57]

Aside from the personal considerations that might have motivated the actions of Gray and his colleagues, Local 208's position certainly had some merit: How could the Black union agree to surrender its assets (which amounted to about $350,000)[58] without assurances of some arrangements regarding benefits and a voice in the workings of the merged local?[59] Gray demanded assurance of equal employment opportunities for Black musicians and guarantees that Black representation would be enacted on a continuing basis "at all levels of the 'power structure of the merged locals.'"[60] Whether that participation would involve the current officers of Local 208 or newly appointed/elected Black members of Local 10, however, was unclear as the increasingly bitter struggle to join forces unfolded. Samuels succinctly summarized their position: "Integration without participation is meaningless," he asserted.[61]

Richards struck back at the tactics of Local 208 by appointing Saunders and another new Black member, Leon D. Washington, as special advisers to assure the new Black members "that their place of employment and prospective employment will be properly policed to provide job opportunities."[62]

By September, increasingly vicious accusations were flying back and forth. James Mack, now the head of CMHI, brought to the surface the long-simmering dissatisfaction of some African American union members with the entrenched leadership of Local 208. Since the time that Gray had been elected president in 1938,[63] asserted Mack, Local 208's leaders had never prioritized the interests of the local's members. In addition to Gray's run-in with Saunders, we have already seen, in chapter 7, his bitter conflict with Marl Young, prior to Young's move to Los Angeles. Officers of the larger Black locals indeed had vested interests in preserving their segregated units; they not only earned substantial salaries but they also occupied positions of authority. Because officers in all locals (both Black and white) were frequently contractors as well as union leaders, rank-and-file members were loath to question their actions. Mack, however, was now in a protected position as a member of Local 10 and apparently felt comfortable speaking out. In fact, his accusations became even more aggressive; he asserted that 208's books would not "stand investigation or examination."[64]

In the Fall of 1963, CMHI brought the issue directly to the membership of Local 208. In a lopsided vote of 276 to 45 on October 6,[65] Local 208 members overwhelmingly chose to amalgamate with Local 10. Kenin then appointed Hal Davis, president of Pittsburgh's (white) Local 60, as mediator, an action loudly opposed by Mack and the CMHI, who had been excluded from the negotiations. They suggested that Davis was unqualified as the head of a white segregated local.[66] CMHI members even picketed the hotel where the talks were held.[67] Davis, however, was a rising star in the federation. The following year he would become one of its vice presidents and in 1970 he would succeed Kenin as AFM president.[68] Kenin, who had set a March 4, 1964, deadline for merger terms to be settled, imposed a blackout on news reporting, and the secret talks went underground for five months.

When an extended deadline of April 1, 1964 to enact voluntary merger passed without results, Kenin issued his own plan and on April 8 the IEB, in a unanimous decision, ordered Locals 10 and 208 to comply.[69] To the frustration of the CMHI, the plan took a go-slow approach, mandating not only that the merger be delayed until January, 1966, but also that the process involve a transitionary phase extending until 1972.[70] According to the plan, from 1966 to 1969, the former members of Local 208 (and *only* those members) would vote on the following ten officials in the merged local: three members of the eight-member executive board, an administrative vice president (a new position), two out of eleven trial board members, one of three examining board members, and three of six convention delegates. Then from 1969 to 1972, those same former 208 members would elect two board members and the administrative vice president.[71] The plan appeared to be a victory of sorts for Gray and the 208 leadership; they immediately complied.[72]

Richards and Mack, on the other hand, were furious, and Richards mounted a challenge at the 1964 national convention in Portland. The *Official Proceedings* of that year present a detailed eight-page report from the Appeals Committee,[73] which includes documents from both parties. Two letters from Gray attest to 208's compliance and report on a membership meeting of May 17 at which a resolution "accepting the terms and conditions of the Executive Board Order" was passed. A lengthy document from Local 10 appealing the order follows. The most important grounds for the appeal were that the IEB did not have the constitutional authority to impose the merger conditions, that by setting up a procedure in which only former members of Local 208 could vote for certain offices set up "a segregated membership within a so-called merged local," that Local 10 would not be able to muster the required two-thirds majority required for approval, and that the plan "practices a reverse discrimination contrary to the spirit of the laws of the United States, of the State of Illinois and of the policy of the Federation." Richards asked instead for the adoption of a plan by Local 10 that would provide for immediate merger with some representation by former 208 members for two years (e.g., two members of the board and an administrative executive officer) and would authorize all members of the merged local to vote. Guaranteeing former 208 members two board positions, wrote Richards, "in effect gives a 25% representation to approximately a 10% membership."[74] On June 13 the Appeals Committee found unanimously that the IEB had acted "with a sensitive regard for the rights of the parties and the realities of the situation." They denied the appeal.[75]

Richards then tried to marshal the Local 10 members and secured a supporting vote on August 7 to defy the IEB's order.[76] Very few members of the giant Local 10 appeared, however. The tally was just 126 to 9. Five days later, on August 12, the federation placed Local 10 in trusteeship (with Pittsburgh's Hal Davis as trustee).[77] Local 10 immediately took the matter to the federal district court, where the judge, on August 14, issued a temporary order blocking the action. Although the court extended the restraining order against the federation for more than a month, the final ruling, on September 25, dismissed the case.[78] The trusteeship took effect.

The formal amalgamation of the Chicago locals, which created a union with a hyphenated number (10-208) to reflect the joining of the white and Black units, took place on January 11, 1966. William Everett Samuels became the new Administrative Vice President and among the three new board members elected by former 208 members was the legendary Chicago educator, Walter Dyett. Harry Gray refused to run for office and did not appear at the ceremonies to install the new officers.[79]

On July 21, 1970, Herman Kenin died suddenly of a heart attack. Hal Davis became the AFM's president and served until he himself died of the same cause in January 1978.[80]

CHAPTER 9

After Chicago

The Chicago model—without the accompanying trusteeship and lawsuits—formed the basis for the numerous mergers that followed in the next five years. That is, the terms for merger not only specified the agreed-upon disbursal of the financial assets and compromises regarding benefits, but also ensured representation in the leadership of the merged locals by members of the now-defunct Black locals. Three cities will serve as representative case studies: Washington, DC, New Orleans, and Boston. The other mergers followed similar paths.

Washington, DC

A year after the Chicago merger, Washington, DC's Local 710 (which had 207 members in 1965) merged with its much larger white counterpart, Local 161 (1,423 members in the same year). Heading 710's merger committee was saxophonist Otis Ducker, who had first joined the AFM in New Orleans in 1947, and moved to Washington in 1954, where he eventually became 710's Business Agent and a member of the board.[1] As records of Local 710 were destroyed after the merger, the following account relies on two extended interviews with Ducker conducted by the author in June and December 2021.

By the time Ducker became 710's business agent, the function of that office had changed from earlier years. No longer were the agents tasked with collecting work dues; instead, Ducker's job primarily involved negotiating conflicts between AFM members and employers. By the 1960s, DC's Black local was doing very well: its officers were paid (which was not the

Figure 9.1. Saxophonist and union leader in Washington, DC, Otis Ducker. (Courtesy of Otis Ducker.)

case with some small locals), it owned its own building with no mortgage, and its growing membership was increasingly multiracial. Whites had begun to join Local 710 for a number of reasons, including lower dues than those in (white) Local 161 and the attraction of jam sessions held at 710's headquarters, which were "available and fun."

Indeed, the local's building on 9th Street was a particular source of pride and warm fellowship. In the basement was a large entertainment space (with a bar) that hosted the jam sessions as well as rehearsals. It also served as a social space; members came to fry fish or chicken, says Ducker, or simply hang out with friends, drink, and play music.

The city's social and entertainment clubs at which members of Local 710 played "were of a different economic ilk" than the clubs run by whites, Ducker recalled. Therefore, Local 710 developed a wage scale that was more economically feasible for these venues. As long as the members played in these clubs, which were patronized primarily by African Americans, Local 161 had no problem with the pay differential. But, as we have seen in other cities, when competition for the same jobs developed, friction ensued. Indeed, Local 710 members increasingly appeared in white-patronized clubs or in big hotels. Local 161's officers worked hard to convince the hiring agents at the hotels to enforce the white local's scale.

In the 1960s, Local 710 set up a merger committee; due to the illness of the president, Lou Aikens, Ducker assumed the duties of chair. The primary concern of the Black musicians was that by merging with a white local seven times its size, former 710 members would not enjoy the consideration for jobs or the influential voice in union activities that they had experienced within a separate entity. "They feared losing identity and representation," says Ducker, "not being able to participate in the deliberations and decisions of the board of directors."

As discussions began, Local 161's officers, like those in Los Angeles and Chicago, simply proposed that 710's members join their union without any further concessions. But Ducker and his team wanted assurance of active participation. To this end they requested: (1) an administrative vice president (as in Chicago), who would be a permanent member of the board of directors; (2) their own business agent; (3) a presidential assistant with an office in the merged local headquarters; and (4) an appointed member on the merged local's board of directors.

In addition to the differing wage scales, other issues also posed stumbling blocks. For example, Local 161 had strict requirements governing the maximum number of working hours and the minimum number of required musicians for each engagement. Ducker recalled that their rules called for ten musicians for a one-night stand. Local 710, on the other hand, typically provided employers with combos of five to seven players.

The merger teams met in New York with Petrillo, who, on December 7, 1964 (two years after he lost the presidency of Chicago's Local 10), had taken on an appointment as head of the AFM's newly established Civil Rights Department.[2] These negotiations eventually led to an agreement. Local 161 acceded to the conditions described above regarding representation on the board; its officers also agreed to allow intact bands of fewer than ten to continue to operate. On the other hand, Local 710 had asked that their representation in the merged union continue for ten years, but yielded to 161's response that the arrangement should expire after five.

In contrast to the agreements in many other cities, Local 710's building was not sold immediately after the merger in 1967. In fact, the union placed a part-time staff person there during the day and African American musicians could choose which facility to use. After about three years, however, this arrangement proved unworkable and the union sold the building.

According to Ducker, the officers of Local 161 had expressed the opinion that after the five-year transitionary period "love would prevail" and African Americans would be elected as leaders. In fact, however, after the mandated positions disappeared, so did Black representation on the board. In 2011 members elected Ducker as vice president of Local 161-710; he was the first elected Black member in the merged local's history. (Hyphenated local numbers such as 161-710 preserved the identities of amalgamated locals; they mostly became the rule after the Chicago merger in 1966.) In 2014 another Black musician, Patty Hurd, replaced Ducker in this position. By this time, Ducker had become very prominent on the national scene. Tom Lee, who was president of the International from 2001 to 2010, asked Ducker to head the federation's Diversity Council, and then in 2006 appointed him to the International Executive Board when one member resigned before completing his term. The IEB ratified Ducker's appointment, making him its first African American member.[3]

New Orleans

There's no need to review here the seminal role that New Orleans played in the history of jazz, or the enormous contributions of its large Black population to that musical revolution. In the nineteenth century, writes historian Henry Kmen, New Orleans had "the largest Negro population, both slave and free, of any American city."[4] That demographic had developed not only from Blacks who were forcibly relocated from Africa to the American South, but also from substantial immigration from the West Indies, which gave rise to the Creoles of Color. As Curtis Jerde, former curator of the Hogan Jazz Archive, reminds us, "the transit of musicians back and forth" from the Caribbean "left a considerable impression upon the city's vernacular musical style."[5] Coupled with the brass band tradition and the string bands playing in the dance culture, the Black population of New Orleans exerted an influence far beyond its size on musical developments in the United States in the early twentieth century.

As noted in chapter 3, the first Black local in New Orleans organized in 1902, the same year as the Chicago local, but dissolved only three years later due to financial difficulties. Stephen Laifer says that thereafter Black musicians in the city had to register with the segregated local in Mobile, Alabama,[6] but that union did not form until 1919. In the interim, Black musicians in the city had no local union representation. As the steamship excursion business, which John Streckfus initiated in 1907, began to mushroom after the First World War, this lack of representation became critical. Blacks wanting to play on the ships needed union membership. The Streckfus Steamer company employed bands of ten to twelve members, not only in St. Louis, "the capital port of riverboat jazz,"[7] but also in NOLA. Bandleader Fate Marable, who "led the most famous hot dance bands for Streckfus Steamers," became the foremost recruiter of Black musicians in both cities. He even brought Streckfus to hear Louis Armstrong, who then started playing on the boats beginning in the 1917–18 winter season on the *Dixie Belle*.[8] Streckfus operated a union shop. "The first thing Marable did with his first New Orleans band," writes William Kenney, "was to take them north by train . . . to Paducah, Kentucky [Marable's home town], where he got them all signed into the local of the black musicians' union." Paducah was hardly convenient to the New Orleans musicians: it is nearly six hundred miles away. Its Black Local 584 was chartered there in 1918, the same year that Armstrong began to play on the Streckfus Steamers. In 1926, Black musicians formed Local 496 in New Orleans, which remained an active force in the community until it merged with white Local 174 in 1969.

Merger negotiations between Locals 174 and 496 (which, like other Black locals, had a few white members as well) began in 1965, but ultimately the two groups held twenty-seven meetings before an agreement emerged, and even then, at the eleventh hour, the International had to mandate approval.[9] During this negotiation period, relations between Locals 174 and 496 appear to have been for the most part cordial and mutually respectful. For example, in two instances, members of Local 496 brought charges against members of 174;[10] in both instances, Local 174's board ruled in favor of the member of Local 496. The minutes confirm that contractors were hiring from both locals and that bands were often racially integrated.

Nor does a differential in pay scale seem to have been a problem. During the negotiation period, Local 496 operated on Local 174's scale. Laifer claims that the Black musicians had a lower scale in force than 174,[11] but notations in the minutes of both locals—in 1966 and again in 1968—confirm that Local 496 was not only operating at 174's scale but also adopting, without discussion or disagreement, increases in that scale and changes affecting the minimum number of players per service. The minutes of Local 496 simply record that its members would be informed of the new regulations.[12]

Despite these friendly interactions, racism within the broader community was commonplace. (White) drummer Barry Martyn, for example, vividly recalls the reaction to his joining (Black) Local 496 after he came to New Orleans from London in 1961. Martyn needed to become a union member in order to make a recording and "naturally I joined the black [local] as I knew only two white musicians in town.... I came here to learn about music from black musicians, not from white players."[13] That evening Martyn received a call from Ku Klux Klan members "threatening to come over and raise my voice a couple octaves. I was worried but replied, 'I don't want you boys hurting yourselves coming up these really narrow stairs and tripping over your robes, and I'll be sitting with a sawed off shotgun to pick you off one by one.' They never showed up."[14]

By June 1966 merger proposals from both locals were on the table and under intensive discussion.[15] Saxophonist David Winstein, who became president of 174 in 1948 and remained in that position for forty-six years,[16] kept the white local's membership updated on progress, as did president Louis Cottrell of Local 496. Winstein was also a member of the International Executive Board, and therefore potentially in a role of significant authority. By July 1967 he projected a target date for the merger of January 1, 1968, and bandleaders of the two groups held a "constructive and informative" meeting. Representatives from the two locals met with Petrillo and Kenin in Atlanta the following month.[17] Reflecting perhaps on the contentious series of events in Chicago, Winstein emphasized to the full membership of Local 174 that "unless agreement is reached, an executive order will probably be forthcoming from the Federation."[18]

The International kept up the pressure, sending the New Orleans unions notice in November 1967 that the Washington, DC, locals had merged and that the two locals in Atlanta had reached an agreement on terms.[19] When negotiations were still stalled in May 1968, Cottrell traveled to Chicago for a meeting of those locals that had not yet merged.[20] Two days after that meeting, he reported on it to the 496 membership: "Decision reached at this meeting was they did not want to merge."[21]

Disagreement over details of the proposed agreement continued to block progress, and by December 1968 the New Orleans locals were at loggerheads. On December 2, officers of Local 496, apparently frustrated by the seeming futility of the process, failed to appear for a scheduled meeting, and Winstein wrote to AFM President Kenin that Local 174 was breaking off negotiations. Local 496 sent its own letter to the AFM president.[22] Six days later Local 496 held a membership meeting at which Secretary Isadore Crump reported that he had been to New York and met with the AFM's Civil Rights Commission. The Black local's membership voted to continue negotiating with Local 174, seeking "an honorable and equitable association; also to settle for nothing less than the tentative plan, with representation with authority in all functioning committees." The implication was that Local 174 was resisting the proposal put forth by Local 496 regarding the role that members of the Black local would play in the governance of the merged body.

The following spring Kenin's assistant, Ernie Lewis, came to New Orleans and met with both groups. With his help (or pressure—or both), they managed on March 30 to develop a plan that addressed the points of disagreement (which are not specified in the minutes). But the fight was not yet over. Local 174 approved the plan in meetings on August 18 and September 2, 1969, but the membership of 496 defeated it on August 31 by an overwhelming majority: fifty-nine votes against merger, eleven in favor, three abstentions (see Figure 9.2).

At this point, federation officials stepped in and mandated acceptance of the terms—just as they had in Chicago. Local 496 did not protest further. The federation's *Charter Book* registers the merger officially on November 1, 1969. On January 20, 1970, after nearly five years of dialogue between two locals that had seemed, from all outward signs, to be cooperative and operating on friendly terms, the merged local held its first general meeting.[23] Following the model in Chicago and other cities, former members of Local 496 thereafter nominated and voted for officers in the new merged organization to serve for a period of three years. The terms were even more favorable than in Chicago; representation in the new body included a dozen members of the now-defunct Local 496, including: one vice president, one business representative, four members of the board of directors, three members of the committee on wages, and three delegates to the convention. These members held their offices until September 30, 1973.[24]

Twenty-eight years later Al Jackson, a local resident from the Tremé district, bought Local 496's vacant building, which was at the time occupied by squatters. He intended to establish a jazz museum there, but the building collapsed before he could renovate it. Jackson opened the one-room "Treme's Petit Jazz Museum" in another location; it features a collection of memorabilia that includes items from the former Local 496.[25]

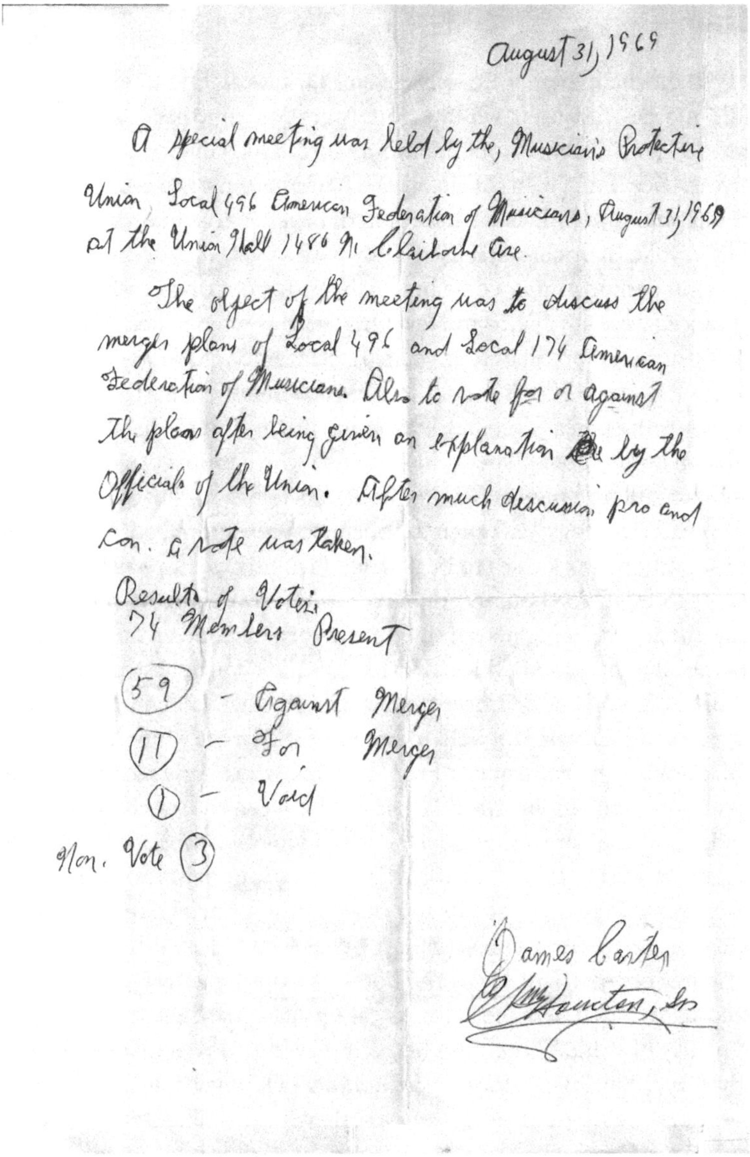

August 31, 1969

A special meeting was held by the Musicians Protective Union, Local 496 American Federation of Musicians, August 31, 1969 at the Union Hall 1486 N. Claiborne Ave.

The object of the meeting was to discuss the merger plans of Local 496 and Local 174 American Federation of Musicians. Also to vote for or against the plans after being given an explanation by the Officials of the Union. After much discussion pro and con. A vote was taken.

Results of Votes:
74 Members Present

(59) - Against Merger
(11) - For Merger
(1) - Void

Non. Vote (3)

James Carter
[signature]

Figure 9.2. Excerpt from the minutes of New Orleans's Black Local 496, August 31, 1969, showing the membership vote opposing merger with (white) Local 174 (59 votes against merger, 11 in favor).

Boston

As 1970 dawned, there were only seven Black locals still in existence. Four would merge with their white counterparts during that year; and Locals 2 and 197 in St. Louis would combine forces on January 1 of the following year. (See Table 8.1a for details.) The remaining two—Cincinnati and Philadelphia—would, as we have noted, never merge and the IEB would finally revoke their charters. (See Table 8.1b.)

Boston demonstrates a case in which the negotiations and resolution of differences were cordial, as in New Orleans, but where once again the process consumed more than four years. In September 1965, (white) Local 9's president, George Harris, began to alert the membership to the projected merger, urging passage of a resolution instituting "work dues" of 4 percent (with a maximum of $40 per year) because "the national office is on record that there will be a merger" and "[Black] Local 535 . . . has a 4% work dues [sic] on ALL earnings."[26] "When this merger is consummated," noted Harris, "the amount of work dues to be collected from traveling bands could well amount to 20 to 25 thousand dollars. . . . Meanwhile many miscellaneous engagements are being played in our territory by bands from neighboring locals because of no work dues." Harris thus took concrete steps to reconcile the differing policies of Locals 9 and 535, but he also emphasized that a merger would enhance the self-interests of the larger white local.

Black multi-instrumentalist Fred Williams, who clearly recalls the merger negotiations, remembers the relationship between the two Boston locals as friendly and nonconfrontational.[27] After living and working in St. Louis, Williams moved to Boston in 1951,[28] where he found far less racial tension. In Boston he joined Local 535 and played in interracial bands, but he also noted that, as in other cities, (white) Local 9 had "first dibs" on the most desirable work, particularly in the hotels. At the same time, says Williams, there was so much demand for musical services that Local 535's members had plenty of work. Sometimes he even played two jobs in a single night.

By June 1966, the two locals were holding talks regarding merger proposals and even taking unified action on other local challenges. For example, Local 138 in Brockton, Massachusetts, requested jurisdictional rights over some territory controlled by Locals 9 and 535. Together the two Boston locals presented their case (through Local 9's president, George Harris) to the IEB at the national convention.[29]

Negotiations moved slowly, however, and finally the International again had to step in to take direct action. Hal Davis, having completed his difficult work in Chicago and now serving as a vice president of the AFM, held negotiation meetings on January 8–9 and February 19–20, 1968, to iron out differences, particularly regarding the pension fund.[30]

Meanwhile, as in other cities, an increasing number of white musicians had chosen to join the Black local. Trumpeter Henry Francis, one of the white members, offers some insight on their motivations.[31] Francis completed his undergraduate degree at Harvard in 1960; during his years there he played in a Dixieland band that performed at parties on campus and in resorts during the summer. Initially he joined Local 9 but then transferred to Local 535. He cites three specific reasons prompting his decision. First, he wanted to protest the existence of two racially separated locals. Second, the dues in Local 535 were lower. Although the wage scale was also lower (as we have seen in many other cities), Francis was not overly concerned, as his livelihood did not depend on his musical work. Finally (and presumably most importantly), he was unhappy with Local 9's "strict enforcement of the bylaws" regarding scale and collaboration with nonunion musicians. He discovered that even though Local 535 ostensibly operated by the same bylaws as Local 9, its officers were more lenient in enforcing them. Therefore, he could have the freedom to choose with whom he played and at what price.

Terms of the merger agreement appeared on the ballot of Local 9 on December 9, 1968, with a tentative date for implementation of January 13, 1969. The plan included the following provisions:[32]

- No members of either local would pay additional initiation fees;
- Local 9's benefits (including hospitalization) would go into effect for all;
- For two years Local 535's members would elect their own officers to serve in the merged union;
- Six positions would be allotted to the former Local 535: two administrative vice presidents, two board members, and two delegates to the national convention;
- Local 9's wage scales and dues would be in effect and its bylaws and constitution used;
- The assets of the two unions would be merged. The building on Massachusetts Avenue belonging to Local 535 would be sold, as it was in need of repairs.

The actualization of this plan, however, consumed another year. In part, the terms required further discussion and ratification; and in part, officers of Local 535—as in Chicago and elsewhere—balked at being absorbed into the much larger white union. Trumpeter Gordon Bowman recalls that Local 535's president, Preston Sandiford, opposed the unification.[33] He was very "entrepreneurial," says Bowman, and "was not eager to lose that edge." In

Figure 9.3. Cover of Boston Local 9-535's magazine, *Interlude*, April–June 1970.

1993, Sue-Ellen Hershman quoted jazz pianist Mabel Robinson as saying, "I had no interest in merging. I just knew that things would never be the same."[34] By 2000, Robinson's recollection was quite different, however. The merger "did give me the advantage of earning a decent wage," she said. "And as the scale went up, my wages went up. That made a difference in my life."[35] As in most other cities, Black musicians saw the handwriting on the wall and negotiated the best terms they could.

Locals 9 and 535 officially amalgamated on April 1, 1970, and held the first joint meeting of their executive boards on the fifteenth of the month. The first meeting of the full joint membership took place in September. Sandiford held one of the vice president's offices in the merged Local 9-535 for several years thereafter.

Summary of the Amalgamation Process (and the Merger in Buffalo)

The case studies described in this chapter and the previous one graphically illustrate the complexity of the AFM's process of extricating itself from its history of segregated locals. In the earliest cases, mergers were instigated by individual locals without pressure from the International. In Los Angeles, the push for amalgamation arose internally, stemming from the particular set of circumstances affecting musicians in the fast-developing media industry. Yet it took the activism of a small group of union members from both Local 767 and Local 47 to move from irritable discontent to aggressive action, leading ultimately to success in 1953. Reflecting the pattern that would develop in the next few years, however, some of the older members of Local 767 expressed opposition; and that sentiment was echoed four years later, when the (now-merged) Local 47 representatives introduced their resolution at the convention to force amalgamation throughout the federation. Representatives from Black locals across the country expressed their opposition, responding vigorously with a petition to defeat the L.A. proposal. The rank and file in their unions thereafter strongly reinforced their stance through direct consultation requested by Petrillo. By this time, however, merger talks were already underway in a number of cities.

San Francisco, by all accounts, appears to have been unusual. Here the Black musicians of Local 669 consistently pressured for absorption into Local 6—and indeed had been doing so since they were forced to become a subsidiary in the mid-1930s—but the white local repeatedly resisted. Only when the state of California made amalgamation mandatory through its Fair Employment Practices Act of 1959 did Local 6 capitulate.

The mergers between 1953 and 1962 in Los Angeles, Seattle, San Francisco, Columbus, Denver, Sioux City, Cleveland, and several other cities mentioned by Petrillo in his letter to George Meany, coupled with numerous articles in the press that exhorted the federation to put an end to segregation, stimulated the national leadership to become increasingly aggressive in pushing the remaining locals to merge.[36] Kenin's announcement in February 1963 that he was "pressing a drive to eliminate segregated locals" reflected the federation's new dedication to freeing itself from its troublesome history. "We want to rid ourselves of this problem because segregation is wrong," said Kenin succinctly. He was, at the time, in Southern California for a convention of the Western AFM locals and he added for emphasis that the incoming president of the Western Conference of Musicians was African American.[37]

The political movements of the 1960s further intensified the pressure on the AFM, and some Black union leaders outside the federation urged merger even in opposition to the expressed wishes of African Americans trying to preserve the organizations they had built up over many decades. The powerful comments of A. Philip Randolph at the 1959 AFL convention challenged these Black leaders to prioritize ending segregation over the possible loss of distinctiveness (and, potentially, jobs) that their members might face.

Chicago proved a testing ground both because of the size of Locals 10 and 208 and because of the history of overt discrimination within the white union. Petrillo's role as president of Local 10 cast a further spotlight on this city, which had often been a hotbed of racial tensions. As in Los Angeles, however, the beginnings of merger activism required overt actions on the part of a group of Black musicians, reinforced by support from some members of Local 10. In this case, the "rebel" members of Local 208 took matters into their own hands by marching in force to the office of the white local and demanding admission. The officers of Local 10 no doubt had some ulterior motives in their ready acceptance of these African Americans. Did they perhaps see the opportunity to eliminate a competing union in their territory? No accusation of such a motivation appeared in the press at the time; but we certainly cannot rule it out. And the resistance to merger on the part of Local 208's officers was, as we have seen, exceptionally robust.

Although the negotiating process in Chicago proved extremely rancorous—to the point of nearly derailing the merger entirely—the ultimate resolution set the pattern for the rest of the federation. The terms of subsequent mergers mirrored those in Chicago by detailing not only the distribution of assets and the standardizing of benefit packages, but also, most importantly, the role that members of the now-defunct Black locals would play in the leadership of the amalgamated union.[38]

For example, in Buffalo, where Lloyd Plummer had been pressuring for equal treatment of Blacks in the federation since his failed resolution demanding an end to subsidiaries in 1937, the amalgamation process followed a path similar to that in Chicago. By the 1960s Local 533 and its white counterpart, Local 43, which was nearly ten times its size, had been cooperating on issues of relevance to both unions and were operating with the same pay scale. Merger discussions began in earnest in June 1964, and both locals ceased being racially exclusive after that time.[39] Nevertheless, the Black musicians were hesitant about the potential loss of voice in the merged union; Buffalo's convention delegates had been among the signatories of the resolution opposing the Los Angeles resolution for amalgamation in 1957. Plummer (who relinquished his position as president and became secretary-treasurer of the local in 1936),[40] along with the then-current president, Perry Gray, met with Kenin and Petrillo repeatedly in 1965, 1966, and 1967.[41] Hal Davis became directly involved again as well. He came to Buffalo to oversee the drafting of the merger agreement when the parties themselves could not formulate a compromise. In March 1968, by a vote of 45–2, Local 533 approved of the draft that had emerged the preceding December. But Local 43 rejected it. As in Chicago, the AFM then took control and imposed compliance,[42] and the merger became effective on January 1, 1969. The agreement in this case created a new local, no. 92, with a constitution and bylaws taken from those of the former Local 43. Assets of the two locals combined. From 1971 to 1974 former members of Local 533 nominated an administrative vice president, an assistant secretary-treasurer, two directors, and one of four convention delegates. The other officers came from Local 43.[43] In 1996, Richard McRae wrote that since free elections had resumed in 1974, no non-white members had won offices.

Notably, merger terms developed independently in the more than fifty cities with dual unions still in existence at the time of the L.A. merger. Although the agreements were similar in their basic objectives, they sometimes varied substantially in detail from one place to another. Federation officials were part of the process in effecting amalgamation in numerous cases. They traveled from city to city, brought local officials to New York for intensive meetings, or both. In some places (e.g., Los Angeles, Washington, DC, Boston, Seattle), the process went relatively smoothly overall; members overcame disagreements through negotiation. In others (notably Chicago), the efforts nearly collapsed; and in some (e.g., Chicago, Buffalo, New Orleans) the federation in the end had to mandate merger. In at least one instance (San Francisco) the state took over, requiring an end to segregation.

Although the Civil Rights Bill of 1964 did not explicitly mandate the elimination of segregated locals (see chapter 1), its passage spurred the amalgamation process. Merging the separate locals conformed to the spirit (if not to the letter) of the new law. Despite the federation's success in helping those locals still existing after the Chicago merger reach satisfactory terms for amalgamation, the two holdouts, Cincinnati's Local 814 and Philadelphia's Local 274, forced the federation to choose between supporting segregation by honoring the wishes of their Black members or defying the wishes of those very members in the name of abolishing the separation between the races. Both Local 814 and Local 274 argued that they were not in fact segregated; their ranks, like those of other locals we have discussed, included a few white musicians. Therefore, they said, they should be allowed to remain intact, or even become the predominant union in the area. Indeed, for the federation there were no good choices; and as we will see in our final chapter, some of the fears expressed by these (and other) local officials about the detrimental effects likely to accrue to Black musicians after merger proved to be justified. In response, the AFM took further steps to support racial equality—or at least racial representation.

CHAPTER 10

Coda

The amalgamation process put an end to segregation in the AFM, but in other respects its effects were decidedly mixed. In Los Angeles, the younger members who had lobbied for merger reported concrete benefits. Buddy Collette says that joining forces "began to make better players out of the good players.... Plus there's better health and welfare and pension benefits. ... Shows began to hire people because they were all in the same union."[1] On the other hand, some of the older musicians saw little improvement in their work situation; they didn't partake of the increased death benefits and they felt swallowed up in a larger impersonal organization. Many members (both young and old) keenly felt the loss of an organization whose primary goal was to "look out" for them. "We had our own local, we had our own money, we owned the building," recalled saxophonist Cecil "Big Jay" McNeely nostalgically.[2] The Central Avenue musical scene itself began to close down, not only due to the union merger, but more importantly because of the relaxation of housing restrictions, which naturally encouraged Black residents to move into less crowded areas of the city. Central Avenue, in fact, had begun to decline well before the 1953 merger, as many of those interviewed for the UCLA oral history project noted. Drug use and crime had increased in the years after the war, stated several of them.[3] Most of those interviewed for the project remarked that the geographic dispersal of the Black population reflected improved economic conditions, but also disrupted the camaraderie of the formerly crowded, tight-knit, segregated district. The UCLA interviews took place between 1989 and 1996; by that time, participants had had many years to reflect on the effects of the merger process. Trumpeter Art Farmer bemoaned the "graveyard" that was left of Central Avenue. "Nothing would give you the impression that this place had ever been anything other than what it is right now," he said. "And you have to stop and ask yourself, 'Well, is it all an illusion?'"[4]

In Chicago as well, the South Side music scene declined due to social developments more significant than the AFM mergers. Indeed, the pressure for amalgamation in the mid-1960s was in tune with changing times. In an eloquent evaluation of the situation, Amy Absher writes that the decline of the lively Black music scene in Chicago was "part of the larger anguish being felt by the Black community caught up in the growth of Chicago's modern ghetto in the 1950s and 1960s. The replacing of the South Side streetscape with housing projects, and the subsequent growth in crime and poverty, became defining characteristics of the South Side in the 1960s."[5]

The loss of clubhouses, with their rehearsal spaces, opportunities for after-hours jamming, and lively social events, is a recurring theme among the reflections of Black musicians in various cities. David Keller even named his pictorial history of Seattle's Black Local 493 after one of these spaces, known as the Blue Note. In a few places the buildings remained and continued to have a life (though less prominent) in the community. In 1985, for example, the *New York Times* ran an article on Buffalo's "Colored Musicians Club." "What keeps the club alive," wrote the author, Edward A. Gargan, "in addition to the jazz that floats from the upstairs windows, are its memories." The venue continued to be "a place where black and white musicians [would] come to practice or just to jam, to talk about music."[6]

The union itself began to lose its grip on casual employment throughout the country. Many young musicians ignored the federation and took jobs at clubs that increasingly hired nonunion personnel. Some of the older musicians simply abandoned attempts to make their living through their profession. To cite but one example, David Keller details the post-merger activities of some of the prominent Seattle players. Pianist Elmer Gill emigrated to Canada, he notes.

> [Saxophonist] Jabo Ward continued playing bebop for two more years at Pete's Poopdeck in an integrated band and then shortly thereafter began working for Texaco. [Sax player] William Funderberg dropped out of 493 for steady work in Seattle's waterfront industry. John Willis . . . went back to school and became a social worker. [Trumpeter] Floyd Standifer, after gigging some and working at Local 76 as an administrator until he quit in disgust over favoritism and unprincipled personality attacks in the early 1960s, became a community college teacher. . . . For

Figure 10.1. The "Colored Musicians Club" of Buffalo in 1985, formerly the headquarters of Black Local 533. (Photo by Andre Carrotflower.)

these black men and for almost all of the minority musician members of former Local 493, a combination of changing musical tastes, economic downturns, and the amalgamation itself combined to render unionism a moot point.[7]

Gordon Bowman estimates that after the merger in Boston only about half of the Local 535 members joined Local 9.[8] As early as 1968, while mergers were still incomplete, *Variety* ran an article under the eye-catching headline "AFM Locals' Integration Backfires." The article opened with a gloomy prediction: "The process of integrating Negro and white locals . . . is not running quite as smoothly as was hoped for by the union's administration. Rumbles of discontent, particularly by Negro musicians, were distinctly heard at the recent AFM convention . . . , where desegregated locals in New Haven and Chicago asked for their charters back." The article highlighted "one local" (not identified) that "originally had 56 members. After the merger, 46 members left the union."[9]

In 1975, at the age of eighty-two, Petrillo left the AFM's Civil Rights Department, "thinking, no doubt, that the task of integration was complete. It was not," says George Seltzer. "Blacks were not integrated into the white locals, they were submerged." Once the dates passed during which members of former Black locals were guaranteed certain official positions in the merged locals, few of them were elected to governing posts. At the 1974 convention, there were only ten Black delegates.

The AFM took steps to counteract this troublesome, but not unexpected outcome of merger. In 1977 the convention approved of a new resolution aimed to increase Black representation. "A merged Local, whose merger was the result of compliance with the Civil Rights policy of the American Federation of Musicians shall be entitled to one additional delegate to be elected from the black membership of said Local."[10] As a result of this change, the number of African American delegates increased, but slowly. In 1993 there were only two Black delegates from Chicago, for instance, and they were, remarkably, the only African Americans to have been elected to such positions in Local 10-208.[11] The 1977 rule has since been broadened to address diversity in general and now reads: "A merged Local, the merger of which was the result of compliance with the AFM Civil Rights policy, shall be entitled to one additional Delegate. *This Delegate shall be elected from the general membership and be identified as the 'Diversity Delegate'* on all election notices and ballots" (italics mine).[12]

Ironically, the dismantling of racist laws in the country and the movement of African Americans outside of ghettoized communities led to a less dynamic, less tightly knit African American cultural scene. That trend then spurred admirable efforts to preserve the distinctive culture by creating Black studies programs; yet these programs also, in some cases, cause increased separation. Amalgamation was definitely a two-edged sword.

Despite the racism that continues to plague American society and the tensions among political factions that sometimes seem insurmountable, there is nevertheless some cause for optimism even though progress seems at times to come at a snail's pace. The AFM, for example, has in recent years established a Diversity Council.[13] The effort originated in 1996 under president Steve Young, who appointed the council "to increase membership, service musicians, and raise the level of participation through affirmative means." The council's eight-member steering committee met with representatives of other trade unions, who offered guidance and pledged cooperation. Five years later, newly elected AFM president Tom Lee appointed a new Council, this one chaired by Otis Ducker from Washington, DC's, Local 161-710. In 2003 the council became a standing committee under the name AFM Diversity Committee. The following year it issued this mission statement:

Our mission is to reflect the diversity of our musical community and further the goal of the AFM to recognize and celebrate the diverse nature of our organization. With the assistance of our International Executive Board, we seek ways to better represent and increase membership by raising the level of participation by all, through affirmative means. This can only be accomplished by organizational educational outreach, recruitment, officer training, and increased leadership opportunities at all levels. The American Federation of Musicians of the United States and Canada is committed to creating an inclusive environment where diversity will be valued and celebrated; where members, leaders, rank and file, and staff are inspired to contribute to the growth of the Federation. We envision our organization as one where the leadership reflects and affirms the diversity of our membership.[14]

Among the most visible actions of the committee is its Diversity Award program, which chooses winners in three categories: The Charles McDaniel Youth Award ($1,000 scholarship for study), the Charles Walton Diversity Advocate Award (given to a member over thirty-five who has contributed to the diversity of the federation), and the President's Award (given to an AFM local that demonstrates it has a diverse executive board). Winners are chosen through a rigorous multistage process. AFM locals nominate candidates, who are vetted by the Diversity Awards Committee in two stages. At the end of the selection process, a panel of independent judges who are not members of the federation choose the winners.[15] Lovie Smith-Wright, from Houston's Local 65-699, who is chair of the Diversity Committee, emphasizes that diversity pertains not only to race but also to gender, age, and musical genre.

As for the historical hesitation of Black workers to join labor unions, recent data suggest attitudes precisely the opposite of those in the early years of the labor movement. Although union membership has declined precipitously in recent years, "Black workers are still more likely than workers of any other race or ethnicity to be unionized," says a recent report from the Center for Economic and Policy Research.[16] "In 2015 14.2 percent of Black workers and 12.3 percent of the entire workforce were represented by unions." The unionized workers "enjoy higher wages, and better access to health insurance and retirement benefits than their non-union peers."

Final Reflections

The history of the AFM's segregated locals—both their formation and their demise—shows that progress comes only through the concurrence of individual action and community validation. Contesting the inequities in society and shaking those inequities loose from their constricting moorings requires the bold activism of individuals such as Marl Young, Buddy Collette, Red Saunders, Powell Barnett, Lloyd Plummer, and many others we have cited in this book. But awakening the conscience of larger bodies such as the federation, or, indeed, of the society at large, also requires outspoken group action. It takes both to bend the "arc of the moral universe . . . toward justice."[17]

Individuals, of course, pursue their own self-interest. In the early years of the twentieth century, Black musicians determined that those interests could best be advanced through separate organizations, even though that segregated structure might result in lower wages and jurisdictional battles with white goliaths. Black locals were, in their estimation, the best alternative available at the time. These locals fostered bonding within a community of like-minded individuals dedicated to realizing the best working conditions possible for their members. In addition, through guaranteed representation on the national scene, these locals stimulated broader discussions outside the core group—discussions that maintained pressure on the federation's officers to find equitable solutions to the problems of racial prejudice.

Indeed, the formation of segregated locals served Black musicians well for several decades, both on the practical and the psychological level. "Monoethnic aggregations," notes African American history professor David Anthony, "while they may often respond to patterns of formal structural exclusion, frequently result from positive determination." Although the formation of such organizations may be motivated by exclusion, they "can also represent an act of volition."[18]

For a time, the system of separate locals worked reasonably well. In many cities, Black musicians managed to find satisfying, if not always lucrative, work. More importantly, perhaps, the communities they formed not only bonded in fellowship and a common cause, but also engaged in productive and satisfying collaborative music-making. Their clubhouses offered venues to rehearse, to jam, to meet after gigs, to share musical ideas, and to learn from one another. The relationships forged in those communities became so tight that dissolution of the Black locals required, in some cases, considerable force.

As wise as the actions of Black musicians seemed in forming separate organizations in the 1910s and 20s, that very separation led to greater conflicts outside of their congenial communities. As jurisdictional disputes became ever more common in the 1930s and beyond, and as the pressure mounted in the society at large to combat racial segregation, Black musicians feared—with justification, as it turned out—the loss of their influence in national decision-making, as well as the possibility of economic damage through their submergence within the majority. Therefore, when amalgamation loomed seriously as a credible threat, they mounted resistance, fearing the potential loss of their distinctiveness and the diminution of their influence within their representative body. David Anthony artfully summarizes the dilemma involved in ending monoethnic entities:

> Decisions to dispense with organizations in which people of African Descent formed majorities in favor of integrated bodies were not always necessarily made easily or comfortably. This is why some have second thoughts about the fruits of integration, reflecting upon a sense of unity of purpose, action, and membership that many perceive to have been lost as a casualty of opening doors to formerly "racially" restricted institutions. This is not to say that there is nostalgia for Jim Crow and all of its attendant violent physical and psychological evils, but that the pervasive perception of a strong "racial" bond uniting African Americans spurred socially cohesive action.[19]

Could the federation have acted differently to prevent the dual union system from collapsing in such a torturous way? The International could, of course, have disallowed Black locals from forming in the first place. There was, as I have emphasized throughout this book, no AFM rule mandating segregation, and many of the locals (such as those in San Francisco and Boston) were racially integrated from the start. Others, it is true, such as Chicago, refused to admit African Americans, or, as with Seattle, imposed conditions draconian enough that there was no incentive for Blacks to join. Honoring the request of Black musicians to form their own locals—in order to allow them to control wage scales, to develop their own audition requirements, and to benefit from a strong voice in the federation through representation at the annual conventions—was the progressive path at the time.

The federation could, and probably did, anticipate that authorizing overlapping jurisdictions with the resulting competition for jobs would lead to disputes that would create headaches for the IEB. What, then, was the board's solution when such conflicts inevitably arose? As we have demonstrated in the discussion of Seattle (and similar decisions are recorded in other cities), the AFM chose at those points to reinforce the authority of the larger white locals over their much smaller Black counterparts. Individual cases could have been decided independently, without mandating overall oversight of one local over the other, but doing so would not have addressed the underlying problem of having two organizations vying for control over the same territory. The federation could have relinquished control over casual engagements entirely, of course, but it is unreasonable to expect it to undermine its own interests.

The solution to formalize the domination of the white locals over Black musicians by creating subsidiaries in a dozen cases during the Great Depression was the most egregious action taken by the federation. The despair of the 1930s was so extreme, the amount of unemployment in the field so debilitating, that the organization succumbed to a racist solution that took a decade or more to undo. The financial woes of the 1930s offer an explanation, but by no means a justification, of this unwise action. By the abolition of subsidiaries in 1944, the federation took responsibility for, and recognized publicly, the error of its prior policy and moved to reverse it. But it was only the insistence of Black musicians such as Lloyd Plummer and Lige Shaw that pressed the IEB to take that action.

At that point, the federation could have taken a different course than it did. Rather than forming still more Black locals out of the abolished subsidiaries, the IEB could have mandated that the parent locals grant full rights to their members, as San Francisco's Black union members requested on several occasions. Perhaps that action might have sent a signal to other segregated locals that they must merge and give Black musicians full rights. But would such a directive have led to the peaceful integration of the dual locals throughout the country? Probably not. There were only twelve subsidiaries, after all, and Black musicians were still advocating—and continued to advocate until the very end of the process—for the separation that would give them greater authority and control over their employment, and, therefore, over their lives. The task of undoing the dual local structure would likely have proven, in the 1940s, as overwhelming as it did in the 1960s.

The Los Angeles merger in 1953 pitted young versus old within the Black local. At this point, the existence of two racially separated locals seemed to the young musicians simply untenable. The youthful rebels there (and later in Chicago and elsewhere) saw their exclusion from work areas such as the entertainment industry as more egregious than the potential loss of power by becoming a minority in a much larger pool. Changes in the composition of musical ensembles supported their cause: multiracial bands were increasingly common, making the separate union structure not only anachronistic, but also burdensome. The changing laws in the country also spurred the cause for amalgamation. Legislation requiring equal pay for equal work, forbidding employment discrimination, and dismantling segregated housing areas offered hope to Black musicians that if they joined forces with their white compatriots they would not be passed over for jobs.

They counted on the proven attraction of Black musical talent (which we have noted repeatedly in this book) and they forcefully proclaimed that equality of rights required a unified labor organization. They were willing to give up the distinctive separateness of segregated musical communities for the rewards of new opportunities.

The merger process proved painful both for the AFM and for many Black musicians. Looking back from the vantage point of more than a half century, however, it appears to have been almost inevitable. History was bending, however slowly, toward interracial cooperation and linkage, but could not do so without determined personal intervention. Those very linkages, new attachments, and professions of cooperation, though, threatened to overpower the attraction of artistic difference, and reduce the colorful fabric woven from disparate musical threads to an undistinguished sameness. The task at hand was, and still is, to find the appropriate balance between individualism and collectivism, to honor difference and highlight individuality while at the same time promoting unification, not just of locals within a labor organization, but also of diverse cultural expressions and their realizations. That task is far from easy. The AFM, and indeed our larger American society, continue the struggle, seeking always to find that elusive balance.

Notes

Chapter 1. Prelude

1. See Shipton, *Groovin'*, 22–23, and Wriggle, "Chappie Willet," 15. The dissertation by Turner, "Organizing and Improvising," deals in great detail with Local 274, but unfortunately also contains quite a number of errors.

2. Wriggle, ibid. See also "Music Union Leader Dies." The Wikipedia article on Fairfax is exceptionally detailed about his role in forming Local 274 and contains many important references; see "Frank Fairfax." Turner, "Organizing and Improvising," 75, erroneously gives Fairfax's year of birth as 1905.

3. Levine, *Highbrow/Lowbrow*.

4. Asian American musicians could join either organization and tended to choose the larger, mostly white locals.

5. See, for example, "Black Officers of Musicians' Local No. 274 Say Whites are Welcome."

6. Turner, "Organizing and Improvising," 284.

7. Title VII of the Civil Rights Act of 1964, Sec. 2000e-2 [Section 703] (c) "Labor organization practices" (2). See https://www.eeoc.gov/statutes/title-vii-civil-rights-act-1964, accessed February 10, 2023.

8. Turner, "Organizing and Improvising," 284.

9. These considerations are specified in "Black Musicians Union Loses Key Legal Battle."

10. See Koshatka, "Musicians' Unions Square Off."

11. Turner, in "Organizing and Improvising" 282–88, discusses in great detail the judge's ruling (*Musicians' Protective Union Local 274, A.F. of M. v. The American Federation of Musicians of the United States and Canada*, U.S. District Court, Civil Action No. 71-809).

12. "Frank Fairfax."

13. Smith-Wright, interview by Miller.

14. I will not cite the many books on this subject, but rather direct readers to Moody and Kessler-Harris, *Perspectives on American Labor History*. The authors provide a good summary of the issues involved and the recent emphases in labor history writings. They cite important works in this evolving field.

15. The AEA is the subject of an in-depth study by Holmes in *Weavers of Dreams*.

16. See, for example, Kibler, *Rank Ladies*, 177–78.

17. In *Rank Ladies*, Kibler addresses Keith's circuit in detail as a primary focus of her book. On the details of how Keith's booking system worked, see Snyder, *Voice of the City*, chapter 4.

18. In addition to numerous books on the histories of individual orchestras, several works trace the development of the symphony orchestra in the United States in general; for example, Mueller, *The American Symphony Orchestra*; Spitzer and Zaslaw, *The Birth of the Orchestra*; and Spitzer, *American Orchestras in the Nineteenth Century*.

19. Miller, "Racial Segregation and the San Francisco Musicians' Union."

20. "Musicians Remembering."

21. Quotations from Fannin, "The Truth in Black and White."

Chapter 2. The Origins of the American Federation of Musicians and Its Place in the History of Organized Labor

1. The MMPU is mentioned in many sources; for example, Spivey, *Union and the Black Musician*, 9; Fink, *Labor Unions*, 241; Kraft, "Artists as Workers," 515–16; and Countryman, "The Organized Musicians," Part 1, 56–57.

2. Fink, *Labor Unions,* 241; Kraft, "Artists as Workers," 523; and Leiter, *Musicians and Petrillo*, 14.

3. Among other sources, see the address of the AFM's first president, Owen Miller, to the membership at the AFM's first convention, printed in the AFM's *Official Proceedings* of its first convention, 39.

4. On the vaudeville performers' union, the White Rats, see Kibler, *Rank Ladies*, 175–78, and Snyder, *Voice of the City*, 74–81.

5. Gompers, *Seventy Years of Life and Labor*, 10.

6. Gompers, *Seventy Years*, 39–41 and 477.

7. Gompers, 469.

8. Kraft, "Artists as Workers," 526.

9. Fink, *Labor Unions*, 241, and Leiter, *Musicians and Petrillo*, 14, claim there were seventy-nine affiliates; Kraft, "Artists as Workers," 524, says there were more than a hundred; Commons, "Types of American Labor Unions," 419, and Countryman, "The Organized Musicians," 58, state that there were 101. For information on the NLM's president, Charles M. Currier, see Seltzer, *Music Matters*, 5.

10. Cobble, "Reviving the Federation's Historic Role," 17.

11. Cobble, "Reviving," lists the name of the group as the "Greater" Western Union of Colored Musicians, but all future references to it in AFM documents use Great Western.

12. Recounted by the AFM's first president, Owen Miller, in a speech to the membership; see AFM, *Official Proceedings* of the 1896 convention, 40.

13. AFM, *Official Proceedings*, 40–41.

14. Kraft, "Artists as Workers," 528. Miller (AFM, *Official Proceedings*, 42) says eighteen rather than seventeen.

15. Fields's attendance at the 1896 convention is mentioned by Kenney, "Just Before Miles," 35, and Cotter, "The Negro in Music in St. Louis," 467; both citations are apparently based on a statement by Elijah Shaw in Johnson, et al., interview by Irene Cortinovis.

16. AFM, *Official Proceedings* of the 1896 convention, 13–29.

17. Countryman, "The Organized Musicians," Part 1, 58, notes that the younger Western affiliates of the NLM, led by Miller and the St. Louis organization, were the strongest advocates for affiliation with the AFL within the NLM, but that the older and larger affiliates, which had the greatest number of delegates at NLM conventions, repeatedly defeated these efforts.

18. Gompers, *Seventy Years of Life and Labor*, 470–71.

19. Fields is listed as a president of the newly formed Local 44—which is identified as the "Great Western Union (colored)"—in the AFM, *Official Proceedings* of the 1896 convention, 54. Also representing this union was the local's secretary R. E. Wilcox.

20. AFM, *Official Proceedings* of the 1897 convention, 36–38, gives the number of members in the various locals.

21. Fredrickson, *The Black Image*, 273.

22. Frederickson, 245.

23. One manifestation of this theory was Frederick L. Hoffman's *Race Traits*, published in 1896. Hoffman tried to prove by statistical means that the smaller growth rate among Blacks stemmed from a higher death rate, which he attributed to certain "race traits and tendencies."

24. The quote, which comes from Hoffman, *Race Traits*, appears in Fredrickson, *The Black Image*, 250.

25. For a perceptive examination of the ambivalent attitudes towards African Americans generated by Blackface minstrelsy in its predominantly white, male, working class audience members during the antebellum period, see Lott, "The Seeming Counterfeit." Lott convincingly demonstrates the contradictory reactions of repulsion and attraction evident in the responses of these audiences.

26. Dorman, "Shaping the Popular Image," 455.

27. Information from Kraft, "Artists as Workers," 529; Seltzer, *Music Matters*, 8–9; and Countryman, "The Organized Musicians," 58–59.

28. Information in this paragraph comes from the original Constitution, By-laws, and Resolutions of the AFM as published in the AFM *Official Proceedings*

of the 1896 convention. The definition of "professional musician" and the requirement for an examining board were the result of resolutions passed at this first convention. Vocalists are not eligible to join the AFM.

29. The AFM *Official Proceedings* of the 1899 convention list locals 1–93, but there is no Local 7.

30. Commons, "Types of American Labor Unions," 419 and 421.

31. Fink, *Labor Unions*, 242. Peretti, *The Creation of Jazz*, 157, gives similar, though not identical numbers.

32. Countryman, "The Organized Musicians," 69.

33. Green, "Musicians' Union of San Francisco," 2–3.

34. Countryman, "The Organized Musicians," 59.

35. See Countryman, 68, for details.

36. The cap of ten votes, part of Article V, does not appear in the constitution until the second convention.

37. The present bylaws, Article 17, Section 4(a), specify the following rules regarding delegates: locals with up to 200 members: 1 delegate; 201–400 members: 2 delegates; 401–1,500 members: 3 delegates; 1,501–3,000: 4 delegates; 3,001–5,000: 5 delegates; 5,001–8,500: 6 delegates; more than 8,500: 7 delegates. Every delegate has one vote.

38. Countryman, "The Organized Musicians," 63, notes that the travel card procedure was initiated in 1902; he gives details about how the process worked. Taxes for radio appearances were 15 percent.

39. Wilkerson, *Caste*. Barbara Fields, "Ideology and Race in American History," summarizes issues surrounding the fluidity of race and cites some important writings on the subject.

40. Wilkerson, Part 3: "The Eight Pillars of Caste."

41. One work that treats the development of the wage-labor economy in the post–Civil War period in critical detail is Moody and Kessler-Harris, *Perspectives on American Labor History*.

42. W. E. B. Du Bois reminds us that a Congress of Trade Unions convened in 1850, attracting 110 delegates, and he provides dramatic statistics that demonstrate the rapid growth of organized labor. By the end of 1863, he reports, there were seventy-nine individual, localized craft unions; the following year there were 270. Ten unions formed national organizations in the period 1863–66; by 1870 there were thirty-two. Du Bois, *Black Reconstruction*, 193.

43. Ibid.

44. Du Bois, *Black Reconstruction*, 192. See also Logan, *The Negro in American Life*, 141.

45. Roediger, *The Wages of Whiteness*, 12–13 and 23. (Part of this material includes Roediger's quotation of Du Bois.)

46. "Bricks Fly," *The Spokesman*, 1.

47. Bloch, "Labor and the Negro," 169.

48. Hill, "The Problem of Race in American Labor History," 193–94.

49. Logan, *The Negro in American Life*, 142.

50. Quoted in Kessler, "The Organization of the Negroes," 274–75; from the *Journal of the Knights of Labor*, Mar. 5, 1891.

51. Kessler, "The Organization of the Negroes," 256.

52. Kessler, 272.

53. McLaurin, "The Racial Policies of the Knights of Labor," 573.

54. Powderly, *Thirty Years of Labor*, 349. Wesley, "Organized Labor and the Negro," 340–41, also recounts this incident in some detail.

55. Powderly, *Thirty Years of Labor,* 350–51. Despite Powderly's remarks, numerous papers in the South asserted that the Knights advocated for social equality, which could lead to miscegenation. For examples, see McLaurin, "Racial Policies," 580.

56. Bloch, "Labor and the Negro," 170.

57. Thomas Barry, for example, reflected on his organizing trips to Virginia, Georgia, and the Carolinas: "Race and labor prejudice ranks there in every phase of life. . . . It is as much . . . as a person's life is worth to be known as a member of the Knights of Labor there." See Kessler, "The Organization of the Negroes," 261, citing *Irish World*, Dec. 31, 1887, as quoted in the Knights' *Proceedings* 1888, Report of the General Executive Board, p. 50.

58. Hild, "Organizing Across the Color Line," 296–301. A host for two of Hover's meetings, Peter O'Neal, was driven out of Milledgeville, Georgia, and his house was burned down. The assassination attempt occurred in Warrenton, Georgia. McLaurin, "Racial Policies," 578, incorrectly states that Hover (called Hoover) was killed in this incident.

59. See McLaurin, "Racial Policies," 569 and 584–85.

60. Quotations in this paragraph come from Washington, "The Negro and the Labor Unions," 756–67.

61. Marshall delves into Washington's views, the AFL's struggles with race, Blacks as strikebreakers, and the disinclination of Black workers to join unions in *The Negro and Organized Labor*, 14–20. See also the very perceptive article by Eric Arnesen on Blacks and strikebreaking, "The Quicksands of Economic Insecurity."

62. AFL, *Proceedings* of the 1890 convention, 31. The matter was then "referred to the Executive Council." Foner and Lewis, *The Black Worker,* vol. 6, present an example of a later citation of this statement: Resolution 72 from the 1925 *Proceedings*, 322–25. The machinists repeatedly projected that the offending restriction would be eliminated, but failed to do so until 1895, when, as noted below, the exclusion was removed from the constitution but retained through ritual. On the machinists' projection that they would omit the color line, see the AFL *Proceedings* of 1891, 12, and the *Proceedings* of 1892, 40. See also the letter from Samuel Gompers to Thomas Talbot in the *Samuel Gompers Papers*, vol. 2, 296–97 and especially the editors' note 3.

63. Taft, *The A. F. of L. in the Time of Gompers*, 309; and Gerald Grob, "Organized Labor," 170.

64. AFL, *Proceedings* of the 1893 convention, 56.

65. AFL, *Proceedings* of the 1891 Convention, 39–40. The situation is described by Grob, "Organized Labor," 170; he presents one of most complete summaries of machinists' case.

66. Grob, "Organized Labor," 171.

67. Letter, Gompers to George Norton, May 17, 1892, printed in the *Samuel Gompers Papers*, vol. 3, 172–73. See also Cobble, "Reviving the Federation's Historic Role," 17.

68. Letter, Gompers to Harry Ives, Nov. 10, 1892, in the *Samuel Gompers Papers*, vol. 3, 235–36. Gompers made a similar appeal to the blacksmiths in an 1893 letter to John C. Knight: "Either you must make friends of [Black workers] or if you will not they will prove enemies to you and play into the hands of employers.... If the question were not a humanitarian one, then enlightened self-interest should prompt us all to declare our desire to organize all our fellow-workers" (quoted in Mandel, "Samuel Gompers and the Negro Workers," 38).

69. AFL, *Proceedings* of the 1925 convention, Resolution 72, recounts these specific occasions; see pp. 322–25. Also reproduced in Foner and Lewis, *The Black Worker,* vol. 6.

70. Taft, *The A. F. of L. in the Time of Gompers*, 315, describes resolutions protesting discrimination presented to the conventions of 1919, 1920, and 1921 that were defeated or not implemented.

71. Prior to 1935, the AFL refused to recognize the BSCP, but permitted some chapters to affiliate as "federated locals" chartered directly by the AFL, allowing Randolph to attend AFL conventions and argue for the admission of the organization as a whole. Arnesen, "A. Philip Randolph," 177–80, summarizes the fight between the Pullman Company and the BSCP, finally resulting in the union's election by the workers as their representative in 1935.

72. Summers, "Admission Policies of Labor Unions," 68. Northrup, *Organized Labor*, chapter 1, describes various levels of racial exclusion by different unions in the same time period and gives details about admission policies.

73. Raskin, "Meany, in a Fiery Debate."

74. See the AFL *Proceedings* of the 1900 convention, 22–23, 112, 129. Northrup, *Organized Labor*, 8, also cites the U.S. Congress, Report of the Industrial Commission, Washington, 1901, 37.

75. AFL *Proceedings* of the 1900 convention, 23.

76. Ibid.

77. Mandel, "Samuel Gompers," 60.

78. Philip Taft, for one, suspects that Gompers regarded the new policy authorizing racially separate AFL locals and central bodies as "a necessity only because integrated locals and central bodies were not found possible" (Taft, *The A. F. of L. in the Time of Gompers*, 314). See also Marshall, *The Negro and Organized Labor*, 20.

79. Cobble, "Reviving the Federation's Historic Role," 13.

80. AFL, *Proceedings* of the 1919 convention, 228 (Resolution 120).

81. For example, two articles in the *Birmingham Reporter*: "A. F. of L. Wipes Out Color Line; Southern Delegates Start War" and "No Color Line, Says the Federation of Labor," both on June 19, 1920, and printed in Foner and Lewis, *The Black Worker,* vol. 6.

82. Resolution 5 and the ensuing discussion appear in the AFL *Proceedings* of the 1920 convention, 307–10. The resolution is also reproduced in Foner and Lewis, *The Black Worker,* vol. 6, Part 4, Section 34.

83. AFL, *Proceedings* of the 1920 convention, 351–52.

84. Taft, *The A. F. of L. in the Time of Gompers*, 315–16.

85. Arnesen, "Following the Color Line of Labor," 61. Arnesen's arguments are explored in more detail in chapter 3.

86. Lewis, *In Their Own Interests*, 16.

Chapter 3. The Formation of Black AFM Locals, 1897–1927

1. Arnesen, "Following the Color Line of Labor," 55.

2. The AFM's monthly magazine, *International Musician*, lists the chartering of 208 in its August 1902 issue, 10 ("Locals admitted since the last report"). Similarly, Local 242 in New Orleans is listed under the same rubric in the November 1902 issue, 7, and Local 253 in East Liverpool in the December issue, 7.

3. *International Musician* 5, no. 3 (Sept. 1905), 9 ("Official Business: Locals suspended for nonpayment of dues: 242 New Orleans. Don't confound this with No. 174 of New Orleans, which is OK.")

4. For example, Turner, "Organizing and Improvising," 57, states that Local 591 in Philadelphia was a subsidiary local. It was not. Similarly, Halker, "A History of Local 208," 215, calls Local 767 in Los Angeles a subsidiary of Local 47. Local 767 was an independent "colored local" and one of the strongest in the country.

5. Randle, interview by Havens, 62 and 63 (two references).

6. See "Buxton: A Lost Utopia."

7. *Iowa State Bystander*, Sept. 6, 1901, quoted in Gray, "The Black Middle Class in Buxton, Iowa." On this newspaper, see the Library of Congress, "About Iowa State Bystander," accessed February 8, 2023, https://chroniclingamerica.loc.gov/lccn/sn83025186/.

8. Local 305 is not designated as "colored" from 1903 to 1910, but it *is* given that designation from 1911 to 1916.

9. Laifer, "Looking Back," 17.

10. Arnesen, "Following the Color Line," 61.

11. Standing resolution no. 2, AFM, *Official Proceedings* of the 1896 convention, 11. In subsequent years, the statement appears in the By-Laws, Article VI ("Miscellaneous"), Section 2.

12. Seltzer, *Music Matters*, 21.

13. *International Musician*, June 1904, 1.

14. These theories form the centerpiece of Levine's arguments in his book,

Highbrow/Lowbrow. Other authors have built on his work. See, for example, Kibler's *Rank Ladies,* which relates the hierarchization of the arts to gender issues (first described in the book on pp. 5–6).

15. Many thanks to Prof. David Anthony for raising this probing issue (email, Jan. 12, 2022).

16. For example, William (Bill) Moriarity, former president of New York's Local 802, recalls that when he joined Local 2 in St. Louis in 1958, the audition committee stopped him after a few bars (Moriarity, personal communication Sept. 24, 2021, and email, Oct. 4, 2021).

17. AFM By-Laws of 1955, Article III, Sec 15 (currently Article IX sec 6). Many thanks to Dan DeRienzo for checking the By-Laws to determine the exact year in which the change occurred.

18. Countryman, "The Organized Musicians," 66.

19. Supreme Court, New York County, *Musical Mutual Protective Union v. [Joseph] Weber,* decided on Apr. 1, 1924. In his decision, the judge reviewed in detail the events of 1920–21 and included the Resolution of May 1922 in full.

20. For a description of the dispute, see Countryman, "The Organized Musicians," 65–67; Leiter, *Musicians and Petrillo,* 28–32; Goldberg, "Swingin' the Color Line," 36–38; and Moriarity, "A Matter of Trust," 6.

21. Leiter, *The Musicians and Petrillo,* 92–93.

22. Smith, interview by Wiley, transcription p. 167.

23. Smith, interview, 168.

24. *International Musician,* Aug. 1946, 26, contains a list of these delegates in support of a resolution thanking Petrillo and the IEB for cancelling a bus ride due to discriminatory policies against African Americans. See the discussion in chapter 6. The number of representatives is greater than the number of locals because the following locals were represented by more than one delegate: Philadelphia (3), Los Angeles (3), St. Louis (2), New Orleans (2), Baltimore (3), and San Francisco (2).

25. Southern, *Music of Black Americans,* 346.

26. Fletcher, *100 Years of the Negro in Show Business,* 261.

27. Johnson, "The Poor White Musician," 617. The editorial, published in the *New York Age,* is dated September 23, 1915; the complaint, by Eugene De Bueris, was contained in a letter to the editor of the *Globe* dated "New York, Sep 8."

28. Walton, "Colored Musicians Invited to Join Musical Union."

29. Ibid.

30. Fletcher, *100 Years,* 262. See also Badger, *A Life in Ragtime,* 121 and 284, n. 36. Bradford, *Born with the Blues,* 31, asserted that Local 310 "tricked the brothers into joining their organization."

31. See the New Amsterdam Musical Association's website, accessed February 8, 2023, https://namaharlem.wixsite.com/namaharlem.

32. Goldberg, "Swingin' the Color Line," 29.

33. May, interview by Miller. Local 16 merged with Local 248 in Paterson in 2013. May became the president of the merged local.

34. May, interview by Miller.

35. McWhirter, *Red Summer*, 26.

36. McWhirter, 28.

37. For some of the most disturbing quotes, see the Civil Rights Heritage Museum Online, "1907: *The Negro, A Menace to American Civilization*," accessed February 8, 2023, https://civilrightsheritage.com/2014/10/03/1907-the-negro-a-menace-to-american-civilization/.

38. Franklin, *From Slavery to Freedom*, 480.

39. Franklin, 481.

40. McWhirter, *Red Summer*, 76.

41. Calverton, *Anthology of American Negro Literature*, 12–13. The poem is included in the anthology on pp. 203–4.

42. Randolph and Owen, "The Negro—A Menace to Radicalism," 20.

Chapter 4. Early Black Locals

1. In addition to the AFM's *Official Proceedings* and *International Musician*, the following sources (listed in alphabetical order) formed the basis for my discussion of the origin, development, and ultimate demise of Local 208: Absher, *The Black Musician and the White City*; Dulf, "A History of Negro Music"; Halker, "A History of Local 208"; Halker, "Banding Together"; Hinton, "Reminiscences"; Lefferts, "A Chronology and Itinerary of the Career of George E. Dulf"; Mazzola, "When Music is Labor"; Peretti, *The Creation of Jazz*; Saunders, "Red: The Reminiscences"; Spear, *Black Chicago*; Spivey, *Union and the Black Musician*; Tuttle, "Labor Conflict and Racial Violence"; and Walton, *Bronzeville Conversations*.

2. Dulf, "A History of Negro Music," 1.

3. "White and Colored Musicians Separate."

4. Dulf, "A History of Negro Music," 2.

5. "White and Colored Musicians Separate."

6. For example, Halker, "Banding Together," 226, describes the credentials of various band members, including Henderson Smith, William Berry, and William Dorsey.

7. Mazzola, "When Music is Labor," 259.

8. Absher, *The Black Musician,* 9. Spear, *Black Chicago*, 30–33 and 152–54, presents detailed tables showing Black employment in Chicago in 1900, 1910, and 1920, separated by gender and occupation. For Blacks making their living as musicians, the numbers are: 1900, 207 men and 49 women, representing 7.7 and 2.4 percent of the total musicians in the city respectively; 1910, 216 men and 136 women (6.3 and 4.2 percent respectively); 1920, 254 men and 134 women (7.4 and 4.4 percent respectively). Of course, the numbers would be much higher if part-timers were included.

9. Halker, "Banding Together," 226.

10. Halker, "A History of Local 208," 212, gives the membership as six hundred

in 1929. Membership numbers in this paragraph come from the AFM *Official Proceedings* in each year.

11. Hinton, "Reminiscences," 15.

12. Hinton, 16.

13. Absher, *The Black Musician*, 37–38.

14. Absher, 38, dates the All-Negro Hour to 1928 (and calls it the Negro Hour), but other sources give 1929. See, for example, "The First Black Radio Show (in America)" and Brenc, "Jack Leroy Cooper."

15. Hinton, "Reminiscences," 16.

16. Tuttle, "Labor Conflict," 410.

17. Local 6, minutes of the meetings of Dec. 21, 1915, and Jan. 13, 1916. Unpublished.

18. Stoddard, *Jazz on the Barbary Coast*, 106–7.

19. Gushee, *Pioneers of Jazz*, 51–52. He found the names in Local 6's report to the International in Jan. 1909, 4 (Gushee, email messages to Miller, Dec. 19 and 21, 2006).

20. Local 6, minutes of the meetings of Apr. 25, May 2, May 9, and May 16, 1916. Unpublished.

21. Stoddard, *Jazz on the Barbary Coast*, 107. The strike involved twelve thousand culinary workers, and also included musicians. By September 8, 150 musicians were striking San Francisco's restaurants. The strike was settled on December 15, 1916 (Green, "Musicians' Union of San Francisco," 76–77).

22. Local 6 minutes, May 18, 2016, unpublished. On these events, see also Miller, "Racial Segregation and the San Francisco Musicians' Union," 165 and 168, and Miller, *Music and Politics in San Francisco*, 96–101.

23. Stoddard, *Jazz on the Barbary Coast*, 98–99. Stoddard gives the date of his interviews with Spikes in his introduction, p. 5.

24. LeProtti, interview by Murphy, 1952.

25. Keller, "Seattle's Segregated Musicians' Union," and his book, *The Blue Note*, provide the source for much of the information on Seattle's Black locals. Keller discusses Barnett's biography in the former on pp. 23–25. *The Blue Note* contains a wealth of fascinating photographs. See also Henry, "Barnett, Powell S."

26. Keller, "Seattle's Segregated Musicians' Union," 25–26, citing the minutes of Local 76, May 28, 1913.

27. Barnett, "The Amalgamation of Local 493 and Local 76." See also Keller, "Seattle's Segregated Musicians' Union," 20–21, citing minutes from Local 76's monthly meetings on Aug. 9, Aug. 20, and Sept. 3, 1918.

28. Frank, "Race Relations and the Seattle Labor Movement," 35.

29. Frank, "Race Relations," 37, and Taylor, *The Forging of a Black Community*, 55.

30. Taylor, *The Forging of a Black Community*, 52, gives the African American population of the city in 1920 as 2,894 within a total population of 315,312 (thus about 0.9 percent). The percentage was about the same in 1910. Wright,

"Organized Labor and Seattle's African American Community," provides the following figures for African Americans in Seattle: in 1900 it was 406 and in 1910 it was 2,206 (a 465 percent increase). The total population of the city in 1910 was 237,194. Taylor gives the 1910 Black population as slightly larger: 2,296 and, thus, a 466 percent increase from 1900 (the period of greatest immigration of Blacks to the city).

31. Keller, "Seattle's Segregated Musicians' Union," 34.

32. Pitts, "Organized Labor and the Negro in Seattle," 68–69. This thesis includes a chapter on the musicians' union, but it should be used with caution, as it contains a number of errors. For example, Pitts consistently refers to the white local in Seattle as Local 7, rather than Local 76.

33. Keller, "Seattle's Segregated Musicians' Union," 37–38.

34. Frank, "Race Relations," 41.

35. Pitts, "Organized Labor," 67–68, dates this matter to 1925–26. Keller, "Seattle's Segregated Musicians' Union," 38, attributes the hesitation on the part of the Park Board partly to an opposition to jazz and implies that the dispute preceded the revocation of Local 458's charter in 1924, but that the resolution of the conflict took place in 1925, when the band was given "a lucrative five-concert, $250 a show contract" (which seems a more logical timeline).

36. Frank, "Race Relations," 39; Keller, "Seattle's Segregated Musicians' Union," 35–37; and Keller, *The Blue Note*, 11.

37. Keller, *The Blue Note*, 15.

38. Information in this paragraph comes from the minutes of the Seattle Labor Council, Feb. 6, Feb. 13, Mar. 12, and Mar. 26, 1924. Frank also refers briefly to this incident in *Purchasing Power*, 233.

39. Keller, "Seattle's Segregated Musicians' Union," 40–57, provides an excellent detailed account of the dissolution of Local 458 and the subsequent establishment of Local 493.

40. Quotations and membership numbers in this paragraph from Keller, "Seattle's Segregated Musicians' Union," 56–57.

41. Minutes of the Seattle Labor Council, Sept. 8, 1926.

Chapter 5. From the Glories of the '20s to the Despair of the '30s

1. Fones-Wolf, "Sound Comes to the Movies," 8–9. See also Joseph Weber's annual report to the membership in 1931, in which he says that the federation has about sixty thousand professionals in its membership, of which about a third had "found employment in the theatres, and this remained so up to the beginning of 1928" (Weber, "President Weber's Annual Report").

2. Riesenfeld, "Music and Motion Pictures," 58.

3. Smith, interview by Wiley.

4. Shipton, *Fats Waller*, especially pp. 10, 13–17, and 31. Machlin, *Stride*, discusses the influence of the pipe organ on Waller's style (see especially pp. 58–62).

5. Riesenfeld, "Music and Motion Pictures," 62.

6. Fink, *Labor Unions*, 242.

7. Fones-Wolf, "Sound Comes to the Movies," 10 and 17.

8. Mermey, "The Vanishing Fiddler," 304.

9. *The Jazz Singer*, released in October 1927 by Warner Brothers, is often cited as the first sound film. It was not in fact the first movie to feature some type of synchronized sound, but it was the first feature-length motion picture to do so. It was for the most part essentially a silent film, but it included several songs and dialogue passages by Al Jolson recorded on the set. *The Jazz Singer*'s phenomenal success (it earned $2.625 million) heralded the beginning of the end of the silent film era. Wikipedia contains a detailed history of the development of sound films (accessed February 14, 2023, https://en.wikipedia.org/wiki/Sound_film). For an interesting discussion of theater musicians as artists vs. workers, their struggle for benefits in Italian court battles, the role of synchronization in defining the legal status of theater musicians, and the prioritization of "high art" in granting such benefits, see Ladd, "Synchronization as Musical Labor."

10. Mermey, "The Vanishing Fiddler," 303.

11. Fones-Wolf, "Sound Comes to the Movies," 18–23.

12. "Owners Close Picture House to Musicians."

13. "Mystery Taxi Traced in Theater Bombing."

14. Hubbard, "Synchronized Sound," 435–39, describes the Chicago local's fight against the talkies in some detail.

15. Leiter, *The Musicians and Petrillo*, 47–48.

16. Spivey, *Union and the Black Musician*, 47. See also Peretti, *The Creation of Jazz*, 165.

17. "Coping with Automation." The article cites exact numbers rather than percentages. In 1930, 99,000 out of 139,000 members were employed full-time; in 1940, 79,000 out of 134,000 members were; in 1954, the number was 59,000 out of 252,000.

18. Peretti, *The Creation of Jazz*, 165, gives the number of members as 146,326 in 1928 and 101,111 in 1934.

19. Erenberg, *Swingin' the Dream*, 13.

20. Hirschmann, "The Musician and the Depression."

21. See, for example, Weber, "President Weber's Annual Report" (June 1931). On the League's campaign, see Novak, "Musicians Wage War Against Evil Robots," and Brackett, "American Federation of Musicians."

22. Weber, "Highly Important for Local Union Officers."

23. Weber, "Living Music Day."

24. Weber, "President Weber's Annual Report," 1931.

25. The six were St. Louis, MO, Paducah, KY, Martins Ferry, OH, Bakersfield, CA, Kansas City, MO, and Denver, CO. The Kansas City local regained its charter in 1933. Data derived from the *International Musician*.

26. Zanesville, OH, Chattanooga, TN, Mobile, AL, Newport News, VA, and Huntington, VA. Data derived from the *International Musician*.

27. Halker, "A History of Local 208," 214, and Halker, "Banding Together," 234.

28. Keller, "Seattle's Segregated Musicians' Union," 82. Keller also says that there was an earlier attempt in 1920 that came to nothing. His source for that information is a paper by Eleanor Siegl, written for a 1966 Sociology class, "The Amalgamation of the Colored and White Musicians' Unions in Seattle" (Keller, "Seattle's Segregated," 37).

29. Barnett, "Musicians Convention L.A.—1933." Despite the document's title, the Los Angeles convention took place in 1932. Keller, *The Blue Note*, 44, reproduces an image of Barnett's Local 493 badge from the convention.

30. Keller, "Seattle's Segregated Musicians' Union," 83. He cites Barnett, "Musicians' Convention L.A.—1933," but these statements do not appear in that source. Keller gives the same quote in *The Blue Note*, 43.

31. Thanks to Bill Moriarity for pointing out this situation to me. The present bylaws of the AFM forbid such conflicts of interest. See By-laws Article 5, Section 40(a).

32. Barnett, "Musician's Convention L.A.—1933" (*recte*: 1932).

33. McRae, "Paying their Dues," 25.

34. Quotations in this paragraph are from McRae, 29 and 32.

35. McRae, 35.

36. McRae, 37, says that Jackson was a cosponsor of this resolution, but he is not listed as such in the *Official Proceedings*, although he was a delegate to the convention.

37. AFM *Official Proceedings* of the 1937 convention, 370–71 ("Resolution 93").

38. The minutes of the meetings are reproduced in the *International Musician*, Feb. 1932, 3, and July 1932, 8, and in the AFM *Official Proceedings* of the 1932 convention, 20.

39. Weber's letter and the subsidiary rules appear in Local 2's newsletter, *The Monthly Synopsis* 31, no. 9, Mar. 1932, reproduced in Rose, "The American Federation of Musicians," Appendix. The St. Louis *Argus* also printed the rules for subsidiaries (but not Weber's letter) in its edition of May 13, 1932, 1 and 5 ("Discrimination by the American Federation of Musicians Opposed").

40. Cotter, "The Negro in Music in St. Louis," 471, note 9.

41. For a photo of the steamer *St. Paul*, see Kenney, *Jazz on the River*, 3.

42. Kenney, *Jazz*, 19 and 46.

43. Cotter, "The Negro in Music in St. Louis," 472.

44. Cotter, 438.

45. Cotter, 473.

46. Johnson, et al., interview by Cortinovis; and Shaw and Oswald, interview by Cortinovis. In the interviews Shaw says that he met with the IEB every year, but a check of the minutes reveals only three meetings.

47. AFM *Official Proceedings* of the 40th convention, 1935, 245; 42nd convention, 1937, 342; and 44th convention, 1939, 412.

48. Shaw and Oswald, interview by Cortinovis.

49. AFM *Official Proceedings* of the 1934 convention, 244.

50. AFM *Official Proceedings* of the 1936 convention, 29.

51. Mitchell, "Musicians' Chatterbox," Sept. 10, 1932.

52. Pillars, interview by Rose (transcript p. 23).

53. Mitchell, "Musicians' Chatterbox," Sept. 9, 1932. Denver's Black local lost its charter in the same year.

54. Cotter, "The Negro in Music," 470–71.

55. In the interview, Shaw erroneously dated the revocation of the charter to 1930 rather than 1932, a mistake repeated by Kenney in his otherwise exemplary accounts of the riverboat jazz culture (see *Jazz on the River*, 107–8 and "Just Before Miles," 35–36).

56. Shaw and Oswald, interview by Cortinovis. Cotter, "The Negro in Music," 469, cites five bands that played on various stations. Smith, interview by Wiley, recalled playing with Eddie Randle's Blue Devils on the radio on Tuesday and Thursday nights.

57. Hubbard, "Synchronized Sound," 435, notes that in 1928 St. Louis "emerged for a short time as the most important battleground in the movie-house musicians' fight against the intrusion of canned music."

58. Smith, interview by Wiley (transcript pp. 13–14 and 98).

59. Randle, interview by Havens (transcript pp. 34–36 and 57–59).

60. Randle, interview by Havens, transcript p. 59.

61. Cotter, "The Negro in Music," 471, note 8.

62. For greater detail on the events recounted in the following section, see Miller, "Racial Segregation."

63. "Appeal for National and State Relief."

64. Data compiled from a detailed examination of the symphony's programs.

65. Passed by a 64 percent margin on May 2, 1935, the tax charged property owners a half-cent per $100 assessed valuation. An excellent summary of the activities supporting the campaign and the vital role played by Local 6 is given in the "Report of Campaign for Charter Amendment Number 3." The symphony began performing again in January 1936 under Pierre Monteux.

66. "Negroes Hit Twice as Hard as Whites." The cities studied were Atlanta, Indianapolis, Richmond, Newark, Charlotte, and Columbus.

67. Broussard, *Black San Francisco*, 114.

68. Harris, The Harder We Run, 104–5. See also Foner, *Organized Labor and the Black Worker*, 200–201.

69. For information on the strike, see *San Francisco: The Bay and its Cities*; Riesenberg, *Golden Gate*; and Quin, *The Big Strike*. Denning considers 1934 a turning point in U.S. labor history, citing not only the general strike in San Francisco, but also strikes in Minneapolis and Toledo (*The Cultural Front*, xiv and 22).

70. Local 6 board meetings of July 14 and 16 (*Musical News* 18, no. 8 [Aug. 1934]: 12–13); and King, "Report of the Delegates of General Strike Committee."

71. The minutes of Local 6's board meetings from October and November record detailed discussions of wage rates. Second-class clubs, for example, were set at $35/week, equivalent to about $770 in 2022. Congress passed the Twenty-

First Amendment on February 20, 1933, but ratification by the states took until December.

72. Love, "The Bubble Bursts."

73. Ibid.

74. Moore, "The End of the War."

75. The Forbidden Territory notices for all clubs in the Local 6 jurisdiction appeared in the local's magazine, the *Musical News*, every month until 1944, when the breadth of this ruling was challenged by a Los Angeles booking agent and the blanket restriction was revoked. See the Local 6 board meeting minutes of June 22, 1944 (*Musical News* 27, no. 8 [Aug. 1944], 3); and July 18 and 21, 1944 (*Musical News* 27, no. 9 [Sept. 1944]: 2, 7). Local 6's protests against the revocation were rejected. See also Moore, "The End of the War."

76. Strather case: board meeting of Dec. 12, 1933 (*Musical News* 17, no. 1 [Jan. 1934], 20); Alameda Walk-A-Way Derby case: board meetings of Apr. 24 and 26, 1934 (*Musical News* 17, no. 6 [June 1934], 7–8).

77. A strong review by critic Alfred Frankenstein appeared in the *Chronicle* ("Negro Vocalist Recital Pleases"). This venue also hosted several of Henry Cowell's avant-garde New Music Society concerts.

78. Metzger, "Roland Hayes Tolerant of Music Ideas"; and "Throng Braves Rain to Hear Roland Hayes" (anonymous). Metzger was editor of the *Pacific Coast Musical Review*. War Memorial Opera House, the first municipally funded opera house in the country, opened on October 15, 1932, after nearly three decades of political struggle to replace the 4,000-seat Grand Opera House that had burned down in fires following the earthquake of 1906. See Miller, "Opera as Politics," for details of the opera house struggle. In 1977, the year of Hayes's death, Marva Carter published a retrospective including photographs, programs, and his writings (Carter, "Roland Hayes").

79. Anderson's 1937 appearance was discussed in the *San Francisco Chronicle* on Feb. 14, D5; Feb. 21, D5; Feb. 24, 9; Feb. 25, 13; Feb. 28, D5; Mar. 1, 28; Mar. 3, 15; Mar. 5, 20 and 36; and Mar. 6, 11. The specific quote is from March 3.

80. Daniels, *Pioneer Urbanites*, 99.

81. Watkins, interview by Miller and Roedig, Aug. 27, 2006.

82. "Bi-Union Discrimination Case."

83. "Coast Musicians Sue White Local."

84. Local 6 board meeting of May 22, 1934 (*Musical News* 17, no. 6 [June 1934]: 12).

85. "Oakland Musicians Go to Law" and "Bi-Union Discrimination Case."

86. Local 6 board meeting of Aug. 7, 1934 (*Musical News* 17, no. 9 [Sept. 1934], 2).

87. "Tip Top Club Features Music" and ad on the same page. The minutes of the Local 6 board meeting of September 11, 1934, state that "Don Regan is granted permission to contract for the engagement at Tip Top Club with five men commencing September 15" (*Musical News* 17, no. 10 [Oct. 1934], 8).

88. Reilly, "Star Stuff."

89. "Bi-Union Discrimination Case."

90. "Negro Musicians Seek Court Ban." ("The Negro plaintiffs charge that the defendants are 'arbitrarily' seeking to bar them from playing in many cafes, night clubs and theaters.") Thanks to attorney Dennis Caspe for helping interpret the court records.

91. Superior Court Record of Action 252613; the case number has since been reassigned to a divorce case from the 1990s. All records below 370000 were destroyed except for probate cases.

92. "Biographical Sketches of Leaders" and "City's Bench and Bar." A "self-made man," Mooslin was educated at Hastings College of Law in San Francisco and Kent Law School in Chicago.

93. The two Dunnes in the firm's name were Arthur and his father Peter, who died in 1933. Arthur was editor of the Harvard Law Review 1921–23. In 1923, he received his LLB cum laude. He became president of the San Francisco Bar Association in 1942 (*Martindale-Hubbell Directory of Experts and Legal Services*, 1970).

94. Local 6 board meeting of Aug. 28, 1934 (*Musical News* 17, no. 9 [Sept. 1934], 10–11), and "Bi-Union Discrimination Case."

95. "Court Bares Threats of Musicians."

96. "White Unions Hit for Discrimination."

97. "Coast Musicians Sue White Local."

98. "White Unions Hit for Discrimination."

99. "NAACP Pickets A. F. of L. Convention."

100. Ibid.

101. "Musicians Balk at Picket Job."

102. Resolution 141; see the AFL *Proceedings* of the 1934 convention, 254–55 and 330–34. The other resolutions (a) opposed wage differentials for blacks and whites, (b) opposed lynching and supported the Costigan-Wagner Federal Anti-Lynching Bill, (c) requested approval of an international charter for the Brotherhood of Sleeping Car Porters, and (d) requested appointment of one or more African American labor organizers.

103. This series of events has been discussed in many sources; see, for example, Harris, *The Harder We Run*, chapter 4 (especially pages 89–91); Sitkoff, *A New Deal for Blacks*, vol. 1, chapter 7; and Foner, *Organized Labor*, 204–12. (Hutcheson's name is misspelled as Hutchinson in some of these sources.)

104. Local 6 board meeting of Oct. 30, 1934 (*Musical News* 17. no. 12 [Dec. 1934], 7).

105. "Union Musicians Drop Job Suit." The timing of this article on October 12 is curious, as several more court actions are registered in the Record of Action before the dismissal on October 22. The article reports that "the musicians of Local 648, through their attorney, A. Mooslin, announced the withdrawal of their petition for an injunction to prevent musicians of white local 6 from closing them out of lucrative jobs in the bay district. . . . From authoritative sources, it is

learned that a local appealing to a civil court from the decisions of the national body is subject to loss of charter. This, it is believed, is the reason for the sudden dropping of the present case from the calendar."

106. Local 6 board meeting of Oct. 30, 1934 (*Musical News* 17, no. 12 [Dec. 1934], 7).

107. Local 6 board meeting of Nov. 13, 1934 (*Musical News* 17, no. 12 [Dec 1934], 9).

108. "Local Musicians May Lose Jobs."

109. Ibid.

110. Ibid.

111. Local 6 board meetings of Nov. 6 and 13, 1934 (*Musical News* 17, no. 12 [Dec. 1934], 8, 12); and "LaFerne Is Our Friend."

112. AFM *Official Proceedings*, 1935, 26; and Local 6 board meeting of Jan. 22, 1935 (*Musical News* 18, no. 1 [Feb. 1935], 9).

113. "Union Offers Olive Twig."

114. "Musicians Must Choose."

115. The minutes of the Local 6 board meeting of April 9, 1935, describe the forthcoming organizational meeting (*Musical News* 18, no. 5 [May 1935]: 11–12).

116. "Baranco Band Loses Out at Dawn Café."

Chapter 6. The 1940s

1. *International Musician* 43, no. 1 (July 1944), 1.

2. "Petrillo Talks!" The quote is on p. 41. Petrillo repeated this claim in his letter to George Meany, Apr. 8, 1958.

3. The 1944 AFM *Official Proceedings* list the membership of Local 10 as 9,853.

4. AFM *Official Proceedings* of 1944, 188 (meeting of June 11, 1944, 8–11:30 p.m.).

5. AFM *Official Proceedings* of 1944, 185 (meeting of June 10, 1944, 7 p.m.–12:30 a.m.).

6. Shaw and Oswald, interview by Cortinovis.

7. King, "The Facts and Correspondence in the Eddie B. Love Case." The specific quote is in the *Musical News* 26, no. 9, 19.

8. Local 6 board meetings of May 7 and 13, 1943 (*Musical News* 26, no. 5 [May 1943]: 15–17 and 18–19).

9. Local 6 board meeting of Oct. 23, 1945 (*Musical News* 28, no. 11 [Nov. 1945]: 12).

10. *Musical News* 27, no. 1 (Jan. 1944): 2.

11. Membership numbers, along with the number of votes and the names of the delegates, appear in the AFM *Official Proceedings* each year for all locals attending the convention.

12. The entire program is given in the AFM *Official Proceedings* of 1944, 29. Anderson sang arias from Donizetti's *La Favorita* and Saint-Saëns's *Samson and*

Delilah as well as the spirituals "The Gospel Train" and "My Soul's Been Anchored in the Lord." The orchestra also performed the overture to Berlioz's *Benvenuto Cellini*, Debussy's *L'après-midi d'un faune*, the prelude to Wagner's *Die Meistersinger*, and Richard Strauss's *Don Juan*.

13. IEB meeting of June 21, 1945, printed in the *International Musician*, Aug. 1945, 19.

14. Minutes of the Local 6 board meeting of Sept. 25, 1945 (*Musical News* 28, no. 10, Oct. 1945: 22).

15. The AFM *Official Proceedings* of 1946 give the membership of Local 669 as 183 and that of Local 6 as 4,010.

16. *Music and Rhythm*, June 1942, 27, 31, and 43.

17. Ibid.

18. The resolution of thanks (Resolution 87, June 6, 1946) appears in both the *International Musician* (Aug. 1946, 26) and the AFM's *Official Proceedings* of 1946, 255–56. These published sources simply state that the event was canceled due to "the colored delegates not being permitted to take part . . . to the same extent as the other delegates," but Petrillo later clarified the details in a letter to George Meany in April 1958, in which the quote in this paragraph appears. (See Petrillo, letter to Meany.)

19. IEB meeting of June 3, 1946, printed in the AFM's *Official Proceedings* of 1946, 298.

20. Information and quotations in this paragraph from "Battle Jim Crow in Miami Locals."

21. The AFM *Official Proceedings* of 1957 list the cancellation of Local 690's charter on p. 136.

22. Dexter, "Kaycee Local 627 Prospered."

23. See, for example, "Jim Crow Issue Grows in Kaycee," "Kaycee Hot Club May Start Again," and Banks, "Police Draw Color Line."

24. Cramton, "Union Wars on Detroit Bashes."

25. The articles cited in this paragraph appeared in *Downbeat* in the following issues (listed in order of mention in the paragraph): Aug. 1939, 1 and 10; Sept. 1939, cover and p. 2; Dec. 1, 1940, 2; May 20, 1946, 13; Dec. 1, 1940, 2 and 23; Dec. 15, 1940, 5. The last two articles were written by R. L. Larkin.

26. On Randolph's influence on Roosevelt's action, see Arnesen, "A. Philip Randolph," 183–84.

27. For more on the FEPC hearings in 1943, see Arnesen, *Brotherhoods of Color*, 181–83.

28. Edises, "Joseph James is a Busy Guy," recounts James's history from his birth in Philadelphia "34 years ago," but is unclear (or erroneous) on the chronology of his cross-country trips. It is likely that James came to Hollywood in 1932 with Johnson's choir, and then returned to the East Coast for *Porgy and Bess* in 1935.

29. Program for the San Francisco production of *Porgy and Bess* that opened

at the Curran Theater on Feb. 14, 1938 (San Francisco Public Library program scrapbooks).

30. For details on this group, see Miller, "Elmer Keeton and His Bay Area Negro Chorus."

31. In addition to the article cited in the previous note, see these sources on the *Swing Mikado*: Fraden, *Blueprints for a Black Federal Theatre,* 139, 169, 187–93; Peterson, *A Century of Musicals in Black and White,* 342; Vallillo, "The Battle of the Black Mikados"; and Woll, *Black Musical Theatre,* 178–83.

32. The best discussion of the court case Joseph James spearheaded is Wollenberg, "James vs. Marinship."

33. Johnson, *The Second Gold Rush,* 71–72.

34. Rubin, Swift, and Northrup, *Negro Employment in the Maritime Industries,* 39–40.

35. The description (with no authorial attribution) appears in a box that identifies Joseph James as the author of an accompanying article. See "Marinship Negroes Speak to Fellow Workmen." The cover of this issue shows a cartoon of workers building and loading a military ship; all the workers pictured are white.

36. "Marinship Walkout Not Demonstration by Majority Group."

37. There was a similar case in Rhode Island resulting in a comparable ruling: *Hill et al., v. International Brotherhood of Boilermakers, Iron Ship Builders and Helpers of America and Local Lodge 308,* 1944. See Harris, *The Harder We Run,* 121 and 208, note 52.

38. Stripp, "The Treatment of Negro-American Workers by the AFL and the CIO."

Chapter 7. Leading the Pack

1. On the development of the Central Avenue music scene, see especially Isoardi, *The Dark Tree,* chapter 2. The author also documents the impressive music education programs characteristic of the area.

2. The five largest U.S. cities in 1950 in descending order were New York, Chicago, Philadelphia, Los Angeles, and Detroit. (Data from the 1950 census.)

3. On the growth of the business and residential community around Central Avenue, see especially Chapple, "From Central Avenue to Leimert Park."

4. Isoardi, *The Dark Tree,* 19.

5. Quotations in this paragraph come from Bryant et al., *Central Avenue Sounds,* 366–67 (Bryant) and 215–16 (Kelson).

6. Data taken from the AFM *Official Proceedings* of 1952.

7. For a succinct listing of the main Central Avenue clubs along with brief descriptions, see Meares, "Central Avenue Swing." On the history of the Club Alabam in particular, see Meares, "Club Alabam."

8. Bryant et al., *Central Avenue Sounds,* 113.

9. See, for example, Eastman, "Central Avenue Blues," 21.

10. In Bryant et al., *Central Avenue Sounds*, 71–72, Lee Young places the incident in 1940, but the account of it in *Downbeat* ("Color Loses Lee Young's Job"), which dates from the time it occurred, appeared in May 1943.

11. Bryant et al., *Central Avenue Sounds*, 72. The interview took place in 1996.

12. *Downbeat* 10, no. 9 (May 1, 1943): 1 and 8.

13. "47 Men Talk 767 Merger at Meeting."

14. The conflicts between the two Los Angeles locals and the merger process are also described in Dickerson, "Central Avenue Meets Hollywood" and, briefly, in Laifer, "Looking Back." My account, however, is based on primary sources, including the detailed writings of Buddy Collette and Marl Young, contemporaneous articles in the local press, and reports and minutes printed in Local 47's monthly newsletter, *The Overture*. Dozens of articles in *Downbeat* recount the process as it unfolded; although I have consulted them all, I reference only the most important of them in this chapter.

15. Collette's account appears in these sources, listed in chronological order: Callender and Cohen, *Unfinished Dream* (1985), 99–107; Collette, *A Jazz Audio Biography* (1994; verbal comments on the recording and written explanations in the liner notes); Bryant et al., *Central Avenue Sounds* (1998), 154–59; and Collette with Isoardi, *Jazz Generations* (2000), 110–20.

16. Collette dates the events related in this paragraph to 1948 or 1949 in various accounts.

17. Callender and Cohen, *Unfinished Dream*, 99.

18. Collette, *Jazz Generations*, 113.

19. Collette, *Jazz Generations*, 115; also see Bryant et al., *Central Avenue Sounds*, 156.

20. "High School Musicians Perform Before Experts."

21. Collette recounts this story in all of the sources cited above, but the exact quotation comes from Collette with Isoardi, *Jazz Generations*, 116.

22. Two articles by Edwin Schallert in the *Los Angeles Times*: "Josephine Baker Will Oo-la-la" and "Josephine Baker Captivates First Audiences" (July 1 and July 5, 1951).

23. Maury Paul, secretary of L.A.'s Local 47, recounted the history of the amalgamation movement in the September issue of local's monthly newsletter, *The Overture*. He dates the start of informal talks to July 1951, just at the time of Baker's appearance (Paul, "From the Boardroom," Sept. 1952, 6).

24. Walton, *Bronzeville Conversations*, 14–15.

25. Bryant et al., *Central Avenue Sounds*, 249, 338–39.

26. Young, "The Amalgamation of Locals 47 and 767."

27. Ibid. See also "Anti-Jim Crow Candidates Win in Local 767 Election."

28. Bryant et al., *Central Avenue Sounds*, 157.

29. Young, "The Amalgamation," confirmed by the minutes of the Local 47 board meeting of Feb. 7. (The *Downbeat* article "L.A. Locals Nearer Union" includes Harvey Brooks but omits Douglass, an apparent error.)

30. Quotations here and in the rest of the paragraph are taken from the minutes of the Local 47 meeting of Feb. 7, 1952, printed in *The Overture*, Mar. 1952, 24.

31. Paul, "From the Board Room," *The Overture*, May 1952.

32. Young, "The Amalgamation."

33. Ibid. Young presents the proposal in full.

34. The relevant parts of the minutes appear in *The Overture* 32, no. 5 (Aug. 1952), 25, and are described by Young in "The Amalgamation."

35. Thanks to Bill Moriarity, former president of Local 802, for clarifying this matter for me (email of Nov. 3, 2021).

36. Young gives the complete list of thirty-five members in "The Amalgamation." In August 1952 *Downbeat* ran an extensive article by Benny Carter in which he reviewed the history of the amalgamation talks and described the efforts to place the merger proposal on Local 47's ballot (see "Benny Carter Sifts L.A. Union Issues").

37. The full discussion of the history of the amalgamation efforts and related documents appears in Paul, "From the Board Room," *The Overture*, Sept. 1952. The resolution to place the proposal on the ballot appears on p. 7.

38. Paul, "From the Board Room," Sept. 1952, 35.

39. Ibid.

40. The anti-merger position is articulated clearly by saxophonist Cecil "Big Jay" McNeely in Bryant et al., *Central Avenue Sounds*, 191–92.

41. *The Overture* 32, no. 7 (Oct. 1952), 22.

42. Collette and Young discuss spreading publicity in the press, involving the local branch of the NAACP, and getting Chet Huntley to announce the situation on his KABC show.

43. Paul, "From the Board Room," *The Overture*, Nov. 1952.

44. "Musicians of Local 47: Amalgamation with Local 767 WILL NOT COST YOU ONE CENT!"

45. The committee from the International working out the details of the merger with the officers of Locals 47 and 767 consisted of IEB members William Harris and Herman Kenin, AFM treasurer George Clancy, and AFM Secretary Stanley Ballard. In 1958 Kenin would succeed Petrillo as president of the AFM, in which capacity he would play a decisive role in overseeing the merger of many of the other dual locals prior to his death in 1970.

46. Many more details are described by Young in "The Amalgamation," but not reported here. See also Young's essay in Bryant et al., *Central Avenue Sounds*, 393–95.

47. Petrillo, letter to Meany, Apr 8, 1958.

48. "47 Men Talk 767 Merger at Meeting."

49. Printed in full in Young, "The Amalgamation."

50. "Disappearing Shadow."

51. E-mail messages from Gordon Stump, former president of Local 5, Sept. 2 and 3, 2006.

Chapter 8. Mergers from 1954 through 1966

1. Petrillo, letter to Meany. Many thanks to Alan Wierdak at the George Meany Archive, University of Maryland, for providing me copies of correspondence between Petrillo and Meany.

2. Candace Lammers, secretary-treasurer of Local 400 in Hartford, notes that prior investigation by that local revealed no merger with Black Local 335; she assumes its members may have simply joined Local 400 (email of Jan. 24, 2022). I have received no response to my inquiries from the Richmond local.

3. Printed in full in the *International Musician,* Nov. 1957, 42–43, and in the *Official Proceedings* of 1957, 81–82.

4. The AFL and CIO merged in 1955.

5. The others were Sioux City, San Antonio, Tulsa, Omaha, Topeka, Montgomery, Dayton, Newport News, and Savannah. Seven others didn't send delegates.

6. Details are found in Seattle Local 76's monthly newsletter, *Musicland,* Dec. 1956, 1–2; Mar. 1957, 1; and Feb. 1958, 1 (courtesy of Local 76's secretary-treasurer Warren Johnson).

7. Petrillo, letter to Meany.

8. Woodward, *The Strange Career of Jim Crow*, 220. In the 1960s and beyond, Woodward began opposing affirmative action and multiculturalism, as well as what he saw as the politicization of the American Historical Association.

9. Janson, "A.F.M. Shelves Bid for Integration."

10. Musicians' Committee for Integration, letter to George Meany, Mar. 17, 1958. See also the report in the *New York Times*: "Meany Urged to Aid A. F. M. Integration."

11. Musicians' Committee for Integration, letter to George Meany, Mar. 17, 1958.

12. Petrillo, letter to Meany.

13. Marshall, *The Negro and Organized Labor*, 103–4. Marshall cites as his source Petrillo's April 8, 1958, letter to Meany, but the numbers do not appear in that letter or in other documents at the George Meany Archive. It is not clear where Marshall got his specific information.

14. Shishkin, memorandum to Schnitzler.

15. Petrillo's statement appears both in Janson, "A.F.M. Shelves Bid" and in "Meany Urged to Aid A. F. M. Integration."

16. Keller, "Seattle's Segregated Musicians' Union," 155.

17. Barnett, "The Amalgamation of Local 493 and Local 76."

18. Keller, "Seattle's Segregated Musicians' Union," 156–57.

19. Watkins, interview by Miller and Roedig, Aug. 14, 2006.

20. AFM, *Official Proceedings* of 1955, 445.

21. The ballot measure, specifying terms of the proposed merger, along with arguments pro and con, is printed in Local 6's monthly newsletter, the *Musical News* 39, no. 11 (Nov. 1956): 6.

22. "Musicians [sic] Union Isn't in Tune with History"; also quoted in *Variety*, Dec. 19, 1956, 58.

23. "Musicians Here Told to End Jim Crow."

24. The story of Browne joining Local 6 is told colorfully by Ralph J. Gleason in "A Blow to Jim Crow."

25. The *New York Times* article "2 Musicians' Locals Agree to Merge" notes that no vote for merger was needed because the California Attorney General simply ordered the action. The article also reports that two members of Local 669 will be paid as coordinators and a third will become a member of the executive board in the merged local.

26. Local 6's newsletter, *Musical News* 43, no. 5 (May 1960): 1.

27. Ohio Fair Employment Practices Act, Ohio Rev. Code §§ 4112.01-.08, .99 (1959).

28. Quotations in this paragraph are taken from "Voluntary Segregation Held Not Illegal Discrimination."

29. Marshall, *The Negro and Organized Labor*, 280, cites cases in Connecticut and Massachusetts in which Fair Labor Practices Commissions requested that white locals accept Black members, but the white locals responded that they were unable to do so without permission from the Black locals in their jurisdictions, and that these Black locals refused to grant permission.

30. Quotations in this paragraph are drawn from Raskin, "Meany, in a Fiery Debate" and "A.F.L.-C.I.O. Race Dispute Flares at Convention End" (anonymous).

31. Saunders tells the story in "Red: The Reminiscences of Red Saunders" (transcript p. 85). For a photo of Baker at the 1960 event, see https://www.pinterest.com/pin/2111131049488204/, accessed February 9, 2023. Absher recounts the story in *The Black Musician and the White City*, 126–27, and Saunders's son, Ted Saunders Jr., also discusses it in Walton, *Bronzeville Conversations*, 4 (but gives an erroneous date of 1961). He says that his father was fined by Local 208 for the offense and that a similar situation arose in 1962 with Black concert pianist Charles Walker, again leading to a reprimand and fine.

32. Absher recounts this story (with a few minor errors) in *The Black Musician and the White City*, 119–21, and cites it as a motivating event. My account, however, is based on seventeen articles from the time in the following publications: *Chicago Tribune, Chicago Defender, New York Times, Hartford Courant, Baltimore Sun*, and the *Atlanta Daily World*, as well as a 2008 retrospective by Ken Trainor in the *Journal of Oak Park and River Forest:* "The Symphony Finds Its Place."

33. "Carol Wins Cheers, Dad Flies Here for Concert." Trainor ("Symphony Finds Its Place") tracked down Anderson in Portland in 2008 and she claimed that she had actually approached Preves and asked to play in Oak Park because she wanted to learn Tchaikovsky's "Pathetique" Symphony. Both versions of the story can, of course, be true (she might have asked Preves to play, and then he issued an invitation).

34. "Symphony Conductor Quits After Negro Musician Row." Almost all the news stories refer to Palmer as "Mrs. Gustave Palmer." Her first name is given as Gertrude in "Rejection of Young Violinist Recalls Marian Anderson Snub," but Trainor ("Symphony Finds Its Place") identifies her correctly as Marie Dock Palmer. See also Deuchler, *Legendary Locals of Oak Park*, 78, which contains a photo of Anderson and Preves.

35. "Village Board Deplores Bias in Orchestra."

36. Janson, "Negro Violinist Wins an Apology."

37. "Barred Violinist Decides Today if She Wants to Return to Symphony."

38. Janson, "Negro Violinist Wins an Apology."

39. Ibid.

40. Whisler, "Applaud Orchestra, Negro Girl"; and "Negro Plays 'First' Violin" (anonymous).

41. "Negro Plays 'First' Violin."

42. "Report: 25 Musicians Quitting Oak Park Symphony."

43. Trainor, "The Symphony Finds Its Place," and Deuchler, *Legendary Locals*, 78.

44. Law, "Creed and Deed in Oak Park."

45. The story of the amalgamation of Locals 10 and 208 is told in some detail by Absher, *The Black Musician and the White City*, chapter 5, and Halker, "Banding Together" and "A History of Local 208." Laifer, "Looking Back," also reviews the merger briefly. My discussion, however, is primarily based on more than fifty articles published in the press from February 22, 1963, to January 22, 1966. The most informative of them are cited in the footnotes that follow.

46. Hunter, "200 Musicians Revolt."

47. Ibid. and Hunter, "Musicians Union Battle Looms."

48. Hunter, "200 Musicians." The accusation is repeated in other reports; see, for example, "Musicians' Merge Halted by AFM."

49. Hunter, "Musicians Union Battle."

50. Ibid. and Hunter, "Tension Mounts."

51. Hunter, "New Charges Aired," and Watson, "Integration Mix-up." The latter article gives the entire contents of Samuels's letter.

52. Walton, *Bronzeville Conversations*, 24.

53. Watson, "AFL Ruling."

54. Bernstein, "Musicians' Head Fights Segregation."

55. "Merger of 2 Musician Locals at Stalemate"; and "Hire Negroes to Help Merge Music Unions."

56. Membership data in this paragraph derived from the AFM, *Official Proceedings* of 1963. In the same year, Local 47 in Los Angeles had a membership of 13,877 and Local 802 in New York had 28,438 members.

57. Hunter, "New Charges Aired"; and Watson, "AFL Ruling."

58. Hunter, "Music Locals Must Merge"; and "Chicago Music Locals Ordered to Merge Soon" (anonymous).

59. See, for example, "Negroes Fight Music Union's 'Raid'" and Newhouse, "An Opinion on Chicago Union Bias."

60. "Negroes Fight Music Union's 'Raid.'"

61. "Chi Negro Musicians Local Resists Integration."

62. "Hire Negroes" and "Musicians Union Names Two."

63. Hunter, "Music Locals Must Merge."

64. "Musicians Adopt 'Watch, Wait Policy.'"

65. The vote is given in "Musicians Vote to Merge"; "Chi Musicians Vote to Merge"; and "Hal Davis Under Fire." Walton, *Bronzeville Conversations*, 6, and Absher, *The Black Musician and the White City*, 132, give it as 283 to 43, but the agreement among the three contemporaneous newspaper sources tends to favor the numbers in those sources as more accurate.

66. Hardy, "Pittsburgh's Harold Davis Under Fire" and Hardy, "Musicians Grapple over Integration."

67. Hardy, "Pittsburgh's Harold Davis."

68. "Hal C. Davis is New Head" and Flint, "Hal Davis."

69. AFM, *Official Proceedings* of 1964, 147–49. The date of the IEB's action appears on p. 149. The entire merger document is printed on pages 149–53.

70. "Order Merger of Two Music Locals"; "Chi's Ofay AFM"; and "Musicians' Merge Halted."

71. The plan appears in full the AFM's *Official Proceedings* of 1964, 149–53, and its terms are summarized in Halker, "Banding Together," 241; Roth, "AFM Rocked by Chi Race Row"; and "Music Locals Continue Dispute."

72. Halker, "Banding Together," 241.

73. AFM, *Official Proceedings* of 1964, 57–64.

74. AFM, *Official Proceedings* of 1964, 62.

75. AFM, *Official Proceedings*, 64.

76. "Music Local Votes to Defy Merger Order."

77. "International Union Seizes Music Local."

78. "Refuse to Bar Music Union Trusteeship"; "Seize Music Union Local"; and "Chi Local 10 Loses Court Bid."

79. Among other articles, see Bliss, "Music Locals Unite"; "Negro, White Musicians in Unison"; "Color Bar Falls"; and "Chi Locals Merge."

80. "Hal C. Davis is New Head" and Flint, "Hal Davis." Davis, a percussionist from Pittsburgh, had served as vice president of the AFM since 1964, and was also a vice president of the Pennsylvania AFL-CIO, a vice president of the national AFL-CIO, and a member National Council on the Arts.

Chapter 9. After Chicago

1. Ducker worked for the National Institute of Health from 1954 to 1984, where he rose from forklift operator to the Director of the Division of Administrative Services. In 1984 he founded the management consulting company Otis Ducker

and Associates. For a history of his musical life, see Bruder and Broven, "The Rocket of Rhythm."

2. The appointment is mentioned in many sources. See, for example, Seltzer, *Music Matters*, 112, and "Petrillo Named Head of AFM's Civil-Rights Department."

3. See "Making Strides: Diversity Expert Elected to IEB." Ducker completed the term of the member who had resigned but then decided not to run for reelection, as his consulting business was consuming so much of his time.

4. Kmen, *Music in New Orleans*, viii.

5. Jerde, "Black Music in New Orleans," 20. Jerde was Curator of the Hogan Jazz Archive from 1948 to 1994.

6. Laifer, "Looking Back."

7. Quotes in this paragraph are taken from Kenney, *Jazz on the River*, 2, 10, 36, and 54.

8. Kenney, *Jazz*, 45.

9. Local 496's newsletter (*Jazz* 36 [Jan. 1966], 2) reports on the meeting of October 10, 1965, in which president Louis Cottrell and other officials gave a presentation on the "effects of a merger," including distribution of assets, terms, and target date. The minutes of Local 174 (AFM Local 174, Aug. 18, 1969), at which the merger proposal was approved by its board, record that agreement was reached at the twenty-seventh meeting between the two unions. I am extremely grateful to Lori Schexnayder at Tulane's Special Collections for providing me with scans of the minutes and newsletters of the two New Orleans locals.

10. The case of Lawrence Guyton vs. Joe Burton was heard on December 6 and 13, 1966; that of Placide Adams vs. Bob Lasley on March 5, 1969 (described in AFM Local 174's minutes on those dates). In a third case, in 1968, Smokey Johnson, a drummer from Local 496, failed to appear repeatedly for contracted work. The contractor had to scramble at the last minute for a replacement. Johnson appeared before the board of Local 174 with the treasurer of Local 496, who concurred in the decision to fine him. Johnson was subsequently expelled from Local 496 for failure to pay the fines (AFM Local 174 minutes of Jan. 2, 16, and 23, 1968). The case confirms that contractors for Local 174 were hiring musicians from both 174 and 496.

11. Laifer, "Looking Back."

12. AFM Local 174, board minutes, May 10, 1966; *Jazz* 38 (July 1966) and 40 (Jan 1, 1967); and AFM Local 496, board minutes, Apr. 2, 1968; and minutes of the general membership meeting of Apr. 7, 1968.

13. Cole, "No Regrets."

14. Ibid.

15. AFM Local 174's board minutes, Jun. 21, 1966.

16. Description of the collection "American Federation of Musicians Local 174–496," Tulane University Special Collections, accessed February 22, 2023, https://archives.tulane.edu/repositories/3/resources/1482/.

17. Winstein projected the January 1968 target date for the merger at a general meeting on July 24, 1967. The meeting of bandleaders from the two locals took place on July 25 (reported in AFM Local 496, minutes of Jul. 18 and Aug. 1). The Atlanta meeting took place on August 30, 1967, and Winstein gave a report on it to the 174 board on September 5 (AFM Local 174).

18. AFM Local 174, minutes of the meeting of the general membership, Oct. 23, 1967.

19. AFM Local 496, minutes of Dec. 5, 1967.

20. AFM Local 496, minutes of May 7 and 28. The Chicago meeting took place on May 26, 1968.

21. AFM Local 496, minutes of May 28, 1968.

22. AFM Local 174, minutes of the board meetings of Dec. 3 and 10, 1968. AFM Local 496, minutes of Dec. 17, 1968.

23. *Prelude,* Jan. 13, 1970.

24. The complete merger document is included in *Prelude,* July 28, 1969.

25. Melendez, "Treme's Petit Jazz Museum."

26. *Interlude,* Sept.–Oct. 1965, 3.

27. Information and quotations in this paragraph from Williams, interview by Miller.

28. Holman, "Mattapan's Maestro." Williams at one point played for the Crown Prince of Norway. He worked with well-known artists such as Jimmy Witherspoon and toured with Jack Benny.

29. Special meeting of the joint boards of Locals 9 and 535, June 12, 1966; minutes printed in *Interlude,* July–Aug 1966, 9.

30. *Interlude,* Jan–Feb 1968, 5.

31. Information and quotations in this paragraph are taken from Francis, interview by Miller.

32. Hershman, "What's in a Number?"

33. Bowman, interview by Miller.

34. "Musicians Remembering," 8.

35. See the obituary, "Remembering Pianist Mabel Robinson Simms."

36. On the Denver merger, see "Musicians Integrate." The article opens with the statement that the "American Federation of Musicians announced another victory yesterday in its effort to promote mergers of Negro and white locals." On the Cleveland merger, see "Kenin Hails Cleve. Tooter Integration."

37. Bernstein, "Musicians' Head Fights Segregation."

38. Seltzer, *Music Matters,* 112, gives the specific terms for the mergers in Louisville (1967) and Dayton (1970).

39. McRae, "Paying Their Dues," 52 and 54.

40. Plummer was elected president in 1930; he became secretary in 1936. See McRae, 35.

41. McRae, 55 and 60–61, describes meetings in July 1965, January and September 1966, and May 1967.

42. McRae, 62–63.

43. McRae, 63, gives the terms.

Chapter 10. Coda

1. Bryant et al., *Central Avenue Sounds*, 158.

2. *Central Avenue Sounds*, 192.

3. For example, Cecil McNeely, Britt Woodman, and William "Brother" Woodman (*Central Avenue Sounds*, 193, 132, and 113, respectively).

4. *Central Avenue Sounds*, 280.

5. Absher, *The Black Musician*, 141 and 143.

6. Gargan, "Past Is Swinging at Club."

7. Keller, "Seattle's Segregated Musicians' Union," 162.

8. Bowman, interview by Miller.

9. "AFM Locals' Integration Backfires."

10. Article 5 of the By-laws, amended Sept. 15, 1985 as Article 26, Section 2. Quoted in Seltzer, *Music Matters*, 114.

11. Walton, *Bronzeville Conversations*, 33. Cited by Absher, *The Black Musician*, 143; she attributes the information to Sam Denov, but in fact it comes from Walton's comments following Denov's interview.

12. In the current By-Laws, the statement appears in Article 17, Section 4(b).

13. Information and quotations in this section come from interviews by the author with Lovie Smith-Wright (June 16, 2021) and Otis Ducker (June 10, 2021), as well as Smith-Wright's article, "A Brief History of the AFM Diversity Committee."

14. Quoted in Smith-Wright, "A Brief History of the AFM Diversity Committee." Smith-Wright was the first African American female elected as president of an AFM local (Houston, 2003).

15. Smith-Wright, interview by Miller, June 16, 2021, and email of Dec. 17, 2021. Only the youth award carries a monetary prize. All winners receive a trophy designed by the Committee in 2004.

16. Bucknor, "Black Workers, Unions, and Inequality."

17. Although this famous quote is generally attributed to Martin Luther King Jr., he in fact was quoting the nineteenth-century clergyman Theodore Parker.

18. David Anthony III, email to Leta Miller, Jan. 12, 2022.

19. Ibid.

References

Absher, Amy. *The Black Musician and the White City: Race and Music in Chicago, 1900–1967.* Ann Arbor: University of Michigan Press, 2014.

"A.F.L.-C.I.O. Race Dispute Flares at Convention End." *New York Herald Tribune,* Sept. 24, 1959, 16.

AFM Locals 174 and 496. Board meeting minutes. Typed or manuscript documents at Special Collections, Tulane University, Collection Identifier HJA-001 (American Federation of Musicians Local 174-496). For an online search tool, see "American Federation of Musicians Local 174-496," Tulane University Libraries. Accessed March 8, 2023. https://archives.tulane.edu/repositories/3/resources/1482.

"AFM Locals' Integration Backfires, N. H. Chi Units Ask Charters Back." *Variety,* July 8, 1968, 47.

Allegro. Newsletter of New York City's Local 802.

American Federation of Labor (AFL). *Report of the Proceedings of the Annual Convention* (various years cited).

American Federation of Musicians (AFM). *Official Proceedings of the Annual Convention* (various years cited).

"Anti-Jim Crow Candidates Win in Local 767 Election." *Downbeat* 19, no. 2 (Jan. 25, 1952), 1.

"Appeal for National and State Relief for Unemployed Musicians." *Musical News* 17, no. 2 (Feb. 1934): 1, 10–11. Newsletter of San Francisco's Local 6.

Arnesen, Eric. "A. Philip Randolph: Labor and the New Black Politics." In *The Human Tradition in American Labor History,* edited by Eric Arnesen, 173–91. Wilmington, DE: SR Books, 2004.

———. *Brotherhoods of Color: Black Railroad Workers and the Struggle for Equality.* Cambridge, MA: Harvard University Press, 2001.

———. "Following the Color Line of Labor: Black Workers and the Labor Movement Before 1930." *Radical History Review* 55 (1993): 53–78.

———. "The Quicksands of Economic Insecurity: African Americans, Strikebreaking, and Labor Activism in the Industrial Era." In *The Black Worker: Race, Labor, and Civil Rights since Emancipation*, edited by Eric Arnesen, 41–71. Urbana: University of Illinois Press, 2007.

Ayer, Julie. *More Than Meets the Ear: How Symphony Musicians Made Labor History*. Minneapolis: Syren Book Company, 2005.

Badger, Reid. *A Life in Ragtime: A Biography of James Reese Europe*. New York: Oxford University Press, 1995.

Banks, Dave. "Police Draw Color Line at K. C. Chez Paree." *Downbeat*, Apr. 22, 1946, 3.

"Baranco Band Loses Out at Dawn Café." *The Spokesman* (San Francisco), May 24, 1935, 1.

Barbash, Jack, ed. *Unions and Union Leadership: Their Human Meaning*. New York: Harper, 1959.

Barnett, Powell. "The Amalgamation of Local 493 and Local 76." Powell Barnett Papers, University of Washington Special Collections.

———. "Musicians Convention L. A.—1933" (*recte*: 1932). Powell Barnett Papers, University of Washington Special Collections.

"Barred Violinist Decides Today if She Wants to Return to Symphony." *Chicago Defender*, Feb. 13, 1963, 3.

"Battle Jim Crow in Miami Locals." *Downbeat* 16, no. 18 (Sept. 23, 1949): 1–2.

"Benny Carter Sifts L.A. Union Issues as Interracial Merger Meets Delays." *Downbeat*, Aug. 27, 1952, 14.

Bernstein, Harry. "Musicians' Head Fights Segregation in Locals." *Los Angeles Times*, Feb. 22, 1963, A2.

Bess, Druie. Interview by Irene Cortinovis and Peter Etzkorn, Nov. 5, 1971. Western Historical Manuscript Collection, University of Missouri-St. Louis.

"Biographical Sketches of Leaders in Professional and Official Fields Tell of Genuine Achievements." *San Francisco Chronicle*, Jan. 16, 1918, 46.

"Bi-Union Discrimination Case Set for Tue.: Showdown Court Trial Follows Music Union's Attempt to Jim-Crow Bay Area." *The Spokesman* (San Francisco), Aug. 30, 1934, 2.

"Black Musicians [sic] Union Loses Key Legal Battle." *Philadelphia Tribune*, July 6, 1971.

"Black Officers of Musicians' Local No. 274 Say Whites are Welcome." *Philadelphia Tribune*, Apr. 24, 1971.

Bliss, George. "Music Locals Unite; Trustee Ends Control." *Chicago Tribune*, Jan. 12, 1966, B9.

Bloch, Herman D. "Craft Unions and the Negro in Historical Perspective." *Journal of Negro History* 43, no. 1 (Jan. 1958): 10–33.

———. "Labor and the Negro 1866–1910." *Journal of Negro History* 50, no. 3 (July 1965): 163–84.

Bowman, Gordon. Interview by Leta Miller, July 14, 2019.

Brackett, John. "The American Federation of Musicians, Robots, and the Roots of an Ideology of Musical Liveness." Paper presented at the annual conference of the Society for American Music (online), March 11, 2022.

Bradford, Perry. *Born with the Blues.* New York: Oak Publications, 1965.

Brenc, Willie. "Jack Leroy Cooper." *Blackpast*, Oct. 19, 2013. https://www.blackpast.org/african-american-history/cooper-jack-leroy-1888–1970/.

"Bricks Fly as 500 Longshoremen Attack Oakland Scabs." *The Spokesman* (San Francisco), May 17, 1934, 1.

Broussard, Albert S. *Black San Francisco: The Struggle for Racial Equality in the West, 1900–1954.* Lawrence: University Press of Kansas, 1993.

Bruder, Jay, and John Broven. "'The Rocket of Rhythm': Otis Ducker at the Dawn of New Orleans R&B." *Blues and Rhythm* 293 (Oct. 2014): 8–13.

Bryant, Clora, Buddy Collette, William Greene, Steve Isoardi, and Marl Young, eds. (Central Avenue Sounds Editorial Committee). *Central Avenue Sounds: Jazz in Los Angeles.* Berkeley: University of California Press, 1998.

Bucknor, Cherrie. "Black Workers, Unions, and Inequality." Washington, DC: Center for Economic and Policy Research, Aug. 2016.

"Buxton: A Lost Utopia." Iowa Department of Cultural Affairs. Accessed February 15, 2023. https://iowaculture.gov/history/education/educator-resources/primary-source-sets/buxton-lost-utopia.

Callender, Red, and Elaine Cohen. *Unfinished Dream: The Musical World of Red Callender.* London: Quartet Books, 1985.

Calverton, V. F. [aka George Goetz], ed. *Anthology of American Negro Literature.* New York: The Modern Library, 1929.

"Carol Wins Cheers, Dad Flies Here for Concert." *Chicago Defender*, Feb. 18, 1963, 1.

Carter, Marva Griffen. "Roland Hayes: Expressor of the Soul in Song (1887–1977)." *The Black Perspective in Music* 5, no. 2 (Autumn 1977): 188–220.

Carter, Robert. Interview by Dan Havens. National Ragtime and Jazz Archive, Elijah P. Lovejoy Library, Southern Illinois University, Edwardsville.

Chapple, Reginald. "From Central Avenue to Leimert Park: The Shifting Center of Black Los Angeles." In *Black Los Angeles: American Dreams and Racial Realities*, edited by Darnell Hunt and Ana-Christina Ramón, 60–80. New York: New York University Press, 2010.

"Chi Local 10 Loses Court Bid to Ax Trustee of AFM's Integration Plan." *Variety*, Oct. 7, 1964, 7.

"Chi Locals Merge After 65 Years." *Philadelphia Tribune*, Jan. 22, 1966, 14.

"Chi Musicians Vote to Merge Tan Local." *Philadelphia Tribune*, Oct. 12, 1963, 24.

"Chi Negro Musicians [sic] Local Resists Integration." *Variety*, Aug. 28, 1963, 1.

"Chicago Music Locals Ordered to Merge Soon." *Atlanta Daily World*, Oct. 10, 1963, A1.

"Chi's Ofay AFM Local Chides Kenin for His '66 Integration Delay." *Variety*, Apr. 15, 1964, 1.

"City's Bench and Bar Boast Great Traditions." *San Francisco Chronicle*, Jan. 18, 1922, 45.

"Coast Musicians Sue White Local." *Chicago Defender*, Sept. 22, 1934, 7.

Cobble, Dorothy Sue. "Reviving the Federation's Historic Role in Organizing." Rutgers School of Management and Labor Relations, Mar. 10, 1996. https://smlr.rutgers.edu/sites/smlr/files/Documents/Faculty-Staff-Docs/ISLO.pdf.

Cole, Thomas. "No Regrets: A Conversation with Barry Martyn." *Offbeat Magazine*, Sept. 26, 2019.

Collette, Buddy. *A Jazz Audio Biography*. Issues Records 1SSCD005, 1994 (Lawndale, CA).

Collette, Buddy, with Steven Isoardi. *Jazz Generations: A Life in American Music and Society*. London: Continuum, 2000.

"Color Bar Falls, Musician Locals Merge in Chicago." *Washington Post*, Jan. 13, 1966, F6.

"Color Loses Lee Young's Job." *Downbeat* 10, no. 9 (May 1, 1943): 1, 8.

Commons, John R. "Types of American Labor Unions—the Musicians of St. Louis and New York." *Quarterly Journal of Economics* 20, no. 3 (May 1906): 419–42.

"Coping with Automation." *Business Week*, June 9, 1956. Reproduced in *Unions and Union Leadership, their Human Meaning*, edited by Jack Barbash, 306–11. New York: Harper, 1959.

Cortinovis, Irene. Interviews she conducted are listed in the references under the names of the interviewees.

Cotter, John Cleophus. "The Negro in Music in St. Louis." MA thesis in Music Education, Washington University, St. Louis, June 1959. https://doi.org/10.7936/qcn0-vf69.

Countryman, Vern. "The Organized Musicians." *University of Chicago Law Review* 16, no. 1 (Autumn 1948): 56—85 and 16, no. 2 (Winter 1949): 239–97.

"Court Bares Threats of Musicians: White Musician's Union Accused of Intimidation, Lose First Court Tilt." *The Spokesman* (San Francisco), Sept. 6, 1934, 1.

Cramton, Lou. "Union Wars on Detroit Bashes, Stiff Fines Set." *Downbeat*, Aug. 27, 1947, 17.

Daniels, Douglas Henry. *Pioneer Urbanites: A Social and Cultural History of Black San Francisco*. Berkeley: University of California Press, 1990.

Denning, Michael. *The Cultural Front: The Laboring of American Culture in the Twentieth Century*. London: Verso, 1996.

Deuchler, Douglas. *Legendary Locals of Oak Park*. Mount Pleasant, SC: Arcadia Publishing, 2013. https://www.google.com/books/edition/Legendary_Locals_of_Oak_Park/PQGpAAAAQBAJ.

Dexter, Dave, Jr. "Kaycee Local 627 Prospered During 1930 Boom Days." *Downbeat*, Jan. 15, 1941, 8.

Dickerson, Lowell Dwight. "Central Avenue Meets Hollywood: The Amalgamation of the Black and White Musicians' Unions in Los Angeles." PhD diss., University of California, Los Angeles, 1998.

"Disappearing Shadow." *Downbeat,* June 12, 1958, 11.

"Discrimination by the American Federation of Musicians Opposed." *St. Louis Argus,* May 13, 1932, 1, 5.

Dixon, Anita. Interview by Leta Miller, June 18, 2021.

Dorman, James H. "Shaping the Popular Image of Post-Reconstruction American Blacks: The 'Coon Song' Phenomenon of the Gilded Age." *American Quarterly* 40, no. 4 (Dec. 1988): 450–71.

Du Bois, W. E. B. *Black Reconstruction: An Essay Toward a History of the Part which Black Folk Played in the Attempt to Reconstruct Democracy in America, 1860–1880.* New York: Harcourt, Brace, and Co., 1935.

Ducker, Otis. Interviews by Leta Miller, June 10 and Dec. 3, 2021.

Dulf, George E. "A History of Negro Music and Negro Musicians in Chicago: A History of Local 208, American Federation of Musicians." Transcript of interview by Louise Henry, Oct. 23, 1939. Chicago Public Library, Harsh Research Collection, Illinois Writers Project, Box 48, folder 11.

Eastman, Ralph. "Central Avenue Blues: The Making of Los Angeles Rhythm and Blues, 1942–1947." *Black Music Research Journal* 9, no. 1 (Spring 1989), 19–33.

Edises, Pele. "Joseph James is a Busy Guy." *People's World,* Jan. 6, 1945, 5.

Eldridge, Roy. "Roy Eldridge Oral History Interview." Jazz Oral History Project, Rutgers University Libraries. Interviewed by Daniel Morgenstern, 1982–1983.

Erenberg, Lewis A. *Steppin' Out: New York Nightlife and the Transformation of American Culture 1890–1930.* Chicago: University of Chicago Press, 1981.

———. *Swingin' the Dream: Big Band Jazz and the Rebirth of American Culture.* Chicago: University of Chicago Press, 1998.

Fannin, Mike. "The Truth in Black and White: An Apology from the Kansas City Star." *Kansas City Star,* Dec. 20, 2020; updated Dec. 22, 2020. https://www.kansascity.com/news/local/article247928045.html.

Fields, Barbara J. "Ideology and Race in American History." In *Region, Race, and Reconstruction: Essays in Honor of C. Vann Woodward,* edited by J. Morgan Kousser and James M. McPherson, 143–77. New York: Oxford University Press, 1982.

Fink, Gary M., editor in chief. *Labor Unions.* Westport, CT: Greenwood Press, 1977.

Fink, Leon. "The New Labor History and the Powers of Historical Pessimism: Consensus, Hegemony, and the Case of the Knights of Labor." *Journal of American History* 75 (June 1988): 115–61.

"The First Black Radio Show (in America) Debuts." African American Registry (AAREG), Nov. 3, 1929. https://aaregistry.org/story/first-exclusively-black-radio-show-goes-on-the-air/.

Fletcher, Tom. *100 Years of the Negro in Show Business.* New York: Da Capo Press, 1984.

Flint, Peter B. "Hal Davis, 63, Head of Musicians Union." *New York Times,* Jan. 13, 1978, B2.

Foner, Philip S. *Organized Labor and the Black Worker, 1619–1973*. New York: International Publishers, 1974.

Foner, Philip S. and Ronald L. Lewis. *The Black Worker,* vol. VI: *The Era of Post-War Prosperity and the Great Depression, 1920 to 1936*. Temple University Press, 1981.

Fones-Wolf, Elizabeth. "Sound Comes to the Movies: The Philadelphia Musicians' Struggle Against Recorded Music." *Pennsylvania Magazine of History and Biography* 118, no. 1–2 (Jan./Apr. 1994): 3–31.

Fones-Wolf, Elizabeth and Kenneth. "Trade-Union Evangelism: Religion and the AFL in the Labor Forward Movement, 1912–16." In *Working-Class America: Essays on Labor, Community, and American Society*, edited by Michael H. Frisch and Daniel J. Walkowitz, 153–84. Urbana: University of Illinois Press, 1983.

"47 Men Talk 767 Merger at Meeting." *Downbeat*, Dec. 3, 1952, 3.

Fraden, Rena. *Blueprints for a Black Federal Theatre, 1935–1939*. Cambridge: Cambridge University Press, 1994.

Francis, Henry. Interview by Leta Miller, July 11, 2019.

Frank, Dana. *Purchasing Power: Consumer Organizing, Gender, and the Seattle Labor Movement, 1919–1929*. Cambridge: Cambridge University Press, 1994.

———. "Race Relations and the Seattle Labor Movement, 1915–1929." *Pacific Northwest Quarterly*, Winter 1994/95: 35–44.

"Frank Fairfax." Wikipedia. Accessed February 3, 2023. https://en.wikipedia.org/wiki/Frank_Fairfax.

Frankenstein, Alfred. "Negro Vocalist Recital Pleases." *San Francisco Chronicle*, Mar. 6, 1933, 5.

Franklin, John Hope. *From Slavery to Freedom: A History of Negro Americans*. Third edition. New York: Alfred A. Knopf, 1967.

Fredrickson, George M. *The Black Image in the White Mind: The Debate on Afro-American Character and Destiny, 1817–1914*. New York: Harper and Row, 1971.

Gargan, Edward A. "Past Is Swinging at Club for 'Colored Musicians.'" *New York Times*, Aug. 7, 1985, B2.

Garlock, Jonathan. "Knights of Labor History and Geography, 1869–1899." University of Washington: Mapping American Social Movement Project. Accessed February 3, 2023. https://depts.washington.edu/moves/knights_labor_map.shtml.

Gleason, Ralph J. "A Blow to Jim Crow." *Downbeat*, Dec. 10, 1959, 14–15.

Goldberg, Jacob. "How Black Musicians Helped Reform Local 802." *Allegro*, Feb. 2020, 31, 33, 35, 37. Newsletter of New York City's Local 802.

———. "Swingin' the Color Line: African-American Musicians and the Formation of Local 802, 1886–1946." Self-published, Amherst, MA, 2008.

Gompers, Samuel. *The Samuel Gompers Papers*. Edited by Peter J. Albert and Grace Palladino. Urbana: University of Illinois Press, 2009.

———. *Seventy Years of Life and Labor: An Autobiography*. With contributions by Florence Calvert Thorne. New York: E. P. Dutton and Co., 1925.

Gray, Phyllis Ann. "The Black Middle Class in Buxton, Iowa." MS thesis in Sociology, Iowa State University, 1984.

Green, Anna Weld. "Musicians' Union of San Francisco." MS thesis in Economics, University of California, Berkeley, 1929.

Grob, Gerald. "Organized Labor and the Negro Worker." *Labor History* 1, no. 2 (1960): 164–76.

Gushee, Lawrence. *Pioneers of Jazz*. Oxford: Oxford University Press, 2005.

"Hal C. Davis is New Head of Musicians' Federation." *New York Times*, July 31, 1970, 27.

"Hal Davis Under Fire by Integrationists." *New Pittsburgh Courier*, Oct. 19, 1963, 20.

Halker, Clark. "Banding Together." In *Black Communities and Urban Development in America 1720–1990: Overviews, Theory and Historiography*, vol. 9, edited by Kenneth L. Kusmer, 224–43. New York: Garland, 1991.

———. "A History of Local 208 and the Struggle for Racial Equality in the American Federation of Musicians." *Black Music Research Journal* 8, no. 2 (Autumn 1988): 207–22.

Hardy, Lester K. "Musicians Grapple over Integration." *New Pittsburgh Courier*, Oct. 26, 1963, 16.

———. "Pittsburgh's Harold Davis Under Fire in Chi Hassle." *Pittsburgh Courier*, Oct. 19, 1963, 1.

Harris, William H. *The Harder We Run: Black Workers Since the Civil War*. New York: Oxford University Press, 1982.

Henry, Mary T. "Barnett, Powell S." HistoryLink.org, Nov. 9, 1998. https://www.historylink.org/File/307.

Hershman, Sue-Ellen. "What's in a Number? The History and Merger of Local 535." *Interlude*, Jan./Feb. 1993, 4–5, 12. Newsletter of Boston's Local 9-535.

"High School Musicians Perform Before Experts." *Los Angeles Times*, Mar. 12, 1950, B1.

Hild, Matthew. "Organizing Across the Color Line: The Knights of Labor and Black Recruitment in Small-Town Georgia." *Georgia Historical Quarterly* 81, no. 2 (Summer 1997): 287–310.

Hill, Herbert. "Labor Unions and the Negro: The Record of Discrimination." *Commentary*, Dec. 1959. https://www.commentary.org/articles/herbert-hill/labor-unions-and-the-negrothe-record-of-discrimination/.

———. "The Problem of Race in American Labor History." *Review in American History* 24, no. 2 (June 1996): 189–208.

Hinton, Milton. "Reminiscences of Milton Hinton." Columbia Oral History Project, 1971. NY: Columbia University.

"Hire Negroes to Help Merge Music Unions." *Chicago Tribune*, June 21, 1963, A2.

Hirschmann, I. A. "The Musician and the Depression." *The Nation* 137, no. 3567 (Nov. 15, 1933): 565–66.

Holman, Tayla. "Mattapan's Maestro: Fred Williams Pays it Forward." *Dorchester Reporter*, Dec. 20, 2012. https://www.dotnews.com/2012/mattapan-s-maestro-fred-williams-pays-it-forward.

Holmes, Sean P. *Weavers of Dreams, Unite! Actors' Unionism in Early Twentieth-Century America*. Urbana: University of Illinois Press, 2013.

Hubbard, Preston J. "Synchronized Sound and the Movie-House Musicians, 1926–29." *American Music* 3/4 (Winter, 1985): 429–41.

Hunt, Darnell, and Ana-Christina Ramón, eds. *Black Los Angeles: American Dreams and Racial Realities*. New York: New York University Press, 2010.

Hunter, Bob. "200 Musicians Revolt, Join Mixed Union." *Chicago Defender*, Mar. 21, 1963, 1.

———. "Music Locals Must Merge by March 4." *Chicago Defender*, Sept. 9, 1963, 16.

———. "Musicians Union Battle Looms Over Integration." *Chicago Defender*, Mar. 23, 1963, 1.

———. "New Charges Aired in Musicians [sic] Hassle." *Chicago Defender*, July 27, 1963, 10.

———. "Tension Mounts as Local 208's Meeting Nears." *Chicago Defender*, Sept. 23, 1963, 20.

Interlude. Newsletter of Boston's Local 9 (later 9-535).

International Musician. Monthly magazine of the American Federation of Musicians (AFM).

"International Union Seizes Music Local." *Chicago Tribune*, Aug. 13, 1964, N11.

Isoardi, Steven L. *The Dark Tree: Jazz and the Community Arts in Los Angeles*. Berkeley: University of California Press, 2006.

Janson, Donald. "A. F. M. Shelves Bid for Integration." *New York Times*, June 14, 1957, 22.

———. "Negro Violinist Wins an Apology." *New York Times*, Feb. 13, 1963, 6.

Jazz. Newsletter of New Orleans's Local 496.

Jerde, Curtis D. "Black Music in New Orleans: A Historical Overview." *Black Music Research Journal* 10, no. 1 (Spring 1990): 18–24.

"Jim Crow Issue Grows in Kaycee." *Downbeat*, Jan. 14, 1946, 17.

Johnson, Eddie, Elijah Shaw, Chick Finney, and Eddie Randle. Interview by Irene Cortinovis, Aug. 20, 1971. Jazzman Project, Oral History Collection (S0829), State Historical Society of Missouri (oral history T-0010).

Johnson, James Weldon. "The Poor White Musician." In *Writings: The Autobiography of an Ex-Colored Man*. New York: Library of America, 2004.

Johnson, Marilynn S. *The Second Gold Rush: Oakland and the East Bay in World War II*. Berkeley: University of California Press, 1993.

"Kaycee Hot Club May Start Again." *Downbeat*, Feb. 25, 1946, 18.

Keller, David. *The Blue Note: Seattle's Black Musicians' Union, A Pictorial History*. Self-published, 2013.

———. "Seattle's Segregated Musicians' Union, Local 493, 1918–1956." MA thesis, Western Washington University, 1996.

"Kenin Hails Cleve. Tooter Integration." *Variety,* Oct. 10, 1962, 49.

Kenney, William Howland. *Jazz on the River.* Chicago: University of Chicago Press, 2005.

———. "Just Before Miles: Jazz in St. Louis, 1926–1944." In *Miles Davis and American Culture,* edited by Gerald Early, 24–39. St. Louis: Missouri Historical Society Press, 2001.

Kessler, Sidney H. "The Organization of the Negroes in the Knights of Labor." *The Journal of Negro History* 37 (July 1952): 248–76.

Kibler, M. Alison. *Rank Ladies: Gender and Cultural Hierarchy in American Vaudeville.* Chapel Hill: University of North Carolina Press, 1999.

King, Clarence. "The Facts and Correspondence in the Eddie B. Love Case." *Musical News* 26, no. 8 (August 1943): 15–25; and 26, no. 9 (September 1943): 15–19. Newsletter of San Francisco's Local 6.

King, Clarence H. "Report of the Delegates of General Strike Committee." *Musical News* 18, no. 8 (Aug. 1934): 1, 6. Newsletter of San Francisco's Local 6.

King, Leon. Interview by Dan Havens. National Ragtime and Jazz Archive, Elijah P. Lovejoy Library, Southern Illinois University, Edwardsville.

Kmen, Henry A. *Music in New Orleans: The Formative Years, 1791–1841.* Baton Rouge: Louisiana State University Press, 1966.

Koshatka, Edgar. "Musicians' Unions Square Off." *Thursday's Drummer,* May 27, 1971, 5.

Kraft, James. "Artists as Workers: Musicians and Trade Unionism in America, 1880–1917." *Musical Quarterly* 79, no. 3 (Autumn, 1995): 512–43.

Kusmer, Kenneth L., ed. *Black Communities and Urban Development in America 1720–1990: Overviews, Theory, and Historiography.* New York: Garland, 1991.

"L.A. Locals Nearer Union." *Downbeat,* Feb. 23, 1952, 18.

Ladd, Marco. "Synchronization as Musical Labor in Italian Silent Cinemas." *Journal of the American Musicological Society* 75, no. 2 (Summer 2022): 273–317.

"LaFerne Is Our Friend, Says Group." *The Spokesman* (San Francisco), Feb. 22, 1935, 1.

Laifer, Stephen. "Looking Back: Merged Locals Are Windows on Changing Times." *International Musician* 101, no. 2 (Feb. 2003): 17.

Law, H. B. "Creed and Deed in Oak Park." *Chicago Tribune,* Feb. 13, 1963, 24.

Lefferts, Peter M. "A Chronology and Itinerary of the Career of George E. Dulf: Materials for a Biography." University of Nebraska, Lincoln, Faculty Publications, School of Music, 57, July 29, 2016. http://digitalcommons.unl.edu/musicfacpub/57.

Leiter, Richard D. *The Musicians and Petrillo.* New York: Bookman Associates, 1953.

LeProtti, Sid. Interview by Turk Murphy, 1952. Stanford University Archive of Recorded Sound.

Levine, Lawrence W. *Highbrow/Lowbrow: The Emergence of Cultural Hierarchy in America.* Cambridge, MA: Harvard University Press, 1988.

Lewis, Earl. *In Their Own Interests: Race, Class, and Power in Twentieth Century Norfolk, Virginia.* Berkeley: University of California Press, 1991.

"Local Musicians May Lose Jobs as Nat. Body Revokes Union Charter." *The Spokesman* (San Francisco), Dec. 14, 1934: 1.

Logan, Rayford W. *The Negro in American Life and Thought: The Nadir, 1877–1901.* New York: Dial Press, 1954.

Long, Sammy. Interview by Irene Cortinovis, April 18, 1973. Jazzmen Project, University of Missouri Oral History Collection (S0829), St Louis. Accessed February 7, 2023. https://shsmo.org/sites/default/files/pdfs/oral-history/transcripts/s0829/t0011b.pdf.

Lott, Eric. "'The Seeming Counterfeit': Racial Politics and Early Blackface Minstrelsy." *American Quarterly* 43, no. 2 (June 1991): 223–54.

Love, Eddie B. "The Bubble Bursts." *Musical News* 18, no. 12 (Dec. 1934): 1–2. Newsletter of San Francisco's Local 6.

Machlin, Paul S. *Stride: The Music of Fats Waller.* Boston: Twayne Publishers, 1985.

"Making Strides: Diversity Expert Elected to IEB." *International Musician,* May 2006.

Mandel, Bernard. "Samuel Gompers and the Negro Workers, 1886–1914." *The Journal of Negro History* 40, no. 1 (Jan. 1955): 34–60.

"Marinship Negroes Speak to Fellow Workmen." *The Marin-er,* Aug. 21, 1943, 5.

"Marinship Walkout Not Demonstration by Majority Group." *Labor Citizen* 4, no. 42 (Dec. 6, 1943): 1, 4.

Marshall, Ray. "The Negro and Organized Labor." *The Journal of Negro Education* 32, no. 4 (Autumn, 1963): 375–89.

———. *The Negro and Organized Labor.* New York: John Wiley and Sons, 1965.

May, Bill. Interview by Leta Miller, July 3, 2021.

Mazzola, Sandy Raymond. "When Music is Labor: Chicago Bands and Orchestras and the Origins of the Chicago Federation of Musicians, 1880–1902." PhD dissertation, Northern Illinois University, 1984.

McLaurin, Melton A. "The Racial Policies of the Knights of Labor and the Organization of Southern Black Workers." *Labor History* 17, no. 4 (Fall 1976): 568–85.

McRae, Richard. "Paying their Dues: Buffalo's African American Musicians Union, Local 533, A. F. M." *Afro-Americans in New York Life and History* 20, no. 1 (Jan. 1996): 7–70.

McWhirter, Cameron. *Red Summer: The Summer of 1919 and the Awakening of Black America.* New York: Henry Holt, 2011.

"Meany Urged to Aid A. F. M. Integration." *New York Times,* Mar. 21, 1958.

Meares, Hadley. "Central Avenue Swing: Mapping the Jazz Clubs that Made Central Avenue Swing." *Curbed LA,* Feb. 28, 2018. https://la.curbed.com/maps/central-avenue-history-jazz.

———. "Club Alabam was the Center of LA's Jazz Scene in the 1930s and '40s."

LAist, Aug. 25, 2020. https://laist.com/news/la-history/club-alabam-central-avenue-center-los-angeles-jazz-scene-history-vintage-black-culture.

Melendez, Steven. "Treme's Petit Jazz Museum Is One Room with 1,000 Stories to Tell." *Very Local,* Oct. 11, 2019. https://nola.verylocal.com/tremes-petit-jazz-museum-is-one-room-with-1000-stories-to-tell/89128/.

"Merger of 2 Musician Locals at Stalemate." *Chicago Defender,* Apr. 16, 1963.

Mermey, Maurice. "The Vanishing Fiddler." *North American Review* 227 (Mar. 1929): 301–7.

Metzger, Alfred. "Roland Hayes Tolerant of Music Ideas." *San Francisco Chronicle,* Dec. 29, 1933, 17.

Middleton, Stephen, David R. Roediger, and Donald M. Shaffer, eds. *The Construction of Whiteness.* Jackson: University of Mississippi Press, 2016.

Miller, Leta E. "Elmer Keeton and His Bay Area Negro Chorus: Creating an Artistic Identity in Depression-Era San Francisco." *Black Music Research Journal* 30, no. 2 (Fall 2010): 303–36.

———. *Music and Politics in San Francisco: From the 1906 Quake to the Second World War.* Berkeley: University of California Press, 2011.

———. "Opera as Politics: The Troubled History of San Francisco's War Memorial Opera House." *California History* 92, no. 4 (Winter 2015): 4–23.

———. "Racial Segregation and the San Francisco Musicians' Union, 1923–60." *Journal of the Society for American Music* 1, no. 2 (May 2007): 161–206.

Mitchell, Frank. "Musicians' Chatterbox." *St. Louis Argus,* Sept. 9, 1932, 5.

———. "Musicians' Chatterbox." *St. Louis Argus,* Sept. 10, 1932, 4.

Montgomery, David. "To Study the People." *Labor History* 21 (Fall 1980): 485–512.

———. *Workers' Control in America: Studies in the History of Work, Technology, and Labor Struggles.* Cambridge: Cambridge University Press, 1979.

The Monthly Synopsis. Newsletter of St. Louis's Local 2.

Moody, J. Carroll, and Alice Kessler-Harris, eds. *Perspectives on American Labor History: The Problems of Synthesis.* DeKalb: Northern Illinois University Press, 1990.

Moore, Ed S. "The End of the War and The State of the Union (Local 6)." *Musical News* 28, no. 9 (Sept 1945): 3, 5. Newsletter of San Francisco's Local 6.

Moriarity, William (Bill). Interview by Leta Miller, Sept. 24, 2021.

———. "A Matter of Trust." *Allegro,* Nov. 1994, 6. Newsletter of New York City's Local 802.

Mueller, John H. *The American Symphony Orchestra: A Social History of Musical Taste.* Bloomington: Indiana University Press, 1951.

"Music Local Votes to Defy Merger Order." *Chicago Tribune,* Aug. 8, 1964, 9.

"Music Locals Continue Dispute." *Los Angeles Sentinel,* Apr. 23, 1964, C19.

"Music Union Leader Dies." *Philadelphia Tribune,* Feb. 5, 1972.

Musical Mutual Protective Union v. [Joseph] Weber. 123 Misc. 182, 205 N.Y.S. 699. Supreme Court, New York County, Apr. 1, 1924.

The Musical News. Newsletter of San Francisco's Local 6.

"Musicians Adopt 'Watch, Wait Policy.'" *Chicago Defender,* Sept. 17, 1963, 20.

"Musicians Balk at Picket Job." *The Spokesman* (San Francisco), Oct. 4, 1934, 1.

Musician's [sic] Committee for Integration (MCI). Letter to George Meany, Mar 17, 1958. George Meany Labor Archive, University of Maryland, College Park. Archive collection reference: "Musicians, American Federation of, 1958–1958, RG1-027.9.17, Box 9, folder 17. AFL-CIO Office of the President, President's Files, George Meany, 0061-LBR-RG1-027. Special Collections and University Archives."

"Musicians Here Told to End Jim Crow." *San Francisco Chronicle,* June 18, 1957, 1, 7.

"Musicians Integrate." *New York Times,* Apr. 22, 1960, 20.

"Musicians of Local 47: Amalgamation with Local 767 WILL NOT COST YOU ONE CENT!" *The Overture* 32, no. 8 (Nov. 1952): 22, 39. Newsletter of Los Angeles's Local 47.

"Musicians' Merge Halted by AFM," *Los Angeles Sentinel,* Apr. 16, 1964, B7.

"Musicians Must Choose Between Jim Crow Union and Scabbing." *The Spokesman* (San Francisco), Apr. 19, 1935, 1.

"Musicians Remembering: The Oral History Project of the Boston Musicians' Association, AFM Local 9-535." *Interlude,* Nov./Dec. 2005, 5–6, 8. Newsletter of Boston's Local 9-535.

"Musicians [sic] Union Isn't in Tune with History." *San Francisco Chronicle,* Dec. 13, 1956, 33.

"Musicians [sic] Union Names Two to Push Merger of Locals." *Chicago Defender,* June 22, 1963, 3.

"Musicians Vote to Merge Chicago Locals." *Los Angeles Sentinel,* Oct. 10, 1963, A18.

Musicland. Newsletter of Seattle's Local 76.

"Must There Be Segregation in the Union?" *Music and Rhythm,* June 1942, 27, 31, 43.

"Mystery Taxi Traced in Theater Bombing." *San Francisco Chronicle,* June 2, 1930, 1.

"NAACP Pickets A. F. of L. Convention." *The Spokesman* (San Francisco), Oct. 4, 1934, 1.

"Negro Musicians Seek Court Ban." *San Francisco Chronicle,* Sept. 2, 1934, 5.

"Negro Plays 'First' Violin: Opponents to Appearance of Musician Apologize." *Baltimore Sun,* Feb. 18, 1963, 11.

"Negro, White Musicians in Unison." *Chicago Defender,* Jan. 12, 1966, 1.

"Negroes Fight Music Union's 'Raid' on Local." *Chicago Tribune,* Sept. 21, 1963, 7.

"Negroes Hit Twice as Hard as Whites by the Depression, Report Shows." *The Spokesman* (San Francisco), Oct. 4, 1934, 5.

Newhouse, Richard H., Jr. "An Opinion on Chicago Union Bias." *Chicago Defender,* Nov. 2, 1963, 9.

Northrup, Herbert R. *Organized Labor and the Negro.* New York: Harper, 1944.

Novak, Matt. "Musicians Wage War Against Evil Robots." *Smithsonian Magazine,*

Feb. 10, 2012. https://www.smithsonianmag.com/history/musicians-wage-war-against-evil-robots-92702721/.

"Oakland Musicians Go to Law When Nordic Group 'Hogs' Good Jobs." *The Spokesman* (San Francisco), Aug. 30, 1934.

Oberdeck, Kathryn J. *The Evangelist and the Impresario: Religion, Entertainment, and Cultural Politics in America, 1884–1914*. Baltimore: Johns Hopkins University Press, 1999.

"Order Merger of Two Music Locals Here." *Chicago Tribune*, Apr. 11, 1964, 12.

The Overture. Newsletter of Los Angeles's Local 47.

"Owners Close Picture House to Musicians." *San Francisco Chronicle*, Mar. 17, 1929, 10.

Owsley, Dennis C. *St. Louis Jazz: A History*. Charleston, SC: The History Press, 2019.

Paul, Maury. "From the Board Room." *The Overture*, May 1952, 11, 37–38. Newsletter of Los Angeles's Local 47.

———. "From the Board Room." *The Overture*, Sept. 1952, 6–7, 35. Newsletter of Los Angeles's Local 47.

———. "From the Board Room," *The Overture*, Nov. 1952, 7. Newsletter of Los Angeles's Local 47.

Peretti, Burton W. *The Creation of Jazz: Music, Race, and Culture in Urban America*. Urbana: University of Illinois Press, 1992.

Peterson, Bernard L., Jr. *A Century of Musicals in Black and White: An Encyclopedia of Musical Stage Works By, About, or Involving African Americans*. Westport, CT: Greenwood Publishing Group, 1993.

Petrillo, James C. Letter to George Meany, April 8, 1958 (unpublished). George Meany Labor Archive, University of Maryland, College Park. Archive collection reference: "Musicians, American Federation of, 1958–1958, RG1-027.9.17, Box 9, folder 17; AFL-CIO Office of the President, President's Files, George Meany, 0061-LBR-RG1-027. Special Collections and University Archives."

"Petrillo Named Head of AFM's Civil-Rights Department." *Downbeat*, Jan. 28, 1965, 10.

"Petrillo Talks!" *Downbeat*, May 16, 1957, 19, 41.

Pillars, Hayes. Interview by Charles E. Rose, 1981. National Ragtime and Jazz Archive, Elijah P. Lovejoy Library, Southern Illinois University, Edwardsville.

Pitts, Robert. "Organized Labor and the Negro in Seattle." MA thesis, University of Washington, 1941.

Powderly, Terence V. *Thirty Years of Labor, 1859 to 1889*. Columbus, OH: Excelsior Publishing House, 1889.

Prelude. Newsletter of New Orleans's Local 174.

Quin, Mike. *The Big Strike*. Olema, CA: Olema Publishing Company, 1949.

Randle, Eddie. Interview by Dan Havens, 1982. National Ragtime and Jazz Archive, Southern Illinois University at Edwardsville.

Randolph, A. Philip, and Chandler Owen. "The Negro—A Menace to Radicalism." *The Messenger,* May/June 1919, 20.

Raskin, A. H. "Meany, in a Fiery Debate, Denounces Negro Unionist." *New York Times,* Sept. 24, 1959, 1, 41.

"Refuse to Bar Music Union Trusteeship." *Chicago Tribune,* Oct. 1, 1964, C7.

Reid, Ira De A. "Lily-White Labor." *Opportunity* 8, no. 6 (June 1930): 170–73, 189.

Reilly, Byron ("Speed"). "Star Stuff: News of Stage, Screen and Radio." *The Spokesman* (San Francisco), Aug. 23, 1934, 2.

"Rejection of Young Violinist Recalls Marian Anderson Snub." *Chicago Defender,* Feb. 11, 1963, 3.

"Remembering Pianist Mabel Robinson Simms." New England Jazz Hall of Fame. Accessed February 7, 2023. http://www.jazzhistorydatabase.com/neja/mabel-robinson-simms.php.

"Report: 25 Musicians Quitting Oak Park Symphony on Race Issue." *Chicago Defender,* Feb. 23, 1963, 4.

"Report of Campaign for Charter Amendment Number 3, 'Save Our Symphony.'" *Musical News* 18, no. 6 (June 1935): 2–3, 5–7. Newsletter of San Francisco's Local 6.

Riesenberg, Felix, Jr. *Golden Gate: The Story of San Francisco Harbor.* New York: Alfred A. Knopf, 1940.

Riesenfeld, Hugo. "Music and Motion Pictures." *Annals of the American Academy of Political and Social Science* 128 (1926): 58–62.

Robinson, Paul. "Race, Space, and the Evolution of Black Los Angeles." In *Black Los Angeles: American Dreams and Racial Realities,* edited by Darnell Hunt and Ana-Christina Ramón, 21–59. New York: New York University Press, 2010.

Roediger, David. *The Wages of Whiteness: Race and the Making of the American Working Class.* London: Verso, 1991.

Rose, Charles Elwin. "The American Federation of Musicians and Its Effect on Black Musicians in St. Louis in the Twentieth Century." MM thesis, Southern Illinois University, 1978.

Roth, Morry. "AFM Rocked by Chi Race Row." *Variety,* Apr. 22, 1964, 129.

Rothstein, Richard. *The Color of Law: A Forgotten History of How our Government Segregated America.* New York: Norton, 2017.

Rubin, Lester, William S. Swift, and Herbert R. Northrup. *Negro Employment in the Maritime Industries: A Study of Racial Policies in the Shipbuilding, Longshore, and Offshore Maritime Industries.* Philadelphia: University of Pennsylvania, 1974.

San Francisco: The Bay and Its Cities. Compiled by Workers of the Writers' Program of the Work Projects Administration in Northern California. New York: Hastings House, 1947.

Saunders, Theodore Dudley. "Red: The Reminiscences of Red Saunders." The Oral History Collection of the Jazz Institute, Rutgers University, 1978.

Schallert, Edwin. "Josephine Baker Captivates First Audiences with Songs, Showmanship." *Los Angeles Times,* July 5, 1951, B9.

———. "Josephine Baker Will Oo-la-la, Bring Rue de la Paix to Coast." *Los Angeles Times*, July 1, 1951, D1.

"Seize Music Union Local." *Chicago Tribune*, Oct. 2, 1964, 3.

Seltzer, George. *Music Matters: The Performer and the American Federation of Musicians*. Metuchen, NJ: Scarecrow Press, 1989.

Shaw, Elijah. Interview by Irene Cortinovis, Aug. 20, 1971. Jazzmen Project, University of Missouri at St Louis.

Shaw, Elijah, and Vivian Oswald. Interview by Irene Cortinovis, May 3, 1972. Jazzmen Project, Oral History Collection (S0829), State Historical Society of Missouri. Accessed February 7, 2023. https://shsmo.org/sites/default/files/pdfs/oral-history/transcripts/s0829/t0109.pdf.

Shipton, Alyn. *Fats Waller: The Cheerful Little Earful*. London: Continuum, 1988.

———. *Groovin' High: The Life of Dizzy Gillespie*. Oxford: Oxford University Press, 1999.

Shishkin, Boris. Memorandum to William F. Schnitzler, Apr. 17, 1958. George Meany Labor Archive, University of Maryland, College Park. Archive collection reference: "Musicians, American Federation of, 1958–1958, RG1-027.9.17, Box 9, folder 17. AFL-CIO Office of the President, President's Files, George Meany, 0061-LBR-RG1-027; Special Collections and University Archives."

Sides, Josh. *L. A. City Limits: African American Los Angeles from the Great Depression to the Present*. Berkeley: University of California Press, 2003.

Sitkoff, Harvard. *A New Deal for Blacks: The Emergence of Civil Rights as a National Issue*, vol. 1, *The Depression Decade*. New York: Oxford University Press, 1978.

Smith, Lloyd. Interview by W. Deane Wiley (1982). National Ragtime and Jazz Archive, Southern Illinois University at Edwardsville.

Smith-Wright, Lovie. "A Brief History of the AFM Diversity Committee and Its Achievements." *International Musician*, Mar. 1, 2021. https://internationalmusician.org/a-brief-history-of-the-afm-diversity-committee-and-its-achievements/.

———. Interview by Leta Miller, June 16, 2021.

Snyder, Robert W. *The Voice of the City: Vaudeville and Popular Culture in New York*. Chicago: Ivan R. Dee, 1989.

"Sound Film." Wikipedia. Accessed February 7, 2023. https://en.wikipedia.org/wiki/Sound_film.

Southern, Eileen. *The Music of Black Americans: A History*. Third edition. New York: W. W. Norton, 1997.

Spear, Allan H. *Black Chicago: The Making of a Negro Ghetto, 1890–1920*. Chicago: University of Chicago Press, 1967.

Spitzer, John, and Neal Zaslaw. *The Birth of the Orchestra: History of an Institution, 1650–1815*. Oxford: Oxford University Press, 2004.

Spitzer, John, ed. *American Orchestras in the Nineteenth Century*. Chicago: University of Chicago Press, 2012.

Spivey, Donald. *Union and the Black Musician: The Narrative of William Everett Samuels and Chicago Local 208*. Lanham, MD: University Press of America, 1984.

Stoddard, Tom. *Jazz on the Barbary Coast.* Berkeley: Heyday Books in conjunction with the San Francisco Traditional Jazz Foundation and the California Historical Society, 1998.

Stripp, Fred. "The Treatment of Negro-American Workers by the AFL and the CIO in the San Francisco Bay Area." *Social Forces* 28, no. 3 (Mar. 1950): 330–32.

Summers, Clyde W. "Admission Policies of Labor Unions." *Quarterly Journal of Economics* 61, no. 1 (Nov. 1946): 66–107.

"Symphony Conductor Quits After Negro Musician Row." *Atlanta Daily World,* Feb. 17, 1963, A6.

Taft, Philip. *The A. F. of L. in the Time of Gompers.* New York: Harper, 1957.

Taylor, Quintard. *The Forging of a Black Community: Seattle's Central District from 1870 through the Civil Rights Era.* Seattle: University of Washington Press, 1994.

"Throng Braves Rain to Hear Roland Hayes." *San Francisco Chronicle,* Dec. 30, 1933, 24.

"Tip Top Club Features Music." *San Francisco Chronicle,* Sept. 20, 1934, 14.

Tournour, Gene. Interview by Leta Miller, June 7, 2021.

Trainor, Ken. "The Symphony Finds Its Place." *Journal of Oak Park and River Forest,* Apr. 15, 2008, updated Feb. 11, 2021. https://www.oakpark.com/2008/04/15/the-symphony-finds-its-place/.

Turner, Diane Delores, "Organizing and Improvising: A History of Philadelphia's Black Musicians' Protective Union Local 274, American Federation of Musicians." PhD diss, Temple University, 1993.

Tuttle, William M., Jr. "Labor Conflict and Racial Violence: The Black Worker in Chicago, 1894–1919." *Labor History* 10, no. 3 (1969): 408–32.

"2 Musicians' Locals Agree to Merge." *New York Times,* Feb. 18, 1960, 15.

"Union Musicians Drop Job Suit." *The Spokesman* (San Francisco), Oct. 12, 1934, 1.

"Union Offers Olive Twig to Oak. Bandmen." *The Spokesman* (San Francisco), Apr. 5, 1935, 1.

Vallillo, Stephen M. "The Battle of the Black Mikados." *Black American Literature Forum* 16, no. 4 (1982): 153–57.

"Village Board Deplores Bias in Orchestra." *Chicago Tribune,* Feb. 12, 1963, 6.

"Voluntary Segregation Held Not Illegal Discrimination." *Ohio State Law Journal* 24 (1963): 412–16.

Walton, Charles E. *Bronzeville Conversations: The Tempo of the Times: The Struggle for an Integrated Musician's Union.* Unpublished manuscript, 1993.

Walton, Lester. "Colored Musicians Invited to Join Musical Union." *New York Age,* Mar. 26, 1914, 6.

Washington, Booker T. "The Negro and the Labor Unions." *The Atlantic,* June 1913: 756–67.

Watkins, Earl. Interviews by Leta Miller and Alyssa Roedig, Aug. 14 and 27, 2006.

Watson, Ted. "AFL Ruling Upsets Unmixed AFM Local." *New Pittsburgh Courier,* Aug. 24, 1963, 20.

———. "Integration Mix-Up Hits Chicago AFM." *New Pittsburgh Courier*, July 27, 1963, 20.

Weber, Joseph. "Highly Important for Local Union Officers and Members Generally to Cooperate with Newspapers Sponsoring Propaganda for Cause of Art—Event Successful in Five Cities." *International Musician* 29, no. 6 (Dec. 1931), 1.

———. "Living Music Day." *International Musician* 29, no. 8 (Feb. 1932), 1–2.

———. "President Weber's Annual Report." *International Musician* 28, no. 12 (June 1931), 1, 8–10.

Wesley, Charles. "Organized Labor and the Negro." In *Anthology of American Negro Literature*, edited by V. F. Calverton, 339–62. New York: Modern Library, 1929.

Whisler, Weldon. "Applaud Orchestra, Negro Girl: Concert Ends Oak Park Row." *Chicago Tribune*, Feb. 18, 1963, 1.

"White and Colored Musicians Separate." *The Presto: A Weekly Music Journal of the Times* 822 (Apr. 10, 1902): 1.

"White Unions Hit for Discrimination by Judge." *California Eagle*, Sept. 21, 1934, 2.

Wilkerson, Isabel. *Caste: The Origins of Our Discontents*. New York: Random House, 2020.

Williams, Fred. Interview by Leta Miller, July 12, 2019.

Wolfe, F. E. *Admission to American Trade Unions*. Baltimore: The Johns Hopkins Press, 1912.

Woll, Allen. *Black Musical Theatre: From Coontown to Dreamgirls*. Baton Rouge: Louisiana State University Press, 1989.

Wollenberg, Charles. "James vs. Marinship: Trouble on the New Black Frontier." *California History* 60, no. 3 (Fall 1981): 262–79.

Woodward, C. Vann. *The Strange Career of Jim Crow*. Commemorative edition, Oxford University Press, 2002. Originally published in 1955, with revisions in 1957, 1966, and 1974.

Wriggle, John. "Chappie Willet, Frank Fairfax, and Phil Edwards' Collegians: From West Virginia to Philadelphia." *Black Music Research Journal* 27/1 (Spring 2007): 1–22.

Wright, Jon. "Organized Labor and Seattle's African American Community: 1916–1920." Civil Rights and Labor History Consortium, University of Washington, 1999. Accessed February 7, 2023. https://depts.washington.edu/labhist/strike/wright.shtml.

Young, Marl. "Amalgamation of Locals 47 and 767." *The Overture* (Los Angeles Local 47), Mar. 1999. Reprinted. Accessed February 7, 2023. https://afm47.org/archives/amalgamation.html.

Index

References in *italics* refer to illustrations and tables.
Bold references (used sparingly) indicate major discussions.
Endnotes are only referenced if they provide supplementary information.
Data in the tables are only referenced for entries cited elsewhere in the text.

Absher, Amy, 164n14, 177nn31–32, 182n11; on Chicago music, 49, 147; on Chicago unemployment, 163n8; on Local 10-208, 178n45
activism, Black: Black locals and, **42–45**; in post-World War I era, **42–45**
actors, as laborers, 6, 11
Actors Equity Association (AEA), 6
Actors' Society of America, 6
Adams, James, 3
Adams, Placide, 180n10
African Americans: of Boston, 8, **140–42**; of Chicago, **46–50**, **124–31**, 147; cohesive action among, 152; following *Plessy v. Ferguson*, 13–14; of Los Angeles, **97–100**, 146–47; of New Orleans, **135–39**; Northern migration of, 44; organized labor and, **16–23**, 45, 48, 54, 55, 150; participation in labor strikes, 8, **19**, 23, 48, 73; of San Francisco, **50–54**, **72–83**; of Seattle, **54–58**, 164n30; of St. Louis, 4, 12–13, **66–72**; World War II service, 90. *See also* bands, Black; locals, Black AFM; musicians, Black

Aikens, Lou, 134
Alley, Vernon, 77; on Local 6 board, 122–23
"The All-Negro Hour" (WSBC, Chicago), 49, 164n14
amalgamation, AFL with CIO, 18, 24
amalgamation, within the AFM, 1–5, *114–16*; AFL-CIO and, 120; AFM mandates for, 6, 111, 136, 143, 145; artistic difference in, 154; Barnett's attempts for, **64–65**, 167n28; benefits of, 2, 47, 127, 132, 144, 146; Black locals' attempts, **64–66**, 89–93; Black locals' disempowerment in, 110–11; Black locals' resistance to, 1, 2–3, 33, 50, 64, 103, **112–13**, *117*, **117–18**, 123, 143; disadvantages for Black locals, 2–3, 47, 90, 104, 110–11, 119, 121, 127, 149; IEB and, 1, 65–66, 111, 137, 140, 179n69; independent negotiations for, 145; individualism/collectivism in, 154; instigated by locals, 142–43; Local 2-197 (St. Louis), 140; Locals 6 and 669 (San Francisco), 7–8, 89, 117, **121–23**, 143, 176n21, 177n25; Local 9-535 (Boston), **140–42**, 148; Local 10-208 (Chicago), 29, 50, 64, 87, **124–31**, 132, 144, 178n45, 179nn65,69; Local 16-248 (Newark), 162n33; Locals 43, 533, and 92 (Buffalo), 65, **144–45**,

amalgamation (*continued*)
181n41; Locals 47 and 767 (Los Angeles), 29, 98, **100–110**, 113, 143, 153, 174nn14–15,21–23, 175nn36–37,45–46; Local 76-493 (Seattle), **64–65, 120–21**; Locals 77 and 274 (Philadelphia), **1, 3–4**; Local 161-710 (Washington, DC), **132–35**; Local 174-496 (New Orleans), **135–38**, *139*, 180n9, 181nn17,24; loss of clubhouses in, 147; loss of identity in, 118, 134, 146; loss of members following, 148; mixed results of, 146; overlapping jurisdictions and, 151, 152–53; petition against, **113, 117–18**; processes of, **142–45**; resolution at convention to mandate, **113, 117, 119–20**

American Federation of Labor (AFL): amalgamation with CIO, 18, 24; Black labor and, **22–27**, 80–81; Committee of Five, 81; Federal Unions policy, 25–26; Federated Unions, 26, 28; founding of, 11, 22; NLM and, 9, 11–12; opposition to racial exclusion, 23–24; race relations within, 8; racial ineffectiveness of, **22–27**; Randolph's protests at, 24, 80–81; role in AFM's rise, 9, 11; whites-only members, 23–24, 26–28, 81

American Federation of Labor (AFL)-CIO: and AFM mergers, 120; constitution of, 113; exclusionary rules, 123

American Federation of Labor (AFL) conventions: anti-discrimination resolutions, 26–27, 160n78, 161n82; Black representatives to, 26–27; Resolution 5 (1920), 26–27, 161n82; Resolution 37 (1920), 27; resolutions of 1934, 81, 170n102

American Federation of Musicians (AFM): aesthetic preferences and, 37; under AFL, 6, 8, **9–14**; agreements with other unions, 16; casual engagements under, 15, 153; challenges to end segregation, **89–93**; *Charter Book*, 29, *32*, 33, 112, *114, 116,* 138; Civil Rights Department, 134, 149; constitution of, 13; contracting method, 15; control over engagements, 14; crisis of 1920s, 37–38; definition of "professional," 14, 35–39, 158n28; Diversity Award program, 4, 150; Diversity Council, 4, 135, 149–50; dominance of, **14–16**; educational outreach, 150; effectiveness for varied ensembles, 15; effect of sound films on, 61–62; ethnic equitability in, 4; founding of, 9, **12–16**; Gompers's initiative toward, 9, 11, 12–13; growth of, 14; institutional history of, 5; local/national balance in, 7, 15; mandates for amalgamation, 6, 34, 58, 111, **113–18**, 143, 145; membership requirements, 14, 36; Music Defense League, 63; negotiations with Ringling Brothers, 39; predecessors of, **10–16**; privileging of white locals, 58, 70, 80, 152; promotion of "Live Music," 63; recruitment efforts, 34; Resolution of May 1922, 38, 162n19; segregation in, 13, 22, 28, 47, 54, 65, 106; systematic racism and, 4, 7–8; traveling musicians under, 16, 92, 119–20, 158n38; unemployment during the Depression, 62, 166n17. *See also* amalgamation, AFM; locals, AFM; subsidiaries

American Federation of Musicians (AFM) conventions: Black representation at, 2, 4, 12, 13, **40–41**, 49, 64, 65, 84, 87, 90–91, 110–11, 117, 119, 121, 130, 138, 141, 145, 149, 152, 162n24; *Official Proceedings* of, 13, 14, *32*, 33, 34, 68–69, 85, 112, *114, 115,* 130; Resolution 34 (requiring amalgamation), **113, 117, 119–20**, 144; subsidiaries' representation at, 70; voting rights, 16, 158n36

American Federation of Musicians (AFM) International Executive Board (IEB), 1, 3, *32*; abolition of Black subsidiaries, **84–91**, *88*, 153; amalgamation efforts, 65–66, 111, 113, *116*; anti-segregation actions, 90–91; dispute with Local 274, **1, 3**; and Locals 6, 648, and 669 (San Francisco), 82, 87, 121; in Local 9-535 (Boston) merger, 140; in Local 10-208 (Chicago) merger, 130–31, 179n69; in Locals 47 and 767 (Los Angeles) merger, 109–10; in Local 174-496 (New Orleans) merger, 137; and Local 814 (Cincinnati), 123, 140; revocation of charters, 29, 33–34; in Seattle locals dispute, **57–58**, 70; segregated locals

and, 70, 152–53; on Subsidiary Local 2, 66, **68–69**
Anderson, Carol, 126, 177n33
Anderson, John, 103
Anderson, Leon, 126
Anderson, Marian, 75, 169n79; with Chicago Symphony, 87, 171n12
Anthony, David, xi; on monoethnic aggregations, 151, 152
Armant, Alexander, 47
Armstrong, Louis, 49; riverboat engagements, 136
Arnesen, Eric, 27, 160n71, 161n85; on biracial unionism, 28; on Black locals' advantages, 35, 38, 39, 40
the arts, hierarchization related to gender, 162n14
the arts, "high": adaptation to audiences, 36–37; AFM's engagement with, 37
auditions: AFM requirement and challenges for Black musicians, **35–39**; classical Western canon in, 36, 37–38, 41, 54; criteria for Black musicians, 38; genre-based, 4; modification of by New York Local 310, 42; as preventing Black membership in Local 6 (San Francisco), **52–54**

Bagley, C. L., 109
Bailey, Edward, 91, 100
Bailey, Lester, *109*
Bailey, William, 91
Baker, Josephine, 102, 124
Ballard, Stanley, 174n45
Bands and orchestras, Black: credentials of, 163n6; movie theater work, 60–61, 63, 165n1; popularity of, 54, 75; radio engagements, 71; on riverboats, 39, 62, 68, 70–71; travel problems, 92; white patrons of, 54, 62
bands, interracial, 3, 67, 92, 140 153
Baranco, Wilbert, 77, 77, 82, 83
Bardi, Gina, xi
Barfield, Bob, 77
Barnett, Powell, 5, *55*, 57, 128, 151; and amalgamation attempts, **64–65**, 119, 167n29,30; and Local 533 (Buffalo), 65; and Local 76 (Seattle), 54, 57, 64; and Local 76-493 merger, **120–21**; and Local 493, 58
Barry, Thomas, 159n57

Basie, Count: movie theater work, 60
Benny, Jack, 181n28
Benny Carter Orchestra, 99
Bigard, Barney, 100
Black Codes, 17, 23
Black Railway Coach Cleaners, challenges to segregation, 27
blacksmiths, whites-only policy, 24, 96, 160n68
Bloch, Herman, 20–21
Blue Devils (band), *71*, 72, 168n56
Boilermakers' Union: Black auxiliaries of, 94; Joseph James's challenge to in *James v Marinship*, **94–95**; Rhode Island lawsuit against, 173n37
booking agencies, national, 6, 16
Boston: AFM locals of, 8, *30*, 40, *115*, **140–42**, 148; symphony, 7
Bowman, Gordon, x, 141, 148
Brotherhood of Locomotive Firemen and Engineers, barriers to Black members, 124
Brotherhood of Railway Carmen, racial exclusion policy, 27, 96
Brotherhood of Railway Clerks, whites-only, 27, 81, 96
Brotherhood of Railway Trainmen, barriers to Black members, 124
Brotherhood of Sleeping Car Porters (BSCP), in AFL, 24, 160n71
Brown, Pat, 122
Browne, Walter, 122, 177n24
Brown v. Board of Education (1954), 2, 118
Bryant, Clora, 5, 98
Bryant, David, 103
Buffalo, AFM locals of, *30*, 65, 84, *115*, **144–48**
Burke, Sonny, 90
Burton, Joe, 180n10
Buxton (Iowa), AFM local in, *30*, **34–35**

Cadrez, Florence, 103
California, Fair Employment Practices Act (1959), 122, 143
California Eagle, on Local 6/648 conflict, 80
Callender, Red, 119
Calverton, V. F. (George Goetz), 44
Camel Caravan (radio variety show), 99
Carter, Benny, 99, 103, 104, 105, 110, 119
Carter, Marva, 169n78

Index   203

Casey, John, 80
Center for Economic and Policy Research, on Black unionization, 150
Charles McDaniel Youth Award (AFM), 150, 182n15
Charles Walton Diversity Advocate Award (AFM), 150
Chesterton, Cecil: *A History of the United States*, 43
Chicago: amalgamation of Locals 10 and 208, **124–31**; Black AFM locals of, 28–29, *30*, **47–50**, 58, 62, *114*, **124–31**; Black employment in, 163n8; Black musicians of, 35; Black population of, 46, 49, 50; club culture of, 46, 49; race riot of 1919, 50; racial exclusion in, 125; South Side music scene, 49, 147; symphony, 7. *See also* Local 10; Local 10-208; Local 208; Petrillo
The Chicago Defender: on Chicago merger, 127; on Local 6/648 conflict, 76, 80
Chicago Musical Society (CMS), NLM affiliation of, 48
Chicago Musicians for Harmonious Integration (CMHI): 127, 129–30
Chicago Musicians for Union Democracy, 128
Chicago and North Western Railroad, 34
Chicago Symphony, 7, 87, 171n12
CIO, 18; amalgamation with AFL, 24; Committee to Abolish Racial Discrimination, 93; formation of, 81, 170n103. *See also* American Federation of Labor (AFL)-CIO
cities, U.S.: desegregation efforts in, 111; housing restrictions in, 110, 146, 149; population of, *51*; ranked by size, 173n2
Civil Rights Act (1964), 2; Title VII, 3
Civil War: Black labor following, 17, 23; wage-labor economy following, 158n41
Clancy, George, 175n45
Clark, John F., 21
classical canon, Western: in AFM entrance exams, 36, **37–38**, 41, 54
Clef Club (New York), labor exchange at, **41**
Cleveland, Ohio, *51*; orchestra, 7; Local 550, *30*, 50, 84, *114*, 143, 181n36
Club Alabam (Los Angeles), 99

Club DeLisa (Chicago), band of, 87, 124, *125*
Cobble, Dorothy, 12, 157n11; on inflated AFL dues for Blacks, 26
Cole, Nat "King," 119; trio of, 99
Collette, Buddy, 110, 119, 151; audition for Million Dollar Theater, 101; on Groucho Marx show, 101; in Local 767 elections, 103; on merger benefits, 146; on merger of Locals 47 and 767 (Los Angeles), **100–104**, 174nn14,21, 175n42
Columbus, Ohio: Local 589, *30*, 40, 47, 50, *114*, 143, 168n66
Commons, John, 14
Compromise of 1877, 17
Congress of Trade Unions, 158n42
Consolidation Coal Company (Buxton, Ohio), 34
Cooke, P. S., 91
coon songs, **13–14**
Cooper, Jack L., 49
Cortinovis, Irene, 68, 70
Cosby, Harper, 110
Cotter, John, 70, 72
Cottrell, Louis, 137, 180n9
Countryman, Vern, 14, 15; on Local 310 dispute, 38; on NLM affiliates, 156n9, 157n17; on travel cards, 158n38
craft unions: admission processes, 36; versus industrial organizations, 18, 81; whites-only, 17, 26
Cramton, Lou, 92
The Crisis (NAACP journal), 42
Crothers, Bob, x

Davis, Hal, 130, 179n80; in Local 9-535 (Boston) merger, 140; in Local 10-208 (Chicago) merger, **129–30, 131**; in Local 43-533 (Buffalo) merger, 144; and Local 274 (Philadelphia), 1
Davis, Leo, 103, 104
Dawn Club (San Francisco), Black musicians at, 82–83
De Bueris, Eugene, 162n27
Denov, Sam, 128
Denver, Black locals of (Locals 753 and 623), *31*, *114*, 166n25, 168n53, 181n36
DeRienzo, Daniel F., ix, *32*
Detroit, Michigan, 11, 47, *51*; Local 5, 42, 92, 110

Dexter, Dave, 92
Dickerson, Lowell Dwight, "Central Avenue Meets Hollywood," 174n14
Dickman, Therese, x
Dietrich, Karl, 78
Dixon, Anita, x
Dorman, James, 14
Douglass, Bill, 103, 104, 110, 119, 174n29
Downbeat, 84, 99; on AFM racial tension, 91, 92; on Los Angeles discrimination, 99–100
Du Bois, W. E. B., 42, 158n42; on Black labor alienation, 48
Ducker, Otis, x, *133*, 179n1, 180n3; Diversity Council chairmanship, 149; on Local 161-710 (Washington, DC) merger, **132–35**
Dulf, George Edmund: on chartering of Local 208 (Chicago), **47–49**
Duncan, James, 23
Dunne, Arthur B., 78, 170n93
Dunne, Peter, 170n93
Dunne and Dunne (law firm), 78, 80, 81
Dwight's Journal, 37
Dyett, Walter, 87, 131

East Bay Chorus, 93–94
Ebbins, Milton, 90
Eckstine, Billy, 101
Edises, Pele, 172n28
Edson, Estelle, 103, 104, *109*; "The Negro in Radio," 102
Eighth Illinois National Guard Regimental Band, 47
Ellington, Duke, 92, 100; in Los Angeles, 99
Elliott, Gretchen, x
eugenics, 43
Europe, James Reese: Clef Club, Tempo Club, and possible Black local in New York, **41**
Eva Jessye Choir, 93
Executive Order 8802 (Fair Employment Act, FDR, 1941), 92–93
Executive Order 9346 (FDR, 1943), 93

Fair Employment Act (Executive Order 8802 by FDR, 1941), 92–93
fair employment legislation, **120–24**, 143, 153, 177n29
fair employment acts: California, 122, 143; Connecticut and Massachusetts, 177n29; Ohio, 123
Fair Employment Practices Committee (FEPC), 93, 120
Fannin, Mike, 8
Farmer, Art, 147
federal government, anti-discrimination acts, 92–93
Federal Unions (AFL), 25–26
Federated Unions (AFL), 26
Ferdon's Quaker Medicine Show Band, 52
Ferrell, Frank J., 20, *21*
Ferrone, Jon, ix
Fielding, Jerry, 101
Fields, John R. (Local 44, Great Western Union of Colored Musicians, St. Louis), 12, 13, 157nn15, 19
Fink, Gary, 14, 156n9
Fisher, Bud, 77
Fletcher, Tom, 41–42
Forbes, Alex, 88, 91
"forbidden territory" rulings (unfair lists): in Miami, 91; in San Francisco, 74, 82, 169n75; in Seattle, 58
Francis, Henry, x, 141
Frank, Dana, 56
Franklin, John Hope, 43
Freight Handlers, Station and Express Employees' Union (Richmond), 26–27

Gargan, Edward A., 147
Garner, George, 75
Gatt Brothers, dance halls of, 56
gender, hierarchization of arts to, 162n14
Gill, Elmer, 147
Gleason, Ralph, 121
Goldberg, Jacob, 42
Gompers, Sadie, 11
Gompers, Samuel, *10*, 55, 67; AFM initiative for, 9, 11, **12–13**; appeal to blacksmiths, 160n68; concern for performers, 11; knowledge of music, 11, 12; and NLM, 12; racial initiatives under, **23–26**, 27, 160n78
Goodman, Benny: interracial orchestra of, 92
Grand Terrace Cafe (Chicago), 102
Grant, Madison: *The Passing of the Great Race*, 43

Graves, Elma, 121
Gray, Harry, 91; conflict with Marl Young, 102, 129; and Local 10-208 (Chicago) merger negotiations, **127–31**; presidency of Local 208 (Chicago), 127
Gray, Perry, 144
Great Depression, 1; AFM during, 4; musicians' unemployment during, **62–64**, 72–73; Locals 6 and 648 (San Francisco) during, 53–54
Great Western Union of Colored Musicians (later Local 44, St. Louis), 12, 13, 28. *See also* Local 44
Green, Anna, 14
Green, William, 81
Green Pastures, 93
Griffith, David Wark: *The Birth of a Nation*, 43
Grimes, John, x
Grob, Gerald, 24
Guyton, Lawrence, 180n10

Halker, Clark, 49, 163nn6,10
Hall Johnson Choir, 93
Hampton, Lionel, 102
Harris, George, 140
Harris, William, 175n45
Harrison, George M., 81
Hayes, Roland, 75
Haywood, Jack, 78
Hershman-Tcherepnin, Sue-Ellen, ix, 8, 142
hierarchies, cultural: Black musicians and, 2, 6, 36
Hill et al., v. International Brotherhood of Boilermakers, 173n37
Hinton, Milt, 5, 49
Hirschmann, I. A., 62
Hodges, Earl, 91
Hoffman, Frederick L.: *Race Traits*, 157n23
Holland, Milt, 101
Holmes, Sean P.: *Weaver of Dreams*, 156n15
Hot Club (Kansas City), interracial events at, 92
House Un-American Activities Committee, 101
housing restrictions, 110; relaxation of, 146, 149
Hover, Hiram F.: assassination attempt on, 21, 159n58

Howard, Paul, 103, 104
Humanist Symphony (Los Angeles), 101–2
Hunter, Bob, 127
Hurd, Patty, 135
Hutcheson, William, 81, 170n103

Imperato, Mimi, 80
improvisation, musical, 7, 37, 54, 59, 101, 121
Interlude (Local 9-535, Boston, newsletter), 8, *142*
International Alliance of Theatrical Stage Employees, 16
International Musician (AFM monthly), *32*, 33, 84, *85*, 161n2
Isoardi, Steven, 98

Jackson, Al, 138
Jackson, Dewey, 68
Jackson, Mr., 52
Jackson, Ray, 65, 84
James, Joseph, *95*, 172n28, 173n35; lawsuit to end segregation in the boilermakers' union, **94–95**; as singer, **93–94**, *95*; as welder, 94
James v. Marinship, **94–95**
The Jazz Singer, 166n9
Jerde, Curtis, 135
Johnson, James Weldon, 41, 42, 43
Johnson, Smokey, 180n10
Johnson, Warren, x
Jolson, Al, 166n9

Kansas City, 8, 90; Black AFM locals of, *30*, 70, 92, 166n25
Kansas City Star, racial reconciliation series, 8
Keeton, Elmer, 93–94
Keith, Benjamin Franklin: booking agency of, 6, 156n17
Keller, David, x, 164n25, 165nn35,39, 167n28; on amalgamation efforts in Seattle, 64; on Barnett, 64, 167n29 167nn29,30; on Seattle, 54–55, 56, 147
Kelso, Jackie (Jack Kelson), 5, 98
Kenin, Herman, 129–30, 143, 175n45; death of, 131; and dual locals, 128; in Local 43/533 merger, 65, 144; in Local 174/496 merger, 137, 138
Kennedy, Charles ("Pop"), 122
Kennedy, Thomas F.: and segregated locals, 47–48

Kerngood, William J., 81–82
Kessler-Harris, Alice, 158n41; *Perspectives on American Labor History*, 156n14
Kibler, M. Alison, 156n17
King, Clarence, 78, 86–87
King, Martin Luther, Jr., 182n17
Kinsler, Julie, 101
Knights of Labor: decline of, 22; progressive agenda of, **19–20**, 159n55; racial inclusiveness of, **20–22**; Southern, 20
Koltun, Alexander, 104
Konrad, Robert, 104
Kraft, James, 156n9
Kuhlau, Friedrich, 101
Ku Klux Klan, 43, 137

labor: immigrant, 17–18; industrial organization of, 18, 81
labor, Black: AFL and, **22–27**; of Buxton, Iowa, 34; collective bargaining by, 27; competition with white workers, 17, 18; following Civil War, 17, 23; in industrial organization, **18–19**, 81; labor relations, 8; during strikes, 8, 19, 23, 48, 73, 159n61; unionization and, **16–22**, 26, 150; under white supremacy, 17
labor, organized: Black distrust of, **20–23**, 45, 48, 54, 55, 150; Black workers in, 58–59; economic class and, **16–17**; race and, **16–22**
laborers: lived experiences of, 5; musicians as, 6, 11
labor history, scholarship on, 5
LaFerne, H., 82–83
Laifer, Stephen, 35, 136
Lammers, Candace, ix, 176n2
Landers, Samuel, 122
Landrum-Griffin Act (1959), 128
Lasley, Bob, 180n10
Law, H. B. "Bob," 127
Lee, Tom, 135, 149
Leiter, Richard D., 39, 156n9
LeProtti, Sid, 5; audition for Local 6, 52, *53*, 54
Levine, Lawrence, 2, 161n14; on artistic eclecticism, 36–37
Lewis, Earl, 27
Lewis, Ernie, 138
Lewis, John L., 81
The Liberator (socialist magazine), 44

Little Rock, subsidiary local of, 88
Living Music Days (LMD), 63
Local 2 (AFM, St. Louis), 13, *30, 88*; subsidiary Local 2, creation of, 34, **66–72**; white membership, 34
Local 5 (AFM, Detroit), discriminatory actions in, 92, 110
Local 6 (AFM, San Francisco), 7, *31*, **72–83**, 96; auditions at, **52–53**, 54, 59; Black members of, 46, 52; blocking of Black local, 41, 46, **50, 52–53**; conflict with Local 648, 72, **74–78**, *79*, **80–83**; control over engagements, 14; death benefits, 121; embezzlement by Eddie Love, **86–87**; in General Strike Committee (1934), 73; during Great Depression, 53–54; lawsuit against Nasser Brothers' theaters, 61; Local 648's injunction against, 78, *79*, 80–82, 170nn90,105; merger with Local 669, 7–8, *31*, 89, 96, 117, **121–23**, 143, 176n21, 177n25; strike by, 52, 164n21; subsidiary Local 6, 34, **82–83**, *89*; subsidiary/parent relationship, **87–89**; unemployment in, 72; unionization requests to, 50, 52
Local 9 (AFM, Boston), *30*, merger with Local 535, **140–42**, 148; pay scale of, 141
Local 9-535 (AFM, Boston), 8, 142
Local 10 (AMF, Chicago), *30*, appeal of merger, 130–31; Chicago Musicians for Union Democracy in, 128; CMHI in, 127; conflict with movie houses, 62; death benefits, 127; exclusion of Blacks, 35, 46, **47–48**, 85; factional dispute within, 48, 58; membership numbers, 85, 128, 171n3; merged officers, 130–31; merger with Local 208, 29, *30*, 50, 64, 87, *114*, **124–31**, 132, 144, 178n45, 179nn65,69; negotiations with Local 208, **128–30**; size of, 87; trusteeship for, 131
Local 10-208 (AFM, Chicago), 131; officers, 130, 179n71
Local 16 (AFM, Newark), 42
Local 30 (AFM, St. Paul), 63
Local 43 (AFM, Buffalo): merger with Local 533, *30*, 65, *115*, **144–45**, 181n41; rejection of merger, 144–45
Local 44 ("Great Western Union of Colored Musicians," St. Louis), *30*, 157nn11,19; AFL charter of, **12–13**,

Local 44 (*continued*)
47; national representation for, 40; revocation of charter, 34, **66–68, 70, 72**, 168n55; subsidiary of Local 2, **66–72**

Local 47 (AFM, Los Angeles): amalgamation resolution, 113, *117*, **119–20**; bylaws of, 107; Committee for Amalgamation, 108; death benefit of, 105; denial of Black members, 100; elections of 1952, 106, 108; financial resources of, 104; initiation fees, 105, 106; Life Membership status, 105; membership numbers, 98, 178n56; merger with Local 767, 29, *31*, 98, **100–110**, 113, *114*, 118, 143, 144, 153, 174nn14–15,21–23, 175nn36–37,45–46; Musician's Committee for Integration (MCI), 119–20; Musicians Club, 105, 106, 107; pay scale of, 107; preferential treatment status, 105–6; property rights of, 106; racism in, 110

Local 76 (AFM, Seattle), *30*, Black members of, 54–55; dispute with Local 458, **54–58**; IEB appeal, 57–58, 70; imposition of conditions on Blacks, 152; merger with Local 493, *30, 114*, 120–21; pay scale of, 55, 56; racism of, 56; segregated facilities of, 54–55; supervision of Local 493, 58, 152

Local 77 (AFM, Philadelphia), **1, 3–4**, *116*, 118, theater work of, 61

Local 92 (AFM, Buffalo), *115*, 145

Local 138 (AFM, Brockton Mass.), jurisdictional rights of, 140

Local 161 (AFM, Washington, DC): merger with Local 710, *31, 115*, **132–35**; negotiations for merger, 134; pay scale of, 134

Local 161-710 (AFM, Washington, DC), 149; officers of, 135

Local 174 (AFM, New Orleans): merger negotiations, 136–38; merger with Local 496, *30, 32, 115*, **135–39**, 180n9, 181nn17,24; pay scale of, 136–37

Local 197 (AFM, St. Louis), *30, 88*, 9, *115*; size of, 87

Local 208 (AFM, Chicago), **28-29**, *30*, 41, 62, 102; assets of, 129; chartering of, *30*, **47–48**, 161n2; dissatisfaction with leadership, 129; formation of, 28, 46; growth and influence of, 29, 49; membership numbers, 40, 48, 49, 87, 98, 112, 163n10, 171n11; merger with Local 10, 29, 50, 64, 87, *114*, **124–31**, 132, 144, 178n45, 179nn65,69; national representation for, 40, 49; negotiations with Local 10, **128–30**; tensions within, 125

Local 242 (AFM, New Orleans), suspension of, 29, *30*

Local 253 (AFM, East Liverpool, Ohio), chartering of, 29, *30*, 161n2

Local 274 (AFM, Philadelphia), *30*, 33; demise of, **1, 4**; formation of, 1, *30*, 155n2; interracial membership, 3–4; resistance to merger, **1, 3–4**, 112, *116*, 140, 145; revocation of charter, 1, 112; segregation lawsuit of, 3–4, 155n11

Local 305 (AFM, Buxton, Iowa), *30*, 34, 161n8

Local 310 (AFM, New York), 162n30; blocking of Black local, **41–42**; entrance requirements, 38, 59; revocation of charter, 38; transfer card dispute of, **38–39**

Local 335 (AFM, Hartford), *32*, 112, *116*, 176n2

Local 400 (AFM, Hartford), 176n2

Local 458 (AFM, Seattle), *30*, **54–58**; competing factions in, 56–57; complaints of racism, 56–57; dispute with Local 76, **54–58**; revocation of charter, 57, 165nn35,39

Local 465 (AFM, Mobile, Alabama), *31, 33, 115*, 136

Local 471 (AFM, Pittsburgh), *30*, 50, 65, *114*

Local 473 (AFM, Dayton), 29, *30*, *115*

Local 493 (AFM, Seattle): amalgamation efforts, 64–65; chartering of, *30*, 58, 165n39; clubhouse of, 147; Local 76's supervision of, 58; merger with Local 76, *114*, **120–21**

Local 496 (AFM, New Orleans), *30, 32*, building of, 138; memorabilia from, 138; merger negotiations, 137–38; merger with Local 174, *30, 115*, **136–38**, *139*, 180n9, 181nn17,24; opposition to merger, 137–38, *139*; pay scale of, 136–37

Local 533 (AFM, Buffalo), *30*, 65; "Colored Musicians Club," 147, *148*; merger with Local 43, *115*, **144–45**, 181n41

Local 535 (AFM, Boston), *30*, 35; merger with Local 9, *115*, **140–42**, 148;

national representation for, 40; opposition to merger, 141–42; pay scale of, 141; white musicians in, 141
Local 584 (Paducah, KY), *30*, 136
Local 587 (AFM, Milwaukee), *32*, 65, *114*
Local 589 (AFM, Columbus, Ohio), *32*, *114*; national representation for, 40
Local 591 (AFM, Philadelphia), 1, *30*, 161n4; suspension of, 33
Local 627 (AFM, Kansas City), membership of, *30*, 92, *115*
Local 635 (AFM, Dayton, then Lexington): merger with Local 554, *115*; suspension of charter, 29, *88*
Local 648 (AFM, San Francisco), *31*, 53; conflict with Local 6, 34, **74–83**; injunction against Local 6, 78, *79*, 80–82, 86, 170nn90,105; Love's attack on, 73; revocation of charter, 70, 72, **81–82**
Local 655 (AFM, Miami), *116,* slowdown tactics, 91
Local 669 (AFM, San Francisco): charter of, *31*, *88*, 91, 122; interracial makeup of, 122; merger with Local 6, 7–8, **89**, *114*, **117**, **121–23**, 143, 176n21; size of, 87, 89
Local 690 (AFM, Miami), 91, *116*; cancellation of charter, 172n21
Local 710 (AFM, Washington, DC), *31;* member/employer negotiations, 132; merger with Local 161, **115,** **132–35**; officers' salaries, 132; pay scale, 134; premises of, 133–34, 135; records of, 132; white members of, 133
Locals 745 and 743 (AFM, Sioux City), *31*, 33, *114*, 143, 176n5
Local 767 (AFM, Los Angeles), *31*, 161n4; Amalgamation Committee, 104, 105, 107; Constitution, 108; death benefits, 105, 110; elections, 103, 108; finances, 104, 105, 107; headquarters of, 99, 110; initiation fees, 108; internal disagreements in, 107; membership size, 87, 98; merger with Local 47, 29, 98, **100–110**, 113, *114*, 118, 143, 153, 174nn14–15,21–23, 175nn36–37,45–46; negative effects of merger, 146; opposition to merger, 143; racial discrimination against, 100; rejection of Local 47 proposal, 106
Local 802 (AFM, New York), 42, 90; dispute with International, 38–39; grants to indigent members, 62; membership numbers, 98, 128, 178n56
Local 814 (AFM, Cincinnati), *31*; opposition to merger, 117, 123, 140, 145; revocation of charter, 33, 112, *116*, 123
locals, AFM: admission requirements, 35–38; audition process, 15, 36, 54; Black/white competition among, 2, 46–47, 54; "clubs" of, 105; constraints over membership, 15; death benefits, 105, 106, 110, 121, 127; denial of membership, 16; dual structure, 28, 47, 90, 92, 106, 119, 128, 152; duplicate numbering of, 29; examination boards of, 36, 38; instigation of mergers, 142–43; membership fees, 106; powers of, 15; property rights, 106, 107, 121; racial composition of, 15; seniority benefits, 106; unequal rights in, 106; voting power of, 16; white dominance of, 152–53. *See also* subsidiaries; individual AFM locals (listed by number)
locals, Black AFM: advantages of, 2, 3, **35–39**, 47, 118, 127; autonomy of, 2, 16, 86, 152; benefits of amalgamation for, 2, 35, 47, 127, 132, 144, 146; Black activism and, 42–45; calls for amalgamation, 89–93; challenges of, 4; chartered 1897–1927, *30*–*32*; under Civil Rights Act, 3; clubhouses, 147, 151; community within, 110, 118, 151; competition with white locals, 2; disadvantages of amalgamation for, 2–3, 12, 35, 47, 90, 104, 110, **118–19**, 121, 127, 146, 154; effectiveness of, 27, 151; entrance exams, 36–38; examination boards, 38; following World War I, 34–35; goals of, 5; impediments to formation, 58–59; impetus for, 28, **34–40**, 58; jurisdictional disputes of, 151; of later twentieth century, 140; local club environments of, 118; of mid-twentieth century, 112–30; numbering system, 29; number of, 29, 120, 140; officials' salaries, 50, 119, 127, 129; origins and growth of, 4, 89; pay scales, 39–40, 85–86; refusal to merge, 33, 143; representation at national conventions, 2, 40–41, 84, 87, 149, 162n24; requirements of, 16; resistance to amalgama-

Index 209

locals, Black AFM (*continued*)
tion, 1, 29, 33, 50, 64, 103, 112–13, *117*, **117–18**, 123, 143, 144, 151–52; size of, 87, *114–16*; successes of, 4, 50; suspension of, 29–30, *30, 32,* 33–34; white acquiescence to, 28, 47, 55; white blocking of, 40–41; white members of, 3, 34, 123, 133, 136, 141; white parent bodies of, 26–27; whites' targeting of, 63–64; workers' control in, 27. *See also* musicians, Black; subsidiaries; and individual listings of Black AFM locals by number

Logan, Rayford, 19

Los Angeles: Black musicians of, 5, **97–99**, 110, 119–20; Black population of, 50, *51*, 146–47; Central Avenue decline, 110, 146; Central Avenue music scene, 97, 98, 99, 110, 146, 173nn1,7; disenfranchisement of Blacks in, 99–100; interracial music making in, 100–102; population growth in, 97–98, *98*; South Central district, 97, 98. *See also* Local 47, Local 767

Lott, Eric, 157n25

Louisville, merger of locals in, *115*, 181n38

Love, Eddie B.: attack on Local 648, **73–74, 77–78**, 86; embezzlement by, **86–87**; Night Club Committee of, 75; on repeal of Prohibition, 73–74; work with Petrillo, 86

Lowe, Curtis, 122

Machinists' Union, "whites only" policy, **23–24**, 159n62

Machlin, Paul S., 165n4

Mack, James, 129, 130

Mancini, Lew, x

Mandel, Bernard, 26, 160n68

Marable, Fate, 5, 39, 136; unionization requirements for, 68

March on Washington Movement (MOWM), 93

Marinship shipyard: firing of black workers, 94; James's lawsuit against, **93–96**

Marshall, Ray, 120, 159n61, 176n13; on Fair Labor Practices Commissions, 177n29

Martyn, Barry: Klan threat to, 137

May, William ("Bill"), x, 42, 162n33

Mazzola, Sandy, 48

McCord, Charles H.: *The American Negro as a Dependent*, 43

McDavid, Russell, 103

McKay, Claude, 44

McKinney, Eddie, 67, 72

McNeely, Cecil "Big Jay," 146, 175n40

McRae, Richard, 145, 181n41

McWhirter, Cameron: *Red Summer*, 43–44

Meany, George, 109, 112; and AFM mergers, **119–20**; and Petrillo, 120, 143, 172n18, 176n13; and Randolph, **123–24**

Medlock, Alan, x

Mermey, Maurice, 61

The Messenger, 44–45

Metzger, Alfred, 75, 169n78

Miami, segregated locals of, **91–92**, 100, *116*

military, desegregation of, 93

Millar, Cynthia, x

Miller, Glenn: on racial equality, 90

Miller, Owen, 13, 156n3, 157nn12,14,17

Million Dollar Theater (Los Angeles), interracial orchestra of, 101

Mingus, Charles, 101

minstrelsy, Black, 14, 157n25

Mitchell, Adam, 52, *53*

Mitchell, Frank, 70

Mobile (Alabama), segregated local of, *31*, 33, *115*, 136, 166n26

Monheim, Allee, x

Monteux, Pierre, 75, 168n65

Moody, J. Carroll, 158n41; *Perspectives on American Labor History*, 156n14

Mooslin, Alexander, 78, 170nn92,105

Moriarity, William (Bill), ix, 162n16

movies, silent: musical employment at, 7, **60–61**, 165n1; musicians' pay scale at, 61; white control of, 71

movies, sound, 2, 59; musicians' unemployment following, **61–64**, 70–72

musical literacy, in AFM entrance exams, **36–38**, 59. *See also* improvisation, musical

Musical Mutual Protective Union (MMPU), 10, 156n1

The Musical News (Local 6 magazine), on forbidden territory, 74

musicians: AFM's definition of "professional," 14, **35–36**, 158n28; effectiveness of unionization for, 6, 15, 38; employment in radio, 7, 61, 71, 99; as laborers, 6, 11, 166n9; protection from amateurs, 11; strikes by, 52, 61, 73; symphony, 7; touring, 16; workplace exploitation of, 9

musicians, Black: audition criteria for, 38; of Boston, 140–42, 148; of Buffalo, 65, 144–45, 147, *148*; of Buxton (Iowa), 34–35, 161n8; of Chicago, 28, 35, 46, 47, 58, 87, 126, 147; cultural hierarchies and, 2, 6, 36; improvisational skills, 7, 37, 59, 101; lived experiences of, 5–6; of Los Angeles, 97–99, 101–2, 110, 146–47; movie theater work, 60–61, 63, 165n1, 168n57; music reading skills, 38, 54; of New Orleans, 28, 135–36; pay scale differentials, 39–40, 59; petitions for locals, 2; representation at AFM conventions, 2, 4, 40–41, 65, 87, 90, 110–11, 149, 162n24; of San Francisco, 46, 50, 52–54, 75, 82; of Seattle, 46, 54–58; self-interest of, 151; silent film work, **60–61**, 165n1; of St. Louis, 4, 39, 66–68, 70, 71; studio work for, 101; traveling, 68, 92, 119–20, 158n38; views of unionization, 6; white imitators of, 49, 71–72; in white locals, 54–55, 127–28, 155n4. *See also* African Americans; bands, Black; locals, Black AFM (listed by number)

Musicians' National Protective Association (MNPA), 10–11

"Must There Be Segregation in the Union" (*Music and Rhythm*, 1942), 89–90

Myers, Isaac, 19

NAACP, 93; founding of, 42

Nasser Brothers, Local 6 (San Francisco) lawsuit against, 61

National Industrial Recovery Act (1933), 73

National Labor Union (NLU): Black members of, **18–19**; segregated locals of, 19

National League of Musicians (NLM), 6, **10–16**, 36, 37, 48, 156n9; AFL and, 9, 12; class concerns of, 12; demise of, 14; local autonomy in, 12

National Negro Congress, 93

Negrophobia, 13–14, 43. *See also* racism

New Amsterdam Musical Association, 42

New Haven, desegregated locals of, 148

New Orleans: Black AFM locals of, 28, 29, *30, 32*, 50; merger of Locals 174 and 496, 112, *115*, 132, **135–38**, *139*, 140, 145; jazz of, 135; population of, *51*

New York City, Musicians' Emergency Fund, 62

Northern states, skilled craftsmen of, 17–18

Northrup, Herbert, 94

Norton, George, 24

Oak Park-River Forest Symphony, racial discrimination incident, **125–27**, 177n33

O'Connell, James, 12

Ohio, Civil Rights Commission, 123

Oliver, King, 100

Olson, David, xi

O'Neal, Peter, 159n58

The Overture (Local 47, Los Angeles, newsletter), on merger with Local 767, 104, 106, 107, 108

Owen, Chandler, 44

Palitzsch, Zachary, x

Palmer, Marie Dock, 126, 178n34

Panic of 1893, 22

Parker, Charlie "Bird": retroactive acknowledgment of, 8

Parker, Theodore, 182n17

Paul, Maury, 104, 108, *109*, 174n23

pay scales, 4, 15; for Black locals, **39–40**, 85–86; Black musicians' differentials, **39–40**, 59; discussions on, 168n71; Local 9 (Boston), 141; Local 47 (Los Angeles), 107; Local 76 (Seattle), 55, 56; Local 161 (Washington, DC), 134; Local 174 (New Orleans), 136–37; Local 496 (New Orleans), 136–37; Local 535 (Boston), 141; Local 710 (Washington, DC), 134; at silent movies, 61

Peretti, Burton W., 166n18

performance, musical: opposing approaches to, 7

Perkins, Terry, x

Petrillo, James C., 62, 162n24; and abolition of subsidiaries, **84–86**; on amalgamation, 112, *116*, 117; with Civil Right Department, 134, 149, 180n2; and Local 6 (San Francisco), 121; and Local 10 (Chicago), **127–28**, 144; and Local 43/533 (Buffalo) merger,

144; and Local 47/767 (Los Angeles) merger, 109, 143; and Local 161-710 (Washington, DC) merger, 134; and Local 174-496 (New Orleans) merger, 137; and Meany, 117, 119, **120**, 143, 176n13; opposition to segregation, **84–85**, **90–91**, 120; ouster from Local 10 presidency, **127–28**; and Resolution 34 (calling for amalgamation), 117, **119**, **120**, 143; resolution of thanks to, 90, 162n24, 172n18

Philadelphia: Locals 77 and 274, **1**, **2**, **3–4**, 112, 117–18, 140, 145, 155n11; orchestra, 7

Pillars, Hayes, 5, 70

Pinto, Mark, ix

Pitts, Robert, 56, 165n32

Plessy v. Ferguson (1896), 13

Plummer, Lloyd, 151, 153, 181n40; resolution to abolish subsidiaries, 65, 70, 84, 144

Porgy and Bess (original production), 93, 172n28

Portola Louvre Café (San Francisco), 52, *53*

Powderly, Terence V., **20–21**, *21*, 55, 67

President's Committee on Fair Employment Practice, 93, 94

Preves, Milton, 126, 177n33

Preyer, Bill, 91–92

professionalism, musical: role in auditions, **35–39**

Prohibition (1920), 56, 60; effect on musicians, 2, 63; musicians' wages following, 73–74; repeal of, 73

race: in AFM admission, 36; fluidity of, 17, 158n39; as labor trait, 18; organized labor and, **16–22**; wage disparity based on, 39

racial Darwinism, 13

racism: in AFM, 4, 7–8; employment issues in, 7; post–Civil Rights Act, 149; of post–World War I era, 43; reconciliation efforts, 7–8

radio, musicians' employment in, 7, 71, 99

railroad unions: challenges to segregation, 26–27; racial exclusion among, 24, 96, 123, 124

Randle, Eddie, 5, *71*, 72, 168n56

Randolph, A. Philip, 24, 160n71; activism of, 44; in AFL-CIO, 123; AFL convention protest, 80–81; on Black labor alienation, 48; challenge to Black leaders, 143; influence on Roosevelt, 172n26; March on Washington Movement (MOWM), 93; and segregated unions, **123–24**

recordings, 49; early quality of, 63

Red Summer (1919), riots of, 43, 50

Regal Theater (Chicago), 124

Reilly, Byron "Speed," 78

Richards, Barney: and Local 10-208 merger negotiations, **127–31**; presidency of Local 10, 127–28

Richmond Dispatch, on Powderly, 20

Riesenfeld, Hugo, 60, 61

riverboats: Black musicians on, 5, 6, **39**, 62, 68, *69*, **70–71**, 136; jazz culture of, 168n55

Robinson, Lester, 78

Robinson, Mabel, 142

Roediger, David, 18

Roosevelt, Franklin Delano: Executive Order 8802, 92–93; Executive Order 9346, 93; Randolph's influence on, 92–93, 172n26

Royal Theater (San Francisco), bombing of, 61

Samuels, William Everett, 87, 128; and CMHI, 127; in Local 10-208 (Chicago), 131

Sandiford, Preston, 141, 142

San Francisco: AFM locals of, 7–8; Black locals of, *31*, **50–54**, *88*; Black population of, *51*, 73, 75; club scene restrictions, **74–75**; exclusionary white unions of, 96; "forbidden territory" venues in, 74, 82, 169n75; general strike (1934), 73, 168n69; lawsuit over racial discrimination in, 72, **73–83**, *79*; Locals 6 and 648 battles, 53–54, **72–83**; Local 6/669 merger, *114*, **121–23**; riots during longshoremen strike (1934), 73; population of, *51*; strike of culinary workers and musicians (1916), 52, 164n21; subsidiary Local 6, **82–83**, **87–89**, *88*, *89*; unionization battles in, 5; Western Addition, 75; white union picketing in, 82

San Francisco Superior Court, in Local 6/648 dispute, **78**, *79*

San Francisco Symphony, 7, 75; "Save

Our Symphony" (S.O.S.) campaign, **72–73**; tax supporting, 73, 168n65
San Francisco War Memorial Opera House, 75, 169n78
Saunders, Red, 5, 87, *125*, 151; and CMHI, 127; conflict with Gray, 102; fining by Local 208, 125, 177n31; in Local 10-208 merger, **124–25**, 129
Saunders, Ted, Jr., 177n31
Sazer, Marc, ix
Schexnayder, Lori, x
Schnitzler, William F., 120
Seattle, 52, 80; AFM locals, 40; Black locals of, *30,* **54–58**, 164n25; Black population of, **55–56**, 164n30; Black unions in, 5, 46, 164n25; jazz scene of, 56; merger of Locals 76 and 493, *114,* 117, **120–21**; symphony, 7
Seattle Central Labor Council, 55; Local 76's appeal to, 57; Local 493's appeal to, 58
Seattle Park Board, 56, 165n35
Shakespeare, William: adaptations to audiences, 36–37
sharecropping, 23
Shaw, Elijah "Lige," 5, *69,* 72, 157n15; on Local 44 (St. Louis), 168n55; meetings with IEB, 68, 167n46; representing Local 197 (St. Louis), 91; Subsidiary Local 2 campaign, **68–70**, 86
Sheklow, Seymour, 104
Shelley v. Kraemer (1948), 110
Shiskin, Boris, 120
Short, John, xi
Shubert Brothers (booking agency), 6
Shufeldt, Robert Wilson: *The Negro, a Menace to American Civilization,* 43
Siegl, Eleanor, 167n28
Simpson, Sammy, 122
Singleton, Zutty, 90
Sioux City, Iowa: Locals 745 and 743, *31, 33, 114,* 143, 176n5
Sky Club (Miami), Black trio at, 91
Smith, Lloyd, 5; movie theater work, 60; on pay scales, **39**; on white imitators, *71,* 71–72
Smith-Wright, Lovie, x, 150, 182n14
So Different Orchestra (San Francisco), 5, *53;* audition for Local 6, 52
soldiers, Black: of World War I, 42; of World War II, 90
Solomon, Izler, 101

sound, mechanized: replacement of live performance, **61–62**. *See also* movies, sound
Southern, Eileen, 41
Spengler, Oswald: *The Decline of the West,* 43
Spikes, Reb, *53,* 164n23; audition for Local 6, 52
The Spokesman (San Francisco): on Local 6/648 conflict, 76, 78, **80–82**; on picketing of AFL, 80–81; on strikes, **19**
Standifer, Floyd, 147
Stanley, Peter, 52, *53*
Stevenson, Dan, x
Stewart, Henry, 54
St. Louis: Great Western Union of Colored Musicians (later Local 44), 12, 13, 28; Local 2, 13; Local 44, 4, **13**, 28, *30,* 40, 47; Local 197, **87**, *88,* 91, *115;* merger of Locals 2 and 197, *115,* 140; movie-house musicians of, 5, 60, 168n57; population of, *51;* riverboat music in, 5, 39, 62, 136; subsidiary Local 2, 33, 34, 64, **66–72**, 86
Stoddard, Lothrop: *The Rising Tide of Color Against White World-Supremacy,* 43
Stoddard, Tom, 54, 164n23
St. Paul (riverboat), musicians on, 68
Strand Dance Hall (Seattle), labor dispute concerning, 57
Strather, Charles W., 74
Streckfus Line Steamers, Black bands of, 68, 70, 136
strikes: Black workers and, 8, **19**, 23, 48, 73; over sound films, 61; in Knights of Labor, 22; by Local 6 (San Francisco), 52; by longshoremen on West Coast (1934), 73; San Francisco general strike (1934), 73; sympathy, 16, 61
Stripp, Fred: "The Treatment of Negro-American Workers...," 95–96
Stump, Gordon, x, 110
subsidiaries, AFM locals, **33–34**, 62, **65–83**, 94, 153; abolition of, **84–89**, *88,* 153; autonomy for, 84–85, *85;* charters for, 84–86; of Little Rock, 88; Local 2, St. Louis, **66–72**; Local 6, San Francisco, 34, **82–83**, **87–89**; Philadelphia, 161n4; representation at conventions, 70, 84; rules for, 66–67, 167n39. *See also* locals

Index 213

Summers, Clyde W., 160n72
Swanberg, Charles, 52
Swing Mikado (1939), 94
symphony orchestras: development in U.S., 7, 156n18. *See also* Chicago Symphony; San Francisco Symphony

Taft, Philip, 160nn70,78
Taft-Hartley Act (1947), 16, 61
Te Groen, John, 109
Tenth Division (Black) Band (Seattle), racial discrimination against, 56
Terrell, John, 75–76, 81
theater, commodification of, 6
Theatrical Syndicate (booking agency), 6
Thomas, Theodore, 37
Tip Top Club (San Francisco), **77–78**, 169n87
Tizo, Juan, 92
Tournour, Gene, x
travel, musicians', 16, 92; segregated, 119–20; travel cards, 16, 38, 158n38
Treme's Petit Jazz Museum, 138
Trocadero (Los Angeles), Black musicians at, 99
Truman, Harry: Executive Order 9981, 93
Turner, Diane Delores, on Local 274, 155nn1,11; on Local 591, 161n4

unionization: benefits of, 6; cultural hierarchies in, 6. *See also* American Federation of Labor; American Federation of Musicians; CIO; labor
urbanization, U.S.: Black labor and, 18

Variety, on amalgamation problems, 148
vocalists, Black: performing in San Francisco, 75

Wagner, Melinda, x
Walker, Charles, 177n31
Waller, Fats: movie theater work, 60, 165n4
Walsh, Alex, x
Walton, Charles E., 182n11
Walton, Lester, 127
Ward, Jabo, 147
Ward, Louis, 78
Washington, Booker T., 44, 159n61; on organized labor, 22–23
Washington, DC, 12, 92–93, 149; amalgamation of Locals 161 and 710, **132–35**, 137, 145; Local 161, *31, 115*; Local 710, *31*, 84, *115*; population of, *51*; social clubs of, 134
Washington, Leon D., 129
Watkins, Earl, x, 5, 75, *76*; on Local 6/669 merger, 121
Weber, Joseph, 84, 162n19; on AFM membership, 36; and Locals 6/648 (San Francisco) conflict, 72, **74**, 77, 78, 81, 82; on Local 76/458/493 (Seattle) conflicts, **57–58**, 80; and Locals 2/44 (St. Louis), **66–67**; promotion of live music, 63; on theater work, 165n1
Weber, Walter, 78; on Local 6 unemployment, 72
Wells, Gerald, 52, *53*
Wesley, Charles, 159n54
Whaley, Wade: band of, 78, 80
White, Walter, 42
Wierdak, Alan, x
Wilkerson, Isabel, 16
Williams, Clarence, 52, *53*
Williams, Fred, x, 140, 181n28
Willis, John, 147
Wilson, Gerald, 103
Wilson, Teddy, 92
Winstein, David, 137, 138, 181n17
Witherspoon, Jimmy, 181n28
Woodman, William "Brother," Jr., 99
Woodward, C. Vann: on integration, 118–19; opposition to affirmative action, 176n8
World War I: Black activism following, **42–45**; Black locals following, 34–35; Black soldiers of, 42
World War II: Black soldiers of, 90; racial equality issues in, 89–90
WPA, Federal Music Project, 93

Young, Lee: racial discrimination against, 99, 174n10
Young, Lester, 99
Young, Marl, *109*, 100, 110, 119, 151; conflict with Gray, 102, 129; meeting with AFL, 108–9; recollections of, 174n14, 175nn36,42,46; role in Local 47/767 merger, **102–5, 108–9**
Young, Steve, 149

LETA E. MILLER is an emerita professor of music at the University of California, Santa Cruz. She is the author, coauthor, or editor of fourteen books, including *Music and Politics in San Francisco*, *Chen Yi*, and *Aaron Jay Kernis*.

The University of Illinois Press
is a founding member of the
Association of University Presses.
———————————————

University of Illinois Press
1325 South Oak Street
Champaign, IL 61820-6903
www.press.uillinois.edu